PRAISE FOR
WHISPERS OF RESILIENCE

"As someone living with MS, this anthology deeply resonated with me. Each personal story showcased the diverse experiences of people like me and the raw emotions shared were both moving and empowering. A must-read for anyone seeking understanding, connection and support." – Anne

"This anthology beautifully captured the multifaceted nature of life with MS. The blend of personal narratives, raw insights and stories from the heart, were inspiring, informative, heartwarming and incredibly moving. A powerful compilation that sheds light on the challenges and triumphs of those impacted by MS." – Suzie

Published in Australia by
Morpheus Publishing
Geelong, Victoria
hello@justinemartin.com.au
www.morpheuspublishing.com.au

First published in Australia 2023
Copyright ©Justine Martin 2023

All rights reserved. No part of this publication may be reproduced, stored in a retrieval system, or transmitted, in any form or by any means without the prior written permission of the publisher, nor be otherwise circulated in any form of binding or cover other than that in which it is published and without a similar condition being imposed on the subsequent purchaser.

National Library of Australia Cataloguing in Publication entry

 A catalogue record for this book is available from the National Library of Australia

ISBN: 978-0-6455375-3-6 (paperback)
ISBN: 978-0-6455375-4-3 (epub)

Anthology Compilation: Justine Martin
Edit and Proofreading: Karen Guest
Copywriting and design: Suzie Veitch
Cover Graphics: Lynette Ingles
Interior layout and design: Sophie White

Printed by Ingram Spark

The information contained in this book is for general informational purposes only. The authors and publisher are not offering any medical, legal or professional advice. While every effort has been made to ensure the accuracy and completeness of the information provided, the authors and publisher assume no responsibility for errors or omissions or for any outcomes or consequences resulting from the use of this book's content.

This book is distributed by Morpheus Publishing and is available through authorised distributors, booksellers and Morpheus Publishing website. For copyright permissions or any other inquiries, please email hello@justinemartin.com.au

Morpheus Publishing acknowledges the Traditional Custodians of the country on which we work, the Wurundjeri Woi-wurrung people of the Kulin Nation and recognises their continuing connection to the land, waters and culture. We pay our respects to their Elders past, present and emerging.

Whispers of RESILIENCE

OUR MS STORIES

COMPILED BY JUSTINE MARTIN

DEDICATION

This book is dedicated to every brave soul living with Multiple Sclerosis, whose strength and resilience continue to inspire us all. Your journey is a testament to the human spirit, and through your courage, you remind us to cherish every moment and embrace life's challenges with unwavering determination.

To the families of the 26 Authors of 'Whispers of MS' Book this book is dedicated to you. Your unwavering support and understanding have allowed these stories to come to life, touching the hearts of countless others facing similar challenges. Your encouragement has nurtured the voices that now whisper loudly, spreading awareness, understanding, and hope. To the loved ones and friends, who stand alongside those living with MS, your care and empathy provide invaluable strength and comfort. This book is a tribute to the unity and resilience of the MS community and those who support them.

And this book is dedicated to Justine Martin's mum, who faced MS with unwavering strength and grace, a true inspiration for us all. Her resilience in the face of adversity taught Justine the power of perseverance and the beauty of a fighting spirit. Her love and determination will forever be etched in Justine's heart and her guiding light.

GIVING BACK
25% OF PROFIT FROM ALL BOOK SALES WILL BE DONATED TO MS RESEARCH

In the pages of this book, you'll find stories of courage, resilience and hope from individuals touched by Multiple Sclerosis (MS). As we delve into the lives of these brave souls, we are reminded of the immense challenges that MS presents and the impact it has on those living with the condition and their loved ones.

It is with a profound sense of purpose that we have chosen to give back to the MS community. With every copy sold, 25% of the proceeds will be dedicated to MS Research. Our commitment is twofold: to raise awareness about MS and its far-reaching effects, and to contribute to the scientific advancements that will one day lead us to a cure!

MS is a disease that can strike at any stage of life, its symptoms unpredictable and diverse. From numbness and tingling to fatigue and mobility issues, the challenges faced by those with MS are as varied as the people themselves. It affects their ability to work, study and engage in everyday activities, taking a toll on physical, emotional and mental well-being.

Our collective efforts matter. By purchasing this book, you become a part of something bigger - a community of compassion and determination. Together, we can make strides in MS research, supporting the scientists and clinicians tirelessly working to improve the lives of those affected by this condition.

Join us on this journey - a journey of giving back, spreading awareness, and inspiring change. Together, we can make a lasting impact on the lives of those living with MS and their families.

With heartfelt appreciation,
The Whispers of MS Authors

CONTENTS

Dedication	5
Giving Back	7
Foreword	10
Introduction	13
1 Emma Archer	15
2 Diane Barclay	27
3 Leanne Boothroyd	37
4 Allyson Brown	47
5 Amanda Campbell	61
6 Don Campanile	77
7 Angharad Candlin	87
8 Nina Crumpton	99
9 Liliana Cuba	111
10 Colleen Daniels	123
11 Laura Di Iulio	135
12 Kim Eagle	145
13 Jayne England	157
14 Penelope Gemmell	169
15 Candice Graham	181
16 Robyn Hart	191
17 Justine Martin	203

18	Stacey Metcalfe	225
19	Elizabeth Neal	235
20	Kristi Paschalidis	245
21	Clare Reilly	259
22	Tanya Rountree	275
23	Kerrie Sculac	285
24	Lachlan Terry	295
25	John Van De Putt	309
26	Beth Wurcker	321

Morpheus Writing Group	333
Justine Martin Keynote Speaker	334
Morpheus Publishing Scholarships	336
Glossary	337

FOREWORD

Whispers of Resilience: Our MS Stories is not just a book. It is a grand symphony of individual experiences bound by one shared reality: living with Multiple Sclerosis (MS). Within this unique anthology, you will discover twenty six diverse and powerful personal stories from across Australia, brought together by the common thread of encounters with MS.

The origin of this book stems from an article[1] I wrote for an Australian women's media group, *Mamamia*, known for its candid discussions. The intention of the article was to raise public awareness about MS—a condition recognised by name but often misunderstood and shrouded in confusion.

MS can manifest in anyone, and being famous does not protect you from acquiring the disease. Alongside celebrities like Christina Applegate and Selma Blair, I share a bond through our individual experiences with MS. Although our stories resonate with similarities, each journey is uniquely our own, reflecting the intricate complexity of this condition.

While it is commonly known that MS affects the nervous system, the practical implications and daily manifestations experienced by those living with the condition remain lesser known. This anthology aims to bridge the knowledge gap by presenting authentic narratives that break stereotypes and demystify the enigma surrounding MS.

The twenty six authors featured in this book contribute unique brush strokes to the canvas of shared experiences while preserving the essence of their individuality. MS is not the sole defining aspect of their lives, but it has certainly left an indelible imprint. *Whispers*

---

1   Martin, J (20 December 2022), 'Christine Applegate and I both have MS. But there's a huge difference in jour journeys', Mamamia, https://www.mamamia.com.au/ms-disease, accessed 28 July 2023.

of Resilience serves as a platform to share their transformative experiences, vocalise their journeys and recount battles, victories, fears, and hopes.

These narratives paint a portrait of resilience—more than tales of suffering or despair—they stand as testimonies of determination, courage, and fortitude. The authors peel back the layers of life with MS, unveiling its gritty reality while shining a spotlight on the incredible resilience of the human spirit. They encapsulate their personal journeys, simplifying the complexities of MS and transforming them into relatable human experiences. These narratives highlight the paradoxical nature of MS—it can incapacitate, empower, alienate, and unite.

Readers are invited to engage with people from all walks of life—young, old, urban, rural, newly diagnosed, and those who have been living with MS for many years. Each account adds a different hue to our collective understanding of MS, demonstrating the myriad of experiences this condition entails. The stories are emotive, inspiring, and thought provoking.

Whispers of Resilience: Our MS Stories is an innovative initiative to expand our collective understanding of MS and foster a sense of community among those living with the condition. It aims to dispel the pervasive sense of isolation, providing comfort and reassurance that their journey is not solitary—they are part of a vast community of individuals, each with a unique story.

This book is also a rallying cry, urging society to empathise, understand, and offer support.

While living with MS is a personal journey, the battle against it is communal. Each author's candid sharing of their experience provides invaluable insights and offers an opportunity for learning.

Each narrative stands as a beacon of human resilience—a testament to the endurance and tenacity of the human spirit in the face of adversity. It serves as a compelling reminder that, despite their unique story, those living with MS are interconnected through shared experiences. Collectively, these narratives offer insightful guidance for those diagnosed with MS and anyone seeking a deeper understanding of this complex condition.

This anthology amplifies the voices often drowned out in the noise of everyday life. It illuminates the lesser known aspects of MS, humanising the otherwise clinical and impersonal diagnosis. With each narrative, the whisper of resilience reverberates louder, affirming that we are more than our diagnosis.

Whispers of Resilience: Our MS Stories will extend its impact by contributing 25% of its sales towards MS research. This philanthropic effort is to fuel the quest for a cure, symbolising a commitment from myself and Morpheus Publishing to the global MS community. It is also an endeavour to drive impactful changes in the MS research landscape.

This anthology aims to serve as a historical record of life with MS when it was an incurable disease. When a cure for MS is found, people won't know anyone who has MS.

As an integral part of this project, I hold a profound sense of pride and admiration for each author involved and what we, as a collective, have achieved.

Justine Martin

INTRODUCTION

Welcome to Whispers of Resilience: Our MS Stories. In curating this collection, we made a deliberate decision to preserve the unique voices of each contributing author. Instead of polishing their chapters to literary perfection, we have left them untouched, so their individual styles and personal voices shine through. As you read, you will find that this choice fosters a deeper connection with each writer, allowing you to engage with their words on a more profound level.

To assist you in your journey through these narratives, a glossary is provided at the back of the book, filled with terms and acronyms that appear throughout the pages. We chose to include this glossary to enhance your reading experience, enabling you to flow seamlessly through each chapter. If you're unfamiliar with the medical terminology that features in our writings, we recommend taking a moment to review the glossary before diving into the stories or flick back and forth between.

Beyond the written word, you will find a more personal connection with each author. Included with their chapter, is a BIO, images and a QR code. Scanning this code will take you to a VLOG with the author, these are available to watch on **https://www.youtube.com/@justinemartincorporation** interview with the author, as well as a podcast episode where we personally explore why each author wanted to write their chapter and what being part of this project means to them.

As you embark on this exploration of resilience, courage and the human spirit, we hope you'll find inspiration, understanding and empathy in the whispers of our shared experiences.

Enjoy the journey.

1

Emma Archer

LIFE AS A JOURNEY, NOT A DESTINATION

I am writing this story because I want to share some of my journey with multiple sclerosis and to give some insights to health professionals, friends and family, colleagues and acquaintances about what it is like to live my MS life. I live in Adelaide, South Australia and was diagnosed with multiple sclerosis in June 2017. I was 37, had two small children, and had a good life. I was training to run a half marathon, was able to drive a manual car, do the gardening and build Ikea furniture. I had my dream job as a clinical midwife in a group practice in regional Queensland when I dramatically lost the feeling in and use of my arms, had numbness from under my breasts to my toes, and had severe pain in my hands and feet, which very quickly led to a diagnosis of MS.

My diagnosis journey only took a couple of weeks, and I've then had six years to adjust. While the initial diagnosis was dramatic and stressful and resulted in me being in hospital on steroids, it was comparatively quick compared to a lot of other people with MS. It took me weeks to recover from that flare. I still have residual numbness in my arms and hands and have been told I have a big lesion on my spine at C3-C4 in my neck, so I have a lot of the same issues that an incomplete quadriplegic would have. Everything below that point in my neck is less reliable than it used to be—limbs, organs, feet and hands—and I noticed some changes in my cognition, memory, and mood. Around this time, I was also diagnosed autistic and ADHD and have been able to embrace having a neurodivergent brain and an autoimmune disease in rapid succession.

As I write this, in 2023, I am still working, although I've had a career change. I am working on a postgraduate qualification in a new field, own my home, drive a car and a power chair, and am still a mama and wife, dog owner, proud plant lady, serial crafty type, and coffee lover. I'm now on my third medication regimen and my fifth neurologist. I've lost count of how many MRIs, blood tests and neurological exams I've had. I can't tell you when it stopped being the hyperfocus of my life, but when I stopped searching for every piece of information I could find, at some point, I accepted it.

In mid-2017, though, this was a crisis that turned my life inside out, and the thing about a crisis is that it's not a neat, planned adventure—it is, by nature, a wild, unpredictable ride. There is no clear start to it, or a pathway through it, which means there's no clear end to it either. My diagnosis didn't mean that my life had ended. I hope you know that it is rare to die from MS and that you are going to learn to live your best life still, with it along for the ride.

I didn't know that. I knew that my life had changed, and there were very few concrete answers, and I wasn't in control. At the same time, I had the cold realisation that I'd never had control, quickly followed by realising I wasn't all that mad about my life direction changing and felt relief and instant guilt about feeling relieved. All of this in a short time was why I cried for two weeks straight. I wanted to bargain my way out of it. I did consider alternative therapies, walking through fire, eating unusual foods, and latching on to any option or supplement that was suggested as a possible cure because hope is what powers you as you come to realise that your diagnosis is now a part of your life.

I've come to make peace with not having to be brave or courageous, or graceful in my journey. I want to tell you it is just a diagnosis, and it will all be okay—different, but okay. I was upset and shocked, of course, and was pretty sure that this diagnosis would be the end of my career, marriage, and life. So far, it's only impacted on one of those domains and helped me realise that my career wasn't the most important thing anyway.

I won't ever forget about how MS came into my life—how I felt when I was diagnosed, how awful and unwell and not okay, and how scared I felt in the MRI machine, hospital room and doctor's office, and how scared I was at seeing my life break apart in front of my eyes with the diagnosis. I might forget now where I put my keys or if I took my meds this morning, but those core memories about MS are tied to a lot of feelings and are a pivotal part of my life, and I can't forget. I don't think I want to forget either, even if I could, like birthing my babies or finishing a marathon.

It took me years to admit to anyone that I was relieved to have a diagnosis rather than a constellation of symptoms that would be dismissed or reduced to a shrug by the doctors. I was relieved I had something mundane and fairly well-known, even though I didn't know much about it. It felt wrong to be relieved when everyone around you was not. This was the first step I took in centreing my own needs rather than trying to support everyone else around me so that I wasn't a burden. But this was the first inkling that I had, even in those first few days, that what people saw on the outside wasn't the same and wasn't going to be the same as what I felt and experienced on the inside.

After maybe six months, I learned as much as I could about this snowflake disease, where everyone's experience, symptoms, diagnosis story and life impact are unique. My experience of being diagnosed is unique, and my experience with disease-modifying drugs is different to others. The journey is truly a different experience for everyone. Even with the same disease and on the same drugs, there is no consistency, and that is what makes connecting to others with MS so valuable as well. This is one of the most frustrating things about MS, and it makes it harder for people to understand our experience of this disease.

Life today

Everything has changed for me in the past few years, but it has also changed for the whole world during and post-pandemic. I feel pretty normal having made adjustments, although mine are because I've embraced having a chronic illness that I'm not out to get better from. I never feel well or great or tickety-boo, just variations of fair to middling or, as the Norwegians say, up and not crying. I get out of the house each day and try to see the sunshine. I tend my plants, pat my dogs, and get some nature input. I connect with people and balance it with alone time, usually with headphones and doing some art practice. I do a night-time routine, including picking a top for the next day, because it reminds me every day that tomorrow is a new one. I am more open now that I have a disability, and I know I have a different version of my life to live. I'm now on the other side of 40, in the throes of postgraduate studies, parenting a tween and a teen, and have a different career to what I had pre-diagnosis.

I plan my day as well, to incorporate less than I used to—everything takes me longer to complete because of fatigue and uncooperative limbs, and often I need a break after doing half a task. I'm more honest and realistic about my capacity than I used to be, but I'm not missing out as much as I feared. My life focuses more on quality over quantity now. I value each intentional hour I spend with people more now than I used to, when I took it for granted that I'd always have more hours to spend. I'm not trying to romanticise the struggles I have when it sucks to not be able to put my socks on or walk my dogs, but I pay more attention to small things now to catch tiny moments of joy and sunshine each day. Otherwise, it's easy for me to go through the motions rather than live the small things to keep myself from giving in to the temptation of crawling into bed and not getting up again.

I go about my morning routine with the help of checklists when my brain fog and pain are bad. Both of them impact my executive function, which is the boss of my brain, and lets me execute tasks or thoughts. Instead of being able to think in a straight line, MS means I struggle to know what to do and how to do it or know that I need to do something fundamental, like drinking water or eating. I use reminders on my home automation AI-supported devices and can pretend, some days, that I'm an early adopter of those technologies rather than needing them to cover for deficits in my brain. Some days I struggle to initiate doing things I know I need to do, something that I'm perfectly capable of doing but can't at that moment. It is infuriating wanting to make a sandwich but being overwhelmed by the one million steps involved in making it and exhausted before I get to the kitchen. So, I now have a support worker who preps fruit and vegetables for me, makes lunch for me, and does the ironing, as I have limited use of my hands and arms for those tasks.

I take the pre-packed medications to manage the symptoms of MS and make sure I don't miss doses or lose scripts or forget to refill a medication. I go at a slower pace some days than others, but I still drink coffee and check the weather and morning news before getting dressed.

The weather has a bigger impact on me now than it used to, so I have to be careful to not get too hot or cold—but I like to pretend I'm fashionable and am picking the right on-trend outfit for all of my appointments and meetings for the day. I drink water with thickener in it and a splash of cordial or a tisane, a herbal or fruit tea, to hide the weird taste—or am I drinking fancy infusion aimed at optimising my body's energy flows?

Mentally, I take a moment when I wake up to assess how I feel for the day. I check in on my mood, motivation, and fatigue levels.

I have a diary for my life and a smart watch to help manage it, which could be because I'm super organised or because I can't remember an appointment if it's not written down, and I have alarms to remind me.

I clearly haven't lost my sense of humour in the process because if I shared these approaches as a serious way of me coping with my experience of the impact of having literal holes in my brain without laughing about them, my psychiatrist tells me I'd be delusional instead of using humour to cope with the morbid.

I use some of these mind tricks to try to refocus my life on the positives and to remind myself that most of what you see in anyone's life is a facade. I work from home flexibly, as many people started doing during the pandemic and continue to do so. Is that because I can't commute and work a full day in the office or because I've negotiated a great arrangement with my workplace? Most of my life now is very much a little of column A, the things I do to look like I have my life optimised, and column B, the things I do to manage the deficits I have because of MS.

It's not fun to choke on water, have bowel issues, walk like I'm drunk, get fatigued by washing my hair, and have issues with breathing while I'm asleep. But there's a silver lining to these realisations. I've found that having always been extremely hard on myself, this diagnosis has meant I have finally found some self-compassion. I've learned to believe in myself and accept when I need support because I am my own leader, coach, and advocate. I have to do these things for myself, or else I add feeling guilty to the list of baggage I'm carrying.

The loud voices in the past that said I wasn't trying hard enough, or achieving enough, are quieter now because I know it is hard and balance needs to be found.

What I have learned is that MS makes you feel so frustrated you want to go and scream at the clouds. Every day is different, and some days you don't want to open your eyes because it's not predictable whether you are going to feel like sludge or doing something fun.

MS makes me angry and sad at the concerns my family and friends have for me, both those they share and those they keep hidden, because they know how many of my own worries I don't share with them and carry alone.

MS sucks, but I have realised that I don't have to like something to accept it and don't get to pick which bits of my life I like. I grieve in my quiet private moments for the life I thought I'd have and can't pursue anymore. MS has often made me really question how I got to this point in my life. When I think about how much I love about my here—my family, my life, myself—I know I wouldn't trade anything in for not having MS if that trade-off was offered.

MS made me try harder to do the things I want to and pare down the list of things I must do. MS means I can accept the things I don't have the energy for and use a heap of gadgets, services, shortcuts and aids instead. MS means I am sensitive to the temperature in a different way from how I used to be, but I also know there's a solution to being too hot and cold, and I'm not weak for needing to use them. In fact, MS gives me a strength that is hard to describe— the strength to say yes, I do need help to pick up my leg to put on my pants, or yes, I do need to wear particular underwear because MS is causing my bladder issues.

The hardest part

The hardest part of being an MS'er is feeling like a burden to other people, so I try to outsource it to paid professionals as much as I can. I have now built an amazing support system to spread that burden. It feels like I've seen every 'ologist in the past few years— exercise physiologist, psychologist, psychiatrist, neurologist, neuroimmunologist, radiologist, radiographer, physiotherapist, orthotist and prosthetist, gastroenterologist, cardiologist, speech pathologist, nutritionist, ophthalmologist, audiologist, occupational therapist, podiatrist, art therapist.... Sometimes it feels like I see my allied health supports more often than my friends.

I have amazing friends who understand that I tell them when it's hard because they remind me I'm doing my best and it's a hard situation. I have a husband who has stuck with me through my dumbest moments of proposing divorce so he can find someone healthy and have a chance to be happy, and the hard times of major side effects from medications and changes in my capacity to be a wife and mama and career-minded all-around badass. I recommend you find your people and be prepared to have external support because it's hard to be the person experiencing this as well as the person who has to support and educate others about it. This is my role in my social situation, and that tension is a very good reason to have good people to share your journey with, in all its gruelling, inspiring, heartbreaking, public, private, scary and positive glory.

It's taken time, therapy, and experience to work out that, for me, there is little to differentiate between severe fatigue when I know I'm toeing the line of burnout and the black dog sniffing around when depression is creeping up on me. It's hard to tell the difference between the two, and for me, the same things that help me manage one manage the other. I can't disentangle them any more than I can tell you where the lesions on my spine stop and the symptoms I experience start.

I know that taking my stupid body to the gym or for a walk for my stupid mental health also helps me manage my fatigue and that cutting back on my commitments reduces my fatigue and the mental strain that makes my depression and anxiety less manageable. If I don't do the small things to smooth out the ups and downs of both, it adds up to me needing a day or two in bed, followed by a very low-demand week to ten days to recover.

It has taken me a long time to work out that I don't have the capacity I used to have. It has taken me repeatedly burning out and being very unwell for weeks at a time to learn this. I'm not a quick learner because it meant I had to accept new limits of what I could do. I have learned that I don't need to complete everything today, I don't have to try extra hard, I don't need to fight constantly, and I don't need to even turn up if it's too much today. I rest when I need to or want to—it is not a bad word or concept to me now.

What's next?

As I write this in winter 2023, I am going through another round of testing to see whether the MS is a progressive form rather than relapsing-remitting. I had to be my own advocate, historian, cheerleader, critical thinker, communicator, educator, and record-keeper to notice these changes and then to try to discuss them with the neurologist I'd been seeing for several years. She was dismissive of my concerns to the point that I lodged a complaint to the health service and paid for a second opinion privately.

I don't have an outcome for the testing, but the new neurologist explained that secondary progressive MS is not a clear-cut clinical diagnosis and doesn't change much in terms of treatment or what my life will look like. I'm not overly concerned about the outcome of this process will be, as again, the overwhelming feeling I have about this information was a relief. The medications I'm on are effective for the lesions, and I'm not imagining that I've got more going on than an MRI can show. While my MRIs have been reassuringly stable since I was diagnosed, I have experienced what's described as the winding path of progression, which is the gradual accumulation of disability between relapses. This is called progression independent of relapse activity (PIRA), and I now use a cane or mobility aid when I used to run 20 km or more a week and do half-marathons for fun.

Shortly after I submitted my final draft, there was a surprise plot twist to my story that I want to add in. Always remember that not everything going on in your body is because of MS, and that you know your body best. If something doesn't sit right with you, please speak up and keep asking for answers until you get them. And also - be honest about what medications, supplements, extra treatments and tablets you are taking because they can cause more harm than help!

In late June 2023 I got a second opinion from a neurologist in the public health system. I had had to put in a complaint and advocate strongly for this due to issues with my previous neurologist dismissing my worsening symptoms for almost 2 years. Turns out that the severe peripheral neuropathy (the pain and numbness and other issues with my feet and lower legs) that I'd developed was not, in fact, MS-related at all and was because of extremely high levels of B6 in my body. The B6 had been included, unbeknownst to me, in magnesium supplements that I took for restless legs!

He told me my MS was stable and I was otherwise healthy, and that the neuropathy should fade over the next year or 2. I've been floating around since this news - I have *hope* for the first time since my diagnosis that MS is going to stop being an interesting part of my life and become a boring side note instead. I have a future to plan, a life to live, races to run, and I am here for it, stronger than ever!

Watch the VLOG/Podcast of Emma on YouTube

ABOUT EMMA

Emma Archer is a writer, educator, artist, public servant and passionate lifelong student. She crams as much into her week as she can while juggling a chronic illness, working, parenting, and studying. She has many talents and hobbies, and isn't letting anything, including Multiple Sclerosis, get in the way of a good life. She is an advocate, leader, loyal friend and mentor as well as a keen, if slow, runner.

Emma loves listening to others share their ideas and stories, and is passionate about expressing herself artistically. She is an alumni of Flinders University, the University of South Australia, and the Sylvia Rodger Academy, and has now added "published author" to her long list of life achievements. She uses her voice to make an impact, is currently working on her writing adventure, and is excited to see what the future holds.

Emma was born in Sydney, Australia and settled in Adelaide after living in several other cities. She lives in organised chaos with her husband and two kids, two dogs, one cat, and many plants. She is building a satisfying and meaningful life, using her experiences to inspire others to find their voices and make their own mark on the world.

2

Diane Barclay

I DON'T GET ANGRY ANYMORE

I was born in 1949. I am 73 years old. My name is Diane Barclay, and I was diagnosed with MS in 2003 when I was 54, not in the typical 20 to 40yearold age group for MS.

I got called back to the neurologist after lots of blood tests, MRIs, and a lumbar puncture. He announced I had MS, and at the time, I had no idea what that even was.

I had started developing strange things with my body. I couldn't run properly anymore. It was an uneven, funny sort of run. I fell over a few times.

One funny time I did fall over was straight in front of the local pub in Geelong on a Monday morning at 9:30 am. I fell over in the gutter and took all the skin off my leg. I continued to deliver my parcel to the pub, looked at the gutter on the way back and thought, *why did I fall over? That was not a big step up.* There were lots of little things that kept happening. Then a few things I couldn't seem to do properly, like swimming—I almost sank because my right leg couldn't keep up with my left leg.

I think I've had MS for a lot longer than 2003, but everything was so very subtle. When I was a lot younger, my daughter and I used to do a lot of horse riding; my right knee would ache, and I couldn't figure out why. Another time I went to a friend's 60th birthday party, and they had rock and roll as the theme. My husband, Peter, and I used to be fairly good rock and roll dancers. I was missing the beat and circle, couldn't quite get around far enough and thought I hadn't had too much to drink, and now I know it all adds up. But when I discussed it with my doctor and told him different things, he would say things like, *you're getting old,* and *you're driving a delivery van for 10 hours a day,* and *you know these things happen.*

The first person I delivered a parcel to after I was diagnosed said their sister died of MS! Not something I needed to hear, nor is it true. But then I went for a blood test, and the nurse there said, *you know it's not a death sentence.* So, I started to look into it a bit and realised it's not actually a death sentence. It can cause a lot of problems down the track that could do it. But I have primary progressive MS, and it's very slow progressing. I can still walk with the help of a mobility walker, and there are a lot of things I can't do now, such as riding a camel or riding a motorbike!

Peter and I were at Cable Beach in Broome, Western Australia. Riding a camel was always on my bucket list. Peter went and tried to book in for the evening ride, which was threequarters of an hour, but it was booked out. So, we had to have the morning ride, which was about 20 minutes. I was so disappointed it was only going to be a short ride after coming all this way. I actually got the biggest and the oldest camel, and as soon as I sat on that camel, I felt the pain in my legs going over the saddle. I asked what happens if I can't make the distance, and the bloke said, *well, the camels aren't used to sitting down halfway through; you're on for the duration*. I thought I would never forgive myself if I didn't try. I completed the camel ride, and then they had to almost lift me off because my legs wouldn't work. The only disappointment is I never got to take a photo of myself riding the camel. It's not something I'll ever be able to do again.

I've always had this little bucket list after being diagnosed that my daughter and I would be on the same motorbike. My daughter and her husband race motorcycles, and, in particular, with sidecars. They used to have a comeandtry day in Broadford, Victoria. I went along and rode in three different types of sidecars. When riding them, you're only about six inches off the ground. It was a dream come true; down the back straight, I knew they weren't going race speed, but it was pretty fast for me. Then when you get to the corners, you've got to move your hands to different hand grips to put your weight on the different sides of the motorbike that go around the corner, or it will tip over. It felt amazing to still be able to do this and tick it off my bucket list. However, my soninlaw bought an exAustralia Post motorbike one day for me to use. So, I rode it down the driveway, then turned around the corner and fell off, so he sold it after that.

I fill my days with knitting or crocheting. Lots of different things help fill my time. Recently I knitted four granny square jackets with matching bags for friends. I've knitted jumpers, crocheted different clothing and knitted lots of toys, for which I have won prizes at the Geelong Show and the MS Art Show; you name it, and I've probably knitted it. I see myself knitting and crocheting in the future until my hands or arms stop working.

My symptoms nowadays are that my right leg is very weak; it only lifts off the ground about four inches. I can't stand on my right leg and balance; I would lose my balance. But I can stand on the left leg for ages and won't lose my balance. MS is basically only affecting my right leg, but not my right arm and I get a bit of backache because I'm not walking properly anymore. I sort of slouch to one side when I walk.

I am no longer on diseasemodifying therapy. The only thing I tried when I was first diagnosed was an infusion that I used to have to go into the private hospital in the oncology department. It took an hour for this little bottle that went in through my wrist as an IV. Once every three months for two years, I had all sorts of heart tests and everything because my neurologist said it could have irreversible damage to my heart. I used to feel rather uncomfortable because I'd be dressed in highvisibility clothes from delivering parcels. I'd go trotting into oncology and see all the people sitting there who obviously looked very sick, had tubes coming out of them, and their hair had fallen out. I'd often wonder what they thought I was in there for as I looked fine. But I wasn't fine. When it was all done, I went back to my neurologist. He said, *we've decided now it doesn't do anything for primary progressive, and I can't do anything for you. If you want to take my advice and do something you really want to do, like climb Mount Everest, do it now because you might not be able to do it in three years.*

He was very abrupt and to the point, but yeah, there have been no medicines to take. I tried a drug once, but I can't remember what it was called. It had a nickname of *the walking drug*; I had to take it at exactly the same time every day. The neurologist, who was different, was a female this time, and she timed me walking up the passage, and I had to turn around and walk back. And then, after I tried this drug for a month, she did it again. There was no improvement, and the drug was extremely expensive. She said *you can get a compound mixture, but it's not as good, and since the real stuff didn't work, the compound one's not going to work either.*

I attend a peer support group on a Wednesday, run by Gen U, for people with MS, and I believe it's very important to keep social. In attending peer support groups for MS, we talk about different issues that people might not talk about, like sex when you have MS and all that sort of thing. You don't feel so alone when you're with peers.

I attend JUZT art for a weekly art wellness class, where I am exploring my creative side. Justine runs the classes, pushing me to try new things, such as painting, and encourages me to enter art competitions around the state.

I also found a craft group of ladies that meet at Cloverdale Community Center on a Thursday, where we do all sorts of crafts, knitting, crocheting, macramé, painting rocks, and lots of other stuff. I like to keep my mind and my hands busy.

With the introduction of NDIS, I now receive a lot of support which has improved my quality of life. One of the tasks they do for me is that I don't have to mow the lawn anymore. I don't do a lot of cooking because the person that comes to clean the house also cooks meals Tuesdays and Thursdays and quite often doubles the quantity so there's enough for another day. I have lots of mobility aids such as walkers, walking sticks, mobility scooters and many things like that, which have made my life a lot easier. I first felt like it was taking away my independence to use these pieces of equipment. I soon realised I was actually gaining back my independence.

I regularly go to the gym. It's mainly cardio stuff to keep me fit, which helps with that. I do lots of stretching of the muscles in my legs that I don't use by just normal walking around the house. I believe if you don't use it, you lose it. And because I can't clone myself and have one person sit around doing nothing, and the person is doing all these exercises. I can't prove that it keeps you walking, but if I'm doing everything I can to keep walking, then hopefully, that is going to continue to happen.

If I meet someone new, I will describe what MS is. My usual comment is, if you're walking down the street, what are you thinking about? You might be thinking, *I've got to get home in time to get the washing off the line*, or *what am I going to have for dinner tonight*? But when I'm walking down the street, I'm actually talking to my right leg, saying lift, extend, down, lift, extend, down. If I forget to do that, that is when I will most likely stumble or trip over and land on the ground.

I've never been good at remembering names, so I can't blame that on MS! My last MRI showed there was no new damage, so I'll take that win.

In the last 20 years, I've actually done some amazing things with my life since having to live with MS. I have tried to not let it stop me from trying to do things such as motorbike riding and camel riding, going on four cruises and on one adventure, I got to ride an elephant.

When travelling on a cruise, I take a walking frame. The biggest problem is the lifts. When you're standing there waiting for the lift, all these nondisabled people come, and as soon as the door opens, everyone rushes in and turns around and looks at you and says, *oh, we're full now, and you can't fit in.* People need to be more considerate of people with disabilities. We went on day tours; usually, there was room to take the walker, or I just took a walking stick. I found getting on and off the boat easy, which was a big fear. There is always somebody holding your hand, so you don't fall over. I would recommend getting a disability cabin when cruising to make your life a lot easier.

I've learned to play the little old lady bit really well. For instance, my phone's got something that's not working properly on it. I walk into the shop, and there are usually some young guys standing there, and I ask, *could you please help an old lady with this stupid phone? I don't know what it's doing.* Then they push a few buttons, and I say, *oh, thank you so much. Oh, geez, you're clever.* Then one day, I went and bought them a little bucket of doughnuts and took it back to them.

I don't get angry anymore, probably because of my age. I don't really think MS stops me from doing a lot of things I would normally do or couldn't do for my age. Bending down and picking up something is the worst of all; I can't quite get down low enough to see if it's going to be picked up with my first finger and my thumb. It's hard to get down that last little bit—I couldn't pick up a fivecent coin the other day, and that made me cross. I always pick them up; you know that oldfashioned saying, look after the pennies and the pounds will look after themselves. Pick up enough five cents, and you've got one dollar.

I do drop a lot of things, such as a lightweight pencil that sort of slips out of my hand, and that's frustrating. But that could be old age too. Who would know?

We tend to think because we have MS that nothing else is going to go wrong in our bodies. I'm also waiting for a hip replacement, which makes me cross, but it's the system. Look out when I get my new hip!

I feel acceptance is very important and helps to keep you moving forward; accept it and keep going. Do whatever you can to overcome it. Maybe you have to do something different from what you used to do to get the same result—but do it.

Nobody has yet found a cure for MS, so there is no point in stewing over something you can't change. I try to keep a positive mindset because then I'm not spending energy fighting something.

My words of wisdom to anyone newly diagnosed are to keep going. There is nothing much you can do about it. So, pick up the pieces and do whatever you can whenever you can.

ABOUT DIANE

Diane Barclay, 73, was diagnosed with MS at 54, not fitting the typical age group. Her journey with MS has been filled with challenges and subtle symptoms. Despite facing difficulties like balance issues and weakness in her right leg, Diane maintains a positive outlook on life. She enjoys knitting, crocheting, and exploring her creative side. Diane embraces various activities and has accomplished incredible feats, like riding a camel and trying motorbike racing. She stays active at the gym and attends support groups to remain social. Diane's determination and acceptance of her condition serve as an inspiration to others with MS, encouraging them to keep moving forward and finding joy in life.

Watch the VLOG/Podcast of Diana on YouTube

3

Leanne Boothroyd

MY MS JOURNEY

To be able to come up with my chapter, I first had to work through the process of deciding what I was going to write about. I found this a little difficult as after 20 years of having MS, I naturally had a lot of stories to share! Like being pregnant and being a mum with MS, having MS for 20 years, navigating the NDIS, my MS moments, symptoms and even sayings and songs that have helped me keep my spirits up when I feel low. I hope my chapter will help other people in a similar situation and, by sharing my story, it can help to normalise your feelings. Happy reading.

I had started my writing earlier but unfortunately got sick, which included an unexpected COVID diagnosis and a stay in the COVID ward in a Melbourne hospital. This had me very fearful, thinking I didn't want to get another infection on top of COVID knowing my compromised immune system or being surrounded by people on ventilators, as shown nightly on the news. I then had a stay at a rehabilitation hospital to rebuild my strength as COVID had given me a flare. During all this, I was finding it difficult to find time to write in between physiotherapy and occupational therapy appointments and regular nursing checks. I knew I wanted to continue to write, but I didn't want it to become a stressful experience on top of trying to get better, so I decided to combine two stories into one. My first story is about my D-Day or my diagnosis day. My second story is about my decision to use mobility aids.

The first story was naturally very emotional as I had to remember quite a stressful time in my life. At times, I wondered if I would be able to write anything at all.

My D-Day. To somebody without MS, they probably don't know what it means, but to somebody with MS, it means the day they were diagnosed. It is basically the day a new normal begins and you get used to saying the words—I have MS. MS is sometimes referred to the snowflake disease, as no two people experience it the same way. After 20 years, I'm still trying to understand. The disease, to me, can change almost hour by hour or minute by minute whether it be movement, a feeling in your hands or feet or even your cognitive function.

My D-Day was somewhere in April 2002. The actual date is a bit of a blur because when you get onto the medical merry-go-round, you can lose track of days very quickly, but I remember the day vividly. I was 28 and was working for a consulting firm in a project support role. I was a bit of a gym junkie, often going to the gym three or four times a week to keep my body in great shape. I loved doing a weight or boxing class and learning the routines. I had my special gym clothes and memberships at the local gym near work and the local YMCA near my flat. I had a routine of working, taking gym classes and going out with friends. On a day that I was working, I remember I used to run from work—yes, I could run then—into the gym to join my class. It was such a thrill when I knew the class routine off by heart and when I became confident enough to move to the front of the class.

Over a few weeks, often at the end of a class, something started to feel off in my body and I knew that something wasn't right. I was really tired and didn't want to go to the gym. As I had had

Glandular Fever in Year 12 and didn't want a repeat of it, I backed off going to the gym, started take it easy and getting more sleep. After a while, I felt better and went back at the gym. All was good, but after a while, I started feeling really hot and couldn't cool down after a class. I also had strange feelings like tingling on the inside of my legs. It was a different tingling from when you've sat in one place too long, and your leg goes to sleep. Whenever I felt it, I tried to shake my legs around to get the blood going, but no matter how many times I would move my legs or rub them, it wouldn't change the sensation. I was scared and frightened and didn't know what was happening to me. As I always put my health first and given the Glandular Fever previously I went to my doctor to get a blood test, and to the chiropractor in case there was something wrong with my back. The blood test and the chiropractor could not detect anything wrong or out of place. So, I went back to the doctor, who suggested an MRI of my brain and spine and suggested it could be something neurological.

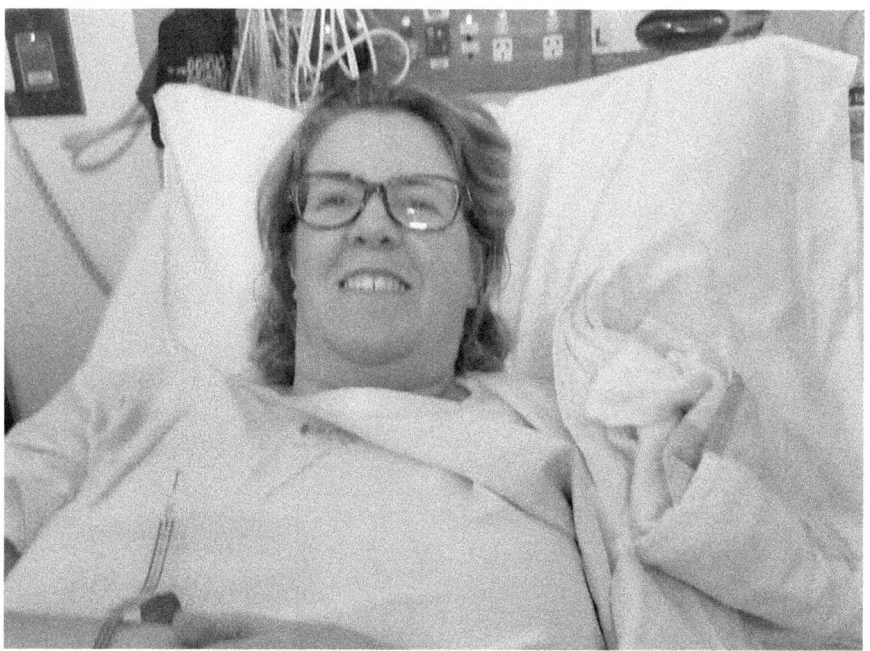

Even to suggest it was something neurological was scary and frightening for me, and I questioned the doctor about what they could be testing for. She responded with transverse myelitis or multiple sclerosis. In the back of my mind—I'm not religious—I was praying for transverse myelitis, as I had no idea about the implications of an MS diagnosis. The only thing I knew of MS was the MS Readathon. I did a little research on both and didn't want to jump to a conclusion. I would wait for the appointment and the results. It was a nervous wait, and I don't even remember the time going by. I tried to busy myself and act like nothing was wrong.

The day came for me to go back to see the neurologist for my results at Monash Hospital. I took my mum with me for support. I was feeling great and even attended a couple of gym classes during the week to deal with the stress. I wanted to cancel the appointment so I could go to the gym or go out with my friends. I even rang the office to see if I could reschedule, but I wasn't allowed to. Instead, the receptionist said *it would be better if you did come in and get the results*. I said, *no, really, I'm good. I feel good. I'll come in another time*, to which she said again, *no, I think it would be good if you came in*.

My mind was going a million miles an hour in every direction. What did she know I didn't? What could they have found on the MRI? The first thing that came to my mind was they had found a brain tumour. I was scared and cried.

I rang my ex-boyfriend and relayed the conversation to him, telling him how nervous I was going to the appointment and what my fear was. He assured me it would all be fine and to ring him afterwards to tell him what happened.

I reluctantly went to the appointment, not knowing it would change my life forever. The building was old and outdated at Monash Hospital. I sat in the neurologist's room painted a funny eggshell yellow with white wooden trim. The room had a funny sterile smell, and there were pictures of the nervous system and certificates of the doctor's credentials on the walls.

Little did I know, it wouldn't be my last time sitting in a neurologist's office. Mum and I traded pleasantries with the doctor, and then the words which I had been dreading came to me from his mouth and lips: *you have multiple sclerosis*. I don't remember what was said next. It was all a blur, and I was confused. I'd been a healthy person, eating well, going to the gym and watching my weight. How did this happen? What did I do to cause this? Sure, I drank sometimes when I was out and ate a little junk food, but surely that wouldn't cause this. I remember there was talk of starting medication straight away and even doing a lumber puncture to confirm the diagnosis as I had lesions on my brain and spine. I was in a state of shock and couldn't say a word. I don't even remember if the doctor asked if I was okay, which I wasn't. Thankfully, Mum took over and said that we won't be making any decisions today and we'll seek a second opinion. We thanked him for his time and took his card. We left the office in the cold and dark—after arriving in the daytime—and we both cried. She held me close and hugged me tightly. Mum drove me back to their house, and I stayed the night as I was in no condition to drive after what I'd just been through. We got home and told my Dad what the doctor said, and we all cried again. I don't even remember if I was hungry. If I was, I probably had a cup of tea and a bowl of cereal—even now, it's still my go-to food when I don't feel like eating. It was the fear of the unknown and later years down the track I recognised as the start of my depression and anxiety.

Dad got out the computer and started reading some things about MS, but I couldn't bring myself to. I was still processing the conversation with the doctor. It was a late and very emotional night in the house. I don't think I slept a wink.

The next day we all struggled to get out to breakfast from the emotional situation we were in the night before. Mum made some calls as she was working for Health Care of Australia and rang someone she knew to put her in contact with the top neurologist in Melbourne. She got the name and rang his office, and we were scheduled to see him in a few weeks. While I had some time, I had to plan my next move. I couldn't even think about going back to work. What am I going to tell them? How am I going to tell my friends what was happening to me, and how will they react and what will they think of me?

One of the first things I wanted to do was tell my best friends of my diagnosis. Mum and I drove to each of their workplaces to tell them the news. I'm not sure what I expected from them, but I just knew I needed to show them I was okay and still the same old me—just with something new going on. I needed time to get my head around it, and probably even telling people and hearing the words was a start to accepting the diagnosis.

I actually quit my job and stopped doing gym for a while. I needed some time to sort things out. Little did I know, I went through grief. Grieving the life I once had and accepting the new life ahead of me. I had actually sunk into a depression and didn't want to see anyone. I did however use Facebook to find MS support groups and people like me. During that time, I met another neurologist who had a better bedside manner and didn't want to rush me into a medication regime or do a lumber puncture. Instead, he wanted to wait and see how things went and, if there was anything new happening, to call him straight away. Sadly, something new happened with my eyes, and I went to see him. A repeat MRI of my brain and spine was ordered, and another lesion showed up. I was given Rebif injectables and scheduled to meet the MS nurse to learn how to administer them. My MS medication journey had just begun—that is another story! Now onto the second part of my story about mobility aids.

One of my first decisions to use a mobility aid was after the birth of my son in 2009. My relapse after I had him affected my mobility and I required the use of a cane to help me walk and safely get around. I was adamant that there was no way I was going to have an older person's cane—despite my using my grandfather's old wooden one prior—and went on the search of finding something younger-looking. The first cane I got was a bright pink one from the chemist.

Having a baby, of course, required me to go into work to show the baby off to my colleagues. I remember the day vividly. We caught the train, arrived at work and entered my office. Friends were delighted to see me again and to meet William. It came as a bit of a shock to some, seeing me with the new baby AND a bright pink cane.

To the people that knew about my MS diagnosis, it was understood that something had happened. I mentioned to them I had a relapse, postnatal depression, and that William was sick with reflux. To others who didn't know, they asked what I had done to myself and how I became injured. I had to explain I had MS, which is hard enough in itself and probably another chapter.

During this time, and even now, I have found that I needed to work through the process of deciding that I actually needed a mobility aid to make things easier and safer for me to get around as the MS was affecting my balance. I found it was a real mental shift and saw it as a way of acknowledging the progression of the disease.

I always thought that I would be bulletproof and was never disabled enough to need one - despite people telling me I needed to get one for my safety. I knew it had to be on my terms and my decision, and I certainly didn't want something that looked like an older person would use it.

I remember many times seeing people in the MS clinic in wheelchairs and with their walkers, and I thought that wouldn't be me. It could never be me. Was this denial? It probably was. I even remember one time when I spoke to someone waiting in another part of the MS clinic, away from everyone else. I asked her why she was waiting out there. She responded by saying she didn't want to be near other people in a wheelchair, as it was too hard for her to look at. I completely understood what she was feeling.

In the earlier days when I was driving, and my son was younger, I often had to pick him up from daycare, school or attend school activities such as assemblies or reading time. I would unpack my mobility scooter from the back of my car and almost didn't want to be seen with it by other mums, teachers, or other children. I was too embarrassed when they looked at me differently, and I didn't want to be judged as less of a mum. My son, however, thought it was cool and would often jump on my scooter to ride it with me until he got too big to do this.

Over the years, I have found different authors and bloggers such as Ardra Shepherd and Zoe Simmons who have written articles about using mobility aids and the freedom they give you as I always thought mobility aids were only for the elderly or people who literally couldn't move without them. I found having articles like this, written by women like me so empowering. https://www.jeanhailes.org.au/news/mobility-aids-are-freedom-machines-zoe-simmons

I now use a number of mobility aids, including several four-wheeled walkers, a mobility scooter and have recently acquired my custom-fit powered wheelchair to use when I get too fatigued to move around.

Using them can be confronting, but they make life a bit easier to do things. It can expose your vulnerability but doesn't change the person you are or the fact that you have a disability and certainly doesn't make you less of a person by using them. Instead it gives you a bit more freedom to do things, like see a concert or a movie or even enjoy a meal at a restaurant. This is so important for your brain and mood to keep your life as normal as possible.

I read something the other day on another MS site called Positive Living with MS - which really resonated with me - Don't get caught up in the negativity of the struggle. Yes, MS is a reality... but there are so many good things in life that are a reality too. Know that what you focus on is what you grow, so if you focus on the negative, that's what will grow. Instead, find something that brings you joy and make that your focus. Find a purpose that's bigger than your struggle. You have one!

MS is not a death sentence. There are great drugs available to help keep your MS at bay and under control. It is scary and daunting and a life changing event. I used it as a wake up call to me. Have I got support in my friends and family that I need? Am I living my best life? Are there things I would/could/should change? Take time to acknowledge how you are feeling, but don't stay there or put your roots down there. Learn and grow from the feelings. Work out what drains you. You have a limited number of spoons now. Check out the spoon theory. How will you spend them? Contact the MS society/Plus for support with your NDIS application. Join other MS groups including the medication you decide to go on and most importantly reach out for help if you need it.

ABOUT LEANNE

Leanne Boothroyd's life took a profound turn on her D-Day - the day of her Multiple Sclerosis (MS) diagnosis. Over the past 20 years, she has faced the ever-changing complexities of MS with remarkable strength and courage. Navigating the challenges of motherhood and MS, she learned to embrace the use of mobility aids as tools for freedom rather than symbols of limitation.

Leanne's journey led her to connect with like-minded individuals, finding solace in shared experiences. Through a positive outlook, she discovered the importance of focusing on joy and purpose amid life's trials.

Leanne's story is a testament to resilience, inspiring others to find strength within themselves and grasp life's joys, even in the face of adversity. By sharing her narrative, she seeks to normalize feelings and provide hope for those on similar paths.

Watch the VLOG/Podcast of Leanna on YouTube

4

Allyson Brown

HOPE EXISTS...

I'm not special. I'm just a woman who was diagnosed with MS and underwent 15 years of immunosuppressant treatment, enduring nearly 20 relapses before stabilising my health through diet. In a strange way, MS has been a blessing in disguise. Without enduring the significant hardships, I wouldn't have discovered invaluable insights that have truly changed my life.

I grew up in Geelong with my family and devoted myself to my studies, excelling throughout my school years. I was accepted into the first intake of forensic science students at Deakin University in 2000. I was one of only three people to graduate with first-class honours, being offered an Australia Postgraduate Award to complete my doctorate. My future looked bright. On 19 July 2005, my life changed forever. At only 23 years old and in the second year of my PhD journey, I received the life-altering diagnosis of relapsing-remitting MS. In an instant, my entire world was upended, leaving me to grapple with the future's uncertainty.

My first symptom occurred while running upstairs, where my right knee collapsed beneath me like a puppet whose strings had been cut. I assumed it was clumsiness. Weeks later, I noticed a strange, numb patch between my shoulder blades. I dismissed it as a pinched nerve. Weeks went by before my doctor's appointment, and during that time, my body became a mysterious puzzle. Normality was a distant memory, as every sensation felt out of place. The right side of my body became a confusing symphony of sensations, oscillating between burning heat and an oddly cool, damp feeling. I endured the unsettling sensation of needles pricking my skin, yet an eerie numbness persisted. It was a dissonant struggle between sharp pain and a feeling of emptiness. My right knee strength had succumbed to an imprisoning weakness, as if shackled by invisible restraints, rendering it a mere shadow of its former strength.

The doctor concluded that a second opinion from a neurologist was needed. The neurologist conducted further neurological assessments of my functional abilities before referring me for an MRI scan of my brain and spine, a vital diagnostic procedure to unravel the mysteries surrounding my symptoms. Instant digital results weren't available in 2005, so I found myself enduring an agonising wait for the printed results of my MRI scan. These precious pieces of paper held the key to my future.

Suddenly, a hospital registrar burst into the room, his voice reverberating with urgency as he called out, "Where's Allyson Brown?" Startled, I hesitantly raised my hand, acknowledging his inquiry.

He responded abruptly, stating, "Right, we need to get you started on treatment straight away!"

I mustered the courage to express my confusion. "Obviously, they found something on the scan, but nobody has told me anything."

The registrar's expression sank, and the wave of dread washed over him as he realised the blunder he had made. He had inadvertently shared details of the treatment prior to revealing the formal diagnosis. Regret was etched across his face as he apologised, informing me that my neurologist needed to convey the results according to hospital policy.

I sat anxiously in the waiting room as terror consumed my every thought—the distant echoes of an argument pierced through the air, further unsettling my already frayed nerves. Overwhelmed by the imminent darkness, tears cascaded down my cheeks, betraying the depth of my fears. The urgency surrounding the treatment implied a grim prognosis: a terminal diagnosis where I had mere days or weeks to live.

After an endless wait, the neurologist finally summoned me. He delivered the news that lesions had been found on both my brain and spinal cord, leading to the diagnosis of multiple sclerosis. The recommended treatment involved a three-day course of methylprednisolone, a potent corticosteroid, aimed at reducing spinal inflammation and alleviating my symptoms.

A wave of relief washed over me. I didn't have a terminal illness! I exclaimed my elation to the neurologist, who stressed the seriousness of the issue. "You realise that this is a lifelong condition? And you'll be on immunosuppressants for the rest of your life?"

Yes, it was a serious condition, but I found solace in the fact that it wasn't terminal. I was grateful to finally have a tangible reason why my body was malfunctioning!

I began immunosuppressant treatment only days after the diagnosis. I was told this would give me the best chance of being as healthy as possible for as long as possible. The initial medication prescribed to me was Betaferon, an injectable treatment that introduced flu-like symptoms, while my body became accustomed to this foreign substance being pumped into my body every second day. Each time, I gathered the courage to plunge the auto-injector into my skin, pressing the button that released the medication. The ensuing moments were met with a piercing sting as the therapeutic agent permeated my skin and coursed through my veins, only to experience sneezing, aching muscles, headaches and fatigue for hours afterwards.

In the following three years, I endured the onslaught of relapses, each wreaking havoc on various aspects of my wellbeing. Walking turned into a daily struggle as if my legs were rebelling against me. My bladder seemed to have a will of its own, disregarding my commands. Even my vision betrayed me, becoming blurry and unreliable. Additionally, I dealt with unsettling sensations of numbness, tingling, and weakness. Vertigo and unsteadiness further added to the challenges, not to mention the persistent brain fog and relentless fatigue that plagued my daily life. These recurrent flares led to frequent visits to the neurology department, where the staff knew me by name. I recall my neurologist cautioning me that if we failed to stabilise these relapses, I would be confined to a wheelchair before reaching the age of 30. The weight of such a prognosis left me grappling with a daunting question. How could I possibly control these relapses? Was it even possible? The uncertainty loomed, overshadowing my journey towards hope and recovery.

After escaping from a toxic personal relationship in 2008 that had been a significant source of stress, a remarkable shift occurred in my battle against relapses. The frequency of these debilitating episodes stabilised, dwindling to approximately one relapse per year. Alongside this pivotal change, I also transitioned to a new medication, Copaxone, which became a constant part of my routine for several years.

Fast-forward to October 2013, when I married a remarkable and compassionate man before embarking on our honeymoon adventure to Bali. My holiday carried an additional responsibility; my Copaxone injections, which required refrigeration. On the second morning of our stay, I reached for a syringe from the mini fridge, only to be met with a horrifying sight. The syringe was an icicle! Panic consumed me as I recalled instructions to discard frozen syringes. Stranded in a foreign country without access to replacements, I faced an overwhelming question, *what do I do?*

I sought advice from my neurologist about whether to risk injecting the once-frozen syringes. His feeling was that the integrity of the solution would be intact. Following his advice, I continued using the syringes and didn't encounter any immediate issues.

However, one month after returning home, I was struck by intense weakness and instability in my legs, leaving me with no choice but to undergo corticosteroid treatment. Sadly, the treatment was ineffective, and I witnessed a further decline in my leg function. It was utterly devastating to experience such a rapid deterioration at the young age of 32, as I was thrust into physical disability, relying on the aid of a walking stick. In a last attempt to stop the relapse and restore my leg function, I was admitted to the hospital only days before Christmas for an experimental treatment called plasmapheresis. It was one of the most traumatic experiences of my life.

The procedure involved pumping my blood out, spinning it down, removing the plasma portion, and then pumping the blood back in with new plasma. Effectively, it's an oil change for the blood. The hope was to remove the active antibodies involved in the overactive immune response. Due to my small veins, the nurses made over a dozen attempts to insert the lines. I was a human pin cushion, with my once smooth skin now adorned with shades of black and purple, scarred by multiple punctures. Eventually, they found a vein large enough to insert the cannula. However, the extensive attempts had caused considerable tissue damage, rendering this method impractical for the next plasmapheresis session three days later.

To allow me to get my remaining treatments, I would need to have a central line guided into my heart, bypassing the need for inserting cannulas into my damaged veins. On Monday, 30 December, at 8:00 am, I underwent surgery. It quickly became apparent that the experience was not going to be smooth, as the nurses failed to identify my medication allergies, despite them being clearly listed on my admission forms. Inside the operating room, I lay on the bed while a nurse attempted to engage in awkward conversation to pass the time as we awaited the arrival of the doctor, who was running late. When he finally entered the room, dressed in a casual Hawaiian shirt, his apology for his tardiness seemed half-hearted as he muttered, "Sorry, I'm late! Thank goodness it's the last Monday before New Year's." It was evident that, mentally, he had already checked out.

After donning his lab coat, the doctor confirmed the procedure.

"I'll make a small incision near your collarbone and insert a line into your heart for faster administration of antibiotics," he stated confidently.

Antibiotics? Wait, something didn't add up. I interjected, "That sounds almost right, but it's for plasmapheresis, not antibiotics."

The doctor appeared puzzled. "No, it's definitely for antibiotics," he insisted, his tone firm.

I shook my head. "Ah, it's definitely plasmapheresis, as I'm booked in straight after this procedure!" I corrected him, growing more frustrated by the minute.

The doctor went back to the paperwork, flipping through the pages and reading them over again. After a moment of silence, he asked hesitantly, "You're Kathleen Brown, right?"

I was in shock. "No, I'm ALLYSON Brown! I understand it's a common name, but we are definitely two different people!" I exclaimed, the disbelief evident in my voice.

The doctor burst into laughter at his mistake.

"Oh, lucky you mentioned something, as it would have been the wrong procedure!"

My confidence shattered like glass on concrete. Moments before, I was to be sliced open by this *medical professional* who failed to confirm the most basic information, like the NAME of the patient!

As the doctor and nurses laughed off their error, I lay on the bed, my head turned to the side, fixated on the rhythmic beeps of the heart-rate monitor. The bed was tilted downward, causing my head to hang lower than my heart. After a small incision, the doctor began feeding the central line down a main artery into my heart.

BOOM! A jolt of terror coursed through my body as a loud, thudding sensation pounded within my chest. My heart erupted in a chaotic dance of palpitations and irregular rhythms, engulfing me in waves of tachycardia and cardiac arrhythmia. The air escaped from my lungs, leaving me gasping for breath—the overwhelming fear of dying washed over me. Strangely, tears defied gravity, rolling upward on my face, mirroring my distress. In a matter of seconds, my heartbeat skyrocketed from 60 to 120 beats per minute.

In a feeble attempt to provide comfort, the nurse patted my trembling hands while uttering the dismissive words, "... it's just a bit of a funny feeling ..." Each condescending word felt like a slap in the face, failing to grasp the gravity of the situation unfolding.

I had entered survival mode. Minutes stretched out like an eternity as panic and despair gripped me. Aware of my escalating panic, I fought to regain control, my heart pounding in my chest like a frantic animal caught in a snare. With every ounce of determination, I attempted to restore rhythm to my breath: in two, three, four ... out two, three, four ... in two, three, four ... out two, three, four ... Slowly, my heart settled, ceasing its tumultuous beating. The procedure was finally over. Physically, it would take weeks for the trauma endured by my heart to heal, but the emotional wounds would last forever.

Months went by, and the ongoing struggle of needing assistance to walk weighed heavily on me. It was during this time that I was prescribed a new oral medication called Tecfidera. As time passed and my body gradually adjusted to my new mobility, I felt a growing desire to return to work. Equipped with my trusty walking stick, I embarked on a daily commute to the office, accompanied by a supportive friend behind the wheel. Though my mobility remained compromised, it did not hinder my mental acuity, so it felt good to engage in meaningful work again.

Little did I know that a life-changing conversation would unfold, ready to redefine the course of my future.

A co-worker with a similar autoimmune condition raised the idea of changing my diet to improve my health. She mentioned how the paleo diet had worked wonders for her. At first, the notion that diet could improve such a serious condition as MS seemed ludicrous to me. But when she presented me with the cookbook, I felt compelled to try it. After all, what did I have to lose? Initially, I felt angry at the thought of giving up food that made me happy. I was reluctant but knew I needed to try. Knowing I couldn't do it alone, I expressed my desire to embark on this new dietary challenge with my husband. Aware of the potential benefits it could bring to my health, my husband offered his unwavering support. Together, we purged our pantry and refrigerator of inflammatory foods, replenishing them with nourishing whole foods.

Months after the treatment and while embracing the new diet, a remarkable transformation unfolded. My leg function gradually restored to its former state, and my overall sense of wellbeing improved. Life had gone back to normal. Yet, amidst this remarkable progress, I failed to recognise the pivotal role that food played in my revitalised health. Tragically, this lack of awareness led me to gradually slip back into my old eating habits over four years. And in 2018, I experienced a monumental relapse that changed everything.

This relapse caused crippling fatigue and cognitive issues, tangling me in a suffocating prison of physical and mental anguish. I was plunged into unparalleled depths of darkness and despair, feeling utterly helpless and disheartened. This persisted for months. The question lingered in my mind: *would I ever get better?* Frequent hospital admissions became a norm as I sought relief from chronic pain. I was also seeing a psychologist for guidance and emotional support in navigating these dark recesses of my mind. Despite working as an analyst, I had moments where simple math, for example, 8 divided by 2, eluded me. I grappled with debilitating fatigue that engulfed every aspect of my existence. Basic tasks became immense challenges as if I were wading through thick mud. The weight of exhaustion was unrelenting, draining any remnants of energy and joy from my life. Alongside the physical burden, I battled devastating anxiety and depression, overshadowing my daily experiences and making each day an arduous journey. These symptoms rendered me incapable of maintaining employment. With a heavy heart, I made the difficult decision to resign, recognising the pressing need to find a way to restore my health.

There was a specific moment etched in my memory when I found myself sitting on the sofa at home, staring blankly out the window like a zombie. It was here that the harsh reality hit me. If I couldn't uncover the path to recovery, this miserable existence would be the best life had to offer. Somewhere in the back of my mind, I recalled the positive impact that eating a healthy diet had on me several years before. Reluctantly, I made the decision to give it another try. With no energy or motivation to fuel these changes, my sole driving force was the fear of being forever imprisoned in my broken body. I held little faith that dietary changes would help. However, with no other avenues left to explore and my health at rock bottom, I felt compelled to try.

I reluctantly started eating healthy again, recording weekly blog videos to hold myself accountable, fully aware that if given the opportunity, I would try to cheat. After two weeks, I felt no improvement and wanted to quit. A Facebook friend who went through a similar journey encouraged me to stick with it for three months, as it could take that long to see positive results. I made a deal with myself: three months was the limit. If I didn't feel improvements by then, I would abandon the diet, satisfied that I had at least tried.

Three months passed before I finally felt it—I could think clearly! The fog in my mind lifted, unveiling a newfound clarity. Energy coursed through my veins, reminiscent of my childhood. The heavy burden of anxiety and depression had vanished, replaced by a sense of positivity and freedom. At that moment, I rediscovered myself. The true essence of who I was. It was an indescribable feeling, a sensation of being whole and alive again. The sheer joy and relief washed over me like a tidal wave, flooding every fibre of my being with hope.

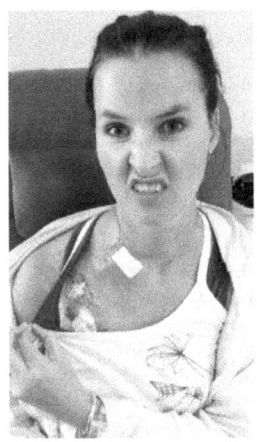

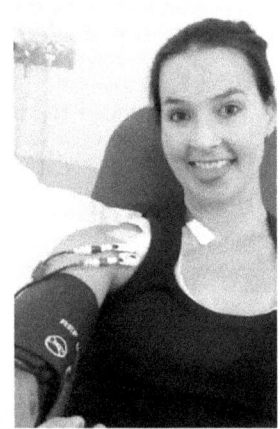

Baffled by the results, I delved into extensive research. I immersed myself in the wisdom of functional medical practitioners, naturopaths, and researchers from around the world. They emphasised a simple yet powerful truth: food can either fuel our bodies or sabotage our health. It can promote healing or trigger harmful inflammation. Sadly, our modern Western diets tend to lean towards inflammation rather than healing. The revelation hit me like a lightning bolt. I'd been addicted to inflammatory foods without realising the toll they were taking on my health and immune system, fuelling chronic inflammation within me. I came to realise that media propaganda had influenced my beliefs, blinding me to the truth.

However, I still needed tangible evidence that changing my diet had actually improved my health. I meticulously analysed my MS journal, documenting my relapses, medications, diet, and symptoms. It became evident that there were some clear correlations between my diet and improvements in my health. My relapses were certainly more pronounced during periods of heightened stress. Conversely, the four-year span from 2014 to 2018, during which I adhered to the paleo diet, showed stability in my condition and no relapse activity. I never realised it! Adopting a healthy diet had played a pivotal role in reducing inflammation within my body and halting the regularity of my relapses. Upon reflection, I realised that the diet I once considered harmless had contributed to my declining health, in addition to my excessive alcohol consumption and 30-year addiction to junk food, sugar and painkillers. I vowed never to return to my old habits, as it was clear that eating an anti-inflammatory diet had genuinely improved my MS.

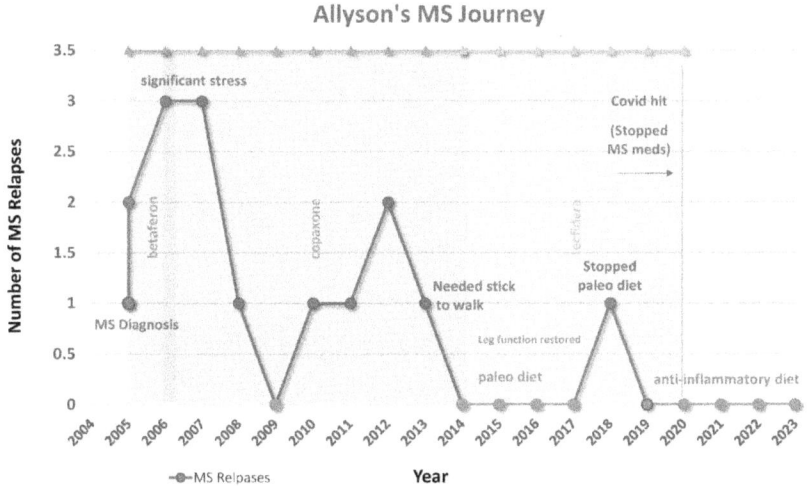

I realised that this is our normal way of living in modern society, and there would be others just like me. People who would be blissfully unaware of the hidden toxic ingredients in our plethora of processed and packaged foods that line our supermarket shelves and creep their way into our mouths, gradually building inflammation in our bodies and leading to serious health consequences. I knew I wanted to help change this.

I'm now dedicated to sharing my extensive research with fellow autoimmune sufferers, aiming to raise awareness and educate them about the profound impact of their dietary choices, empowering them to improve their health naturally to regain control. In 2020, I created my business, *everheal*, containing transformative programs designed to educate, motivate, and empower those with autoimmune conditions to adopt an anti-inflammatory diet. I've been fortunate to witness life-changing client results again and again, which reaffirm that I'm now on the right path, providing guidance, support, education, and the development of healthy daily habits so others can live the life they deserve.

Had I not endured the relapses and health struggles associated with my MS and hitting rock bottom with my health, I wouldn't have discovered the life-changing impact that simple dietary improvements can have on inflammatory conditions like MS. I wholeheartedly recommend for anyone to embrace an anti-inflammatory diet and lifestyle to improve their health, allowing them to live their best lives. I know that change is scary. As someone who once thought dietary changes were impossible, believe me when I say that if I can successfully implement them into my life, then I know you can too!

Best wishes on your journey. Always remember to aim high, follow your dreams and never give up on yourself!

Watch the VLOG/Podcast of Allyson on YouTube

ABOUT ALLYSON

Allyson Brown is an accomplished visionary, revered for her expertise and transformative approach. As the Director of everheal www.everheal.com.au, she leads the innovative LIFE Formula Program, leaving a profound impact on countless lives across the globe. Allyson's journey into Analytical Research led to the completion of her PhD in 2010 and exploration into functional medicine, a testament to her unwavering commitment to continuous learning and development.

Her influence extends both nationally and internationally, as she captivated audiences at the 2020 Virtual Disability Expo with her innovative and educational presentation. Allyson's thought-provoking talks gained her further acclaim at the esteemed 2022 & 2023 Symptom Free MS Summit, establishing her reputation as a global authority.

Her remarkable contributions have been recognised by reputable publications such as TickerNews, TickerInsights, GT Magazine, and MS InTouch Magazine, further establishing her as a leader in her field. Driven by an unyielding passion to enhance the lives of individuals grappling with chronic illnesses and autoimmune disease, Allyson goes above and beyond to educate, uplift, and empower them on their journey to cultivate natural health, enabling them to unlock their full potential.

Email: info@everheal.com.au
Website: www.everheal.com.au
Facebook group: https://www.facebook.com/groups/autoimmunediet/

Facebook: https://www.facebook.com/allyson.everheal/
Instagram: https://www.instagram.com/everheal_/
LinkedIn: https://www.linkedin.com/in/allyson-brown-everheal/

5

Amanda Campbell

BENDING LIKE BAMBOO

When we are tired, stressed, and anxious, we tend to overthink the future, and we can become stuck in the past, living on autopilot. You know how it feels when you are checked out, disengaged, and not your best self. This impacts our ability to be at our best, at home, at work and within our relationships. Every single day we are going through change. Sometimes, life brings bigger changes, like a diagnosis, illness, divorce, or death.

No matter what I have been through, a paralysis, MS, the ending of a business or a relationship, grieving after losing my Mum from cancer only four weeks after her diagnosis. I have learned that when we feel well, we can adjust and adapt. With a more flexible mindset, we can be more solution-focused, confident, and resilient. Being able to navigate solutions through the more difficult times we face can reduce our stress levels, promoting more repair in our minds and bodies. It is with a more elevated mindset that we can access more elevated emotions of love, joy, compassion, courage, and resilience; letting go of fear, anger, worry and overthinking.

I believe that flexibility in our mindset impacts everything that matters, our body's ability to repair, how happy and resilient we are, and how we show up in our lives. I would love to share my story with you about how I learned to Bend Like Bamboo.

Nearly 20 years ago, life was not the same.

At age 24, I was diagnosed with multiple sclerosis (MS), and five years later, I was paralysed in a wheelchair.

I had to learn how to rebuild my mind, body, and life. This was the hardest and darkest time of my life. It was like looking at a candle in a well-lit room; you don't really notice the light. It's when everything becomes dark that is a time when you find your light and what you are truly capable of.

On this journey, I had to learn how to believe in myself and face my fears. I discovered that a flexible mindset was the key to overcoming my biggest challenges. I know first-hand how stressful and overwhelming it can be when diagnosed to live with an autoimmune disease.

Paralysed down the entire left-hand side of my body, unable to wash, walk or feed myself, I was given only a 50% chance of ever walking again.

With no choice but to succeed, I channelled my energy with a mountain of determination and a balanced approach, adopting Eastern and Western medicines and recovering. When I got my strength back, I hit the books and began to research, and I managed to find other stories of recovery. I studied for a Diploma in Sports Kinesiology in 2011 and opened Bend Like Bamboo in 2013. In 2014, I had an amazing opportunity to co-found a business called Nourissh that delivered fresh and healthy ready-made meals.

When I needed repair, or to perform at work, I discovered that a flexible mindset impacts everything that matters: our body's ability to repair, how happy and resilient we are and how connected we feel.

My diagnosis

When I was young, I was always a motivated, happy, and driven girl. My twin sister Nicole and I were lucky to attend schools that offered not only academics but also sports and music. We had a passion for music, which led us to pursue a music career, and we wrote our own music with producers. We were living the dream. I was enjoying life in every way possible, working in the fashion industry, a career I loved. I was happy, dating and going out with my friends.

At age 19, we were studying music theatre and dance full-time. This was the year I first experienced pins and needles down the left-hand side of my face and fingertips. I went to my local doctor, who then ordered an MRI. They found one lesion on my brain, but there was no diagnosis. My symptoms eventually resolved, and I just got on with my life.

I fell into the fashion industry, a career I loved throughout my 20s. At age 24, my symptoms came back. But this time, the numbness progressed to weakness on the left side of my body. Another MRI showed two new lesions in my brain, and I was diagnosed with multiple sclerosis. From that moment on, everything just stopped. Feeling stressed and uncertain about my future, I began to focus on what I didn't want and what I feared; that I might end up disabled, bedridden, or worse. So, I went out later, I worked harder and disconnected more and more from the inner conflict that was brewing in my body. I lost hope in the future and what could be possible in my life. Externally, I was still driven; I worked and played hard. But on the inside, I was terrified and wanted to disconnect from the fear and pain.

I had a few minor symptoms over the next few years, including numbness, balance issues, and weakness on the left-hand side of my body. But they were often years apart, so this allowed me to live in denial of my diagnosis. The symptoms returned at age 29, and I had a big relapse. Gradually, over a slow, cruel 10 days, the entire left-hand side of my body became completely paralysed. My face dropped, my left arm twisted, and my hip, leg and foot completely stopped working on the left side of my body. I lost the ability to walk, wash and feed myself, and I couldn't get dressed without help. I lost my financial independence, my ability to work and life as I knew it. I had to completely stop and reset.

I went from running around, enjoying my life, to standing still and paralysed. I was living life to its fullest and suddenly found myself in turmoil and darkness. I went from feeling in complete control of my future to feeling totally helpless.

In less than 10 days, my whole world had crumbled as my body slowly, day by day, became paralysed. I could not feel or move the left-hand side of my body. It became dead and heavy. My sister literally had to drag me, on her back, up and down stairs along the carpet to see my doctor. They checked me into the hospital at the beginning of January 2009, and I knew going in that I wasn't going to be leaving anytime soon. They started me on a high dose of steroids for three days to reduce the inflammation in my brain. I was not responding—so they continued for five days, but I still could not move.

I was transferred into rehab at Epworth Richmond in Melbourne, and the work began. I stayed for two months. I hit rock bottom, and I had to ask myself, *am I ever going to walk again?* I was stretched to my limits emotionally and physically, beyond normal comprehension, and everything stopped.

In one of my first rehab sessions, I was given an exercise by my neuro-physiotherapist. I had to try to make my fingers open and close, and tears ran down my face because it was so hard. I knew that, at that moment, I had a choice. I could either give up or I had to change my mind about what I believed could be possible to get different results.

Typically, we had Tuesday night girls' night, but I could not be there because I was living in the hospital. One week, all the girls came in with my sister, and they wheeled me across the road to a restaurant, and we all had dinner together. It was so wonderful laughing, connecting, and feeling normal again for a few hours. Perhaps because of the polarity of going through such a difficult time, the joy I felt in those moments, being present with my friends, was profound. I will never forget how elevated and connected my mind and body felt that night.

I returned to my room after dinner, and my toe moved for the first time! At that moment, I found hope, and as a result, I started to channel my energy differently. Feeling hope, I had more courage to believe that I could possibly walk again. I began to shift what I believed; I started to focus on what I wanted rather than what I didn't want. I wanted to get my life and body back.

Like a woman on a mission, I was first in at physio and the last to leave, three sessions a day, five times a week. There were many weeks of no change, and that was a very difficult time contemplating living the rest of my life so disabled. Alone in my thoughts, sitting in my wheelchair, or lying in my hospital bed, a new girl inside me began to emerge.

It is amazing what can happen to us when we have no choice but to succeed. The neurologists predicted that I may never walk again, as my lesions were in the motor skill area of my brain, and my prognosis was not good. But I was determined to leave the hospital, not only walking but running! I had to learn how to use my hand again. I was taught all over again how to pick things up, and I had to learn how to walk again. Week by week, I started to get movement back in my toes and fingers, then arms and legs and my face. I started to walk with a foot brace. Then I progressed from walking with my knee taped up to walking on my own. And those first few steps to freedom were indescribable.

I left there running. It wasn't the most graceful of runs. I won't win medals for it. It was an awkward-looking run. But I did it in 6 weeks.

It wasn't just me; far from it. I had an amazing team of people who helped me. These people made me believe I could do it. They stood with me when I couldn't stand and helped me to believe in myself. I was blessed. I had neuro-physiotherapists, speech therapists, counsellors, occupational therapists, neurologists, kinesiologists, family, and friends. I could not have come through this with the courage and determination that I had, had it not been for my loving, supportive family and friends, particularly my twin sister, Nicole.

She was there every day and night. On some nights, she slept beside me in my single hospital bed. I cannot begin to explain how much I appreciate her and count my lucky stars for her kindness and unconditional love through the hardest time of my life.

As horrific as it was—the experience of paralysis—it was equally joyful taking those first few steps to walk again. It was in my sessions that I met and spent every day with other patients going through similar things, car accidents and strokes—so many stories and so much suffering. I found I had re-evaluated my life, and I was grateful to be getting better, finally. This sort of stuff changes you; it humbles you.

One year on, I now had full function back in my body. I took some time off and studied for a Diploma in Sports Kinesiology. I learned how to nourish my mind, body, and soul, and I began to

feel happier and more connected, and I began to repair.

Experiencing such a rapid recovery, I researched how other individuals had recovered when they were not *supposed to* and why some of us get sick, even when we seem to be eating well and exercising. Now, as the practitioner and the patient, what did I learn?

Food is medicine

When we eat better, we feel better. When we nourish our bodies on a cellular level, we can maximise repair, allowing transformation in our minds, bodies, and lives. I believe that every meal can be an opportunity to renew ourselves. Nutrition is the foundation for the health of our brain, hormones, and gut health, as well as our emotional and physical wellbeing.

I came across Dr Terry Wahls, a neurologist with secondary progressive MS. She had been confined to a tilt recline wheelchair for a few years. As a professor of medicine at the University of Iowa USA, Dr Wahls has a sound scientific background. On her journey, she discovered that if she fed the mitochondria—energy centre—of her cells, deficient in those with an autoimmune disease, she would recover from being paralysed in a wheelchair. After adopting *Wahl's Protocol*, she went from being in a wheelchair for three years to bike riding a marathon in nine months.

I had the pleasure of meeting Dr Wahl face-to-face in 2013 in Iowa, USA! A moment I'll truly never forget. I thanked her for giving me my life back.

It was an absolute game changer when I optimised my nutrition. Within a few months, my health and overall feeling in my mind and body had vastly improved. I no longer had to lie down for half the day, which was life-changing. I had more energy to walk and jog every few days. My MS symptoms started to completely subside. Emotionally, I started to get the spring back in my stride, the sparkle back in my eye. I began to fall in love with cooking and nourishing my body, a habit and attitude that translated into other areas of my life.

I learned about the science behind nutrient-dense foods from the research and personal experience of doctors. I was particularly inspired by the ones that had been through their own journey of recovery from disease. With medical backgrounds, they have managed to research their results, and some have also conducted clinical trials. In particular, I combined the work of Professor George Jelinek[1], Dr Terry Wahls[2], Dr Roy Swank[3], Dr John McDougal[4] and Dr Robynne Chutkan[5]. Their amazing work has gone on to help many people worldwide.

Destress and reset

In our modern lives, our bodies can experience high levels of stress from problems like financial worries, family issues, relationships or overworking to live up to someone else's expectations. As a result, an alarmed state can remain switched *on* in a stress response for long periods. Add to this the external stimulation from our addiction to digital media, and you have a perfect storm for anxiety, disconnection, stress, inflammation, and disease. When we are in a survival and stress response, this can lead to overthinking, stress, and a rigid mindset—not the best environment to be solution focused and to heal.

When we are calmer, happier, and less stressed, we can prioritise pathways of growth and repair. When we promote growth and repair pathways, we can feel more calm, resilient, and open to change. What we believe is what matters; our thoughts, feelings, and emotions are all connected to how our biochemistry fires.

1 https://overcomingms.org/about-us/professor-george-jelinek
2 https://terrywahls.com/
3 http://www.swankmsdiet.org/
4 https://www.drmcdougall.com/
5 https://robynnechutkan.com/

When we manage our stress better and develop a deeper anchor and connection within ourselves, this becomes integrated through our relationships and work culture. We can receive feedback more constructively, and we are less reactive. An elevated and positive state becomes contagious as we are all so connected. When we feel like a leader, we will also think and act like one.

The power of kinesiology

A kinesiologist and physiotherapist helped me walk again, which inspired me to go back to school to study sports kinesiology. I learned about Chinese medicine concepts of the mind-body connection, anatomy, and physiology.

My studies explored the body's connection structurally, biochemically, emotionally, and electromagnetically. This was the first time I had understood the body in an integrated way rather than seeing it in isolation. I discovered we don't think or function in isolation; there are many moving, dynamic parts, all connected in a very powerful way that we are yet to fully understand. Learning the traditional Chinese medicine technique and how our bodies are so connected has been an amazing experience.

Kinesiology works with the muscles connected to the brain via the nervous system. Kinesiologists use the muscles to understand the health and state of our organs and systems of the body. When tested, the integrity of our muscles gives the practitioner feedback and an insight into the mind-body connection and any imbalances that need to be assessed.

Taking a holistic approach helps a trained practitioner to find the cause of stress. I find kinesiology to be effective for both physical and emotional disorders. Some examples include relief from symptoms of disease, fertility issues, addiction, menopause, anxiety, worry, stress, pain, allergies, digestion, injuries, weight loss, grief, and inflammation.

Kinesiology is also effective for optimising performance and learning and identifying barriers to achieving our goals. After a session, I feel lighter, clearer, and more relaxed. I am better able to manage stress and take on life's challenges with an elevated and, therefore, more positive and resilient mindset.

The art of bending like bamboo

When we *Bend Like Bamboo,* we are anchored like a bamboo tree. When we discover our inner anchor, this allows us to be more flexible and resilient.

To *Bend Like Bamboo* is the ability to be flexible and adaptable in times of change. It is the ability to adapt and see our situation with fresh eyes. It is the ability to re-imagine what can be possible in our minds, bodies, and lives. It is the ability to see our obstacles as opportunities from a higher perspective. It is the ability to get out of our comfort zone to grow.

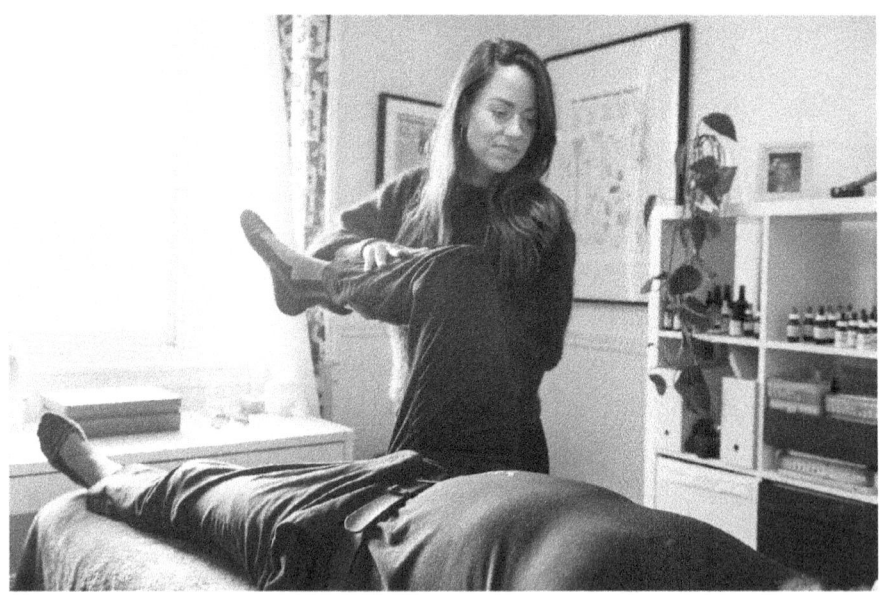

When we *Bend Like Bamboo*, we can let go of rigidity and stress and become more flexible. Just like a bamboo tree is anchored in the soil, it can bend in direct proportion to the wind without snapping. Anchored and flexible, we can change our minds about old stories and let go of what is old and redundant.

When we are flexible, we can elevate our mindset, see our situation from a higher perspective, and think in new and innovative directions. When the wind comes in life, we are prepared and believe in our ability to keep going and overcome. As resilience builds up, we can lean into uncertainty with confidence, getting out of our comfort zone, where we will grow.

With an elevated mindset, we can access more elevated emotions such as joy, compassion, forgiveness, and courage. Letting go of lower and denser emotions such as guilt, shame, anger, and worry. When we are in this more flexible state, we are more adaptable. We can optimise creativity, performance, and wellbeing.

Where I am now

2023 marked my fourteenth year of clear MRIs, no disease progression, and every year keeps getting better and better. I continue to work with a great team; I have loved specialists such as kinesiologists, naturopaths, nutritionists, acupuncturists, functional trainers and functional medical practitioners, neuro-physiotherapists, and neurologists. In my experience, having a great doctor who supports a balanced approach can be helpful.

What maximised my recovery was not just one thing. It has been a personal journey with a lot of help from many different people I have had the privilege of working with. This continues in my current maintenance program.

Taking a balanced approach has helped me to cover the broad range of moving parts I believe contribute to optimising wellness. I have an incredible neurologist who takes the time to listen to my questions and supports my initiative to be proactive and my balanced approach.

I believe that conventional medicine works well in conjunction with natural medicine. I've found that educating myself about the various fields of repair and recovery has empowered me and made me become an active and informed patient, reaping benefits from all approaches available in the field of medicine. Knowledge is power and only improves patient care. Educating ourselves about wellness prevention and dealing with the cause of disease, as well as treating symptoms, is what I hope for the future of medicine.

I hope this chapter inspires you to promote self-care and prevention, as I believe they are key to optimising wellness. I think that illness, setbacks, and changes in life are there to help us grow. As we push ourselves out of our comfort zone more and more, we realise how resilient we are and what we are truly made of. This births joy and an inner belief within us that literally changes us forever.

When you really believe in yourself, others will believe in you, too. My message is what we believe is what matters, and with flexibility, we can change our minds about what can be possible in our minds, bodies, and lives. We can re-imagine what can be possible for us, rise to our challenges with courage and resilience, and discover what we are made of. This is the space where miracles happen, where our superpower is revealed, and where we can let go of the world as we knew it and step into a new reality of possibility.

Thank you for your time and for listening to my story and the lessons I've learned along the way. I am honoured to share them with you. No matter what you are going through, I believe you can overcome it and discover just how powerful you really are.

My book *Bend Like Bamboo* will be available in 2023-2024. You can sign up on my website to receive announcements and inspiration.

May the force be with you.

Amanda x

Watch the VLOG/Podcast of Amanda on YouTube

ABOUT AMANDA

As a trained Sports Kinesiologist and MS Ambassador, Amanda specialises in multiple sclerosis and autoimmune disease. As a resilience trainer and keynote speaker, she works with leaders at work and children at school, helping them to destress and reset, and uncover blind spots to achieve their personal and professional goals.

How does she do this? Amanda teaches individuals to *Bend Like Bamboo*, via in-person and virtual kinesiology sessions, in-person and virtual workshops, online courses and retreats.

After her diagnosis of multiple sclerosis at age 24 and overcoming a left-hand side body paralysis at age 29, Amanda discovered that a flexible mindset impacts everything that matters: our body's ability to repair, how happy and resilient we are and how connected we feel.

Amanda believes that flexibility builds resilience in people, and building resilience in our mindset improves our physical wellbeing. Available in-person and online, the *Bend Like Bamboo* program is customisable for individuals, schools, and workplaces nationally.

The clinic:

Website: www.bendlikebamboo.com
Facebook: www.facebook.com/BendLikeBamboo
Instagram: www.instagram.com/bendlikebamboo

Amanda's blog, podcast, courses, and workshops:

Website: www.amandacampbell.com.au
Facebook: www.facebook.com/amandacampbellspeaker
Instagram: www.instagram.com/amandacampbell_speaker/
Twitter: twitter.com/AmandaC_health
LinkedIn: www.linkedin.com/in/amandacampbellau
Blog: www.amandacampbell.com.au/blog
Podcast: www.amandacampbell.com.au/podcasts
YouTube: www.youtube.com/user/BendLikeBamboo

6

Don Campanile

ASKING FOR HELP IS A SIGN OF STRENGTH, NOT WEAKNESS

At the age of 50, I never thought this would be the life that I would be living. But I am, and I am sure making the best of it.

By the end of November 2016, I had headaches for a good two weeks. One morning I woke up seeing a grey spot in my eye. After going to my doctor, I was referred to a hospital in Melbourne. After all the tests they did, they were pretty sure it was optic neuritis. They did an MRI, although they didn't find any lesions. However, they said that it was the start of MS. So, I ended up having the three days steroid treatment while I was there.

So yeah, that is when it all started. It was funny when they did the MRI when it was optic neuritis. They didn't find anything to suggest it was MS. It's just funny how, in a matter of nine months after that, they found six lesions. I didn't realise you can develop symptoms without it showing like Christmas lights in your brain.

From that point on, I was having MRIs every six months, and then I think it wasn't even a year after that. They found some lesions, three on the brain and three down the spinal cord. It all started from that damage to my body.

I was diagnosed by a different specialist but have been fortunate to have a great relationship with my neurologist ever since being diagnosed at the Geelong University Hospital. I didn't realise when I was diagnosed that there were even different types of MS. I have RRMS. When I was diagnosed, I was terrified. Did I say I was terrified? I knew I would never get better, as there was no cure. I got used to the idea, but it was just terrifying. I wasn't having too many symptoms to start with; then you do the worst thing you could ever do and jump on Dr Google. All I read were negative things. A lot that I now know was just false information. You won't see many positive things online, with very few concerning this disease. Hopefully, this book changes people's perspective that there are plenty of good things in all our lives despite having MS. I am very careful nowadays about what I read. If I want to find out something about MS, I ask my neurologist.

I went into a deep depression after being diagnosed, then adding to that, Dr Google. Depression kicked in big time, and there have been some very dark days.

I had been married, and we divorced in 2013. Then I met another woman I wanted to spend the rest of my life with. We were engaged, and life was good. We had been planning our wedding to happen in 2018, but she couldn't deal with the MS thing.

I couldn't believe someone who was supposed to love me and spend the rest of their life with me had little support or compassion. I turned around and said, *what if you went through this sh*t? I'd be supporting you. I would one hundred per cent support you.* She said *yes, but what if you end up in a wheelchair?* What if this? What if that? What if, what if! All these what ifs. Everyone knows someone that's got it, and we are all different. MS affects people differently, depending on the lesions where they are. We can't compare our journeys with MS; we are all different.

Every night she got into bed, she would be crying. I'd ask *what's wrong with you?* And she would start again and carry on with the what ifs. Some people handle it better than others. None of us know what tomorrow will bring, so we live the best day and each day we possibly can. She broke it all off and left. I let her go. If a person can't handle your diagnosis, how will they ever stand by you when sh*t gets real.

Often, it's easier to be there for yourself and not have to worry about how someone else will react when things go wrong. In saying that, I put myself back out into the dating pool.

Before being diagnosed, my only knowledge of MS was I remember as a child doing the MS Readathon at primary school. I took that sheet of paper around the neighbourhood, collecting signatures and a promise of money for each book I read. Never did I think I'd ever get it.

Telling my family was tough, I told them, and they were there for me, unconditionally to support me and still are. A different type of support that I had and have today is just amazing with MS Connect. MS Connect came along at the right time for me. They helped me with counselling, some therapy with walking and balancing, and all that kind of stuff.

I still try and do as much as I can. I'm part of a car club and am the president. It's a nonprofit club called Geelong Car and Bike

Club. I have my own business and am working for myself, which gives me the freedom and flexibility I need for my disabilities. I was a prison guard for 12 years before being diagnosed and thought I would see out that job until retirement when all this started around that time. I started becoming a liability at work because I couldn't perform my job well. Life was hell for the next two and a half to three years. My depression skyrocketed.

One day, I thought I had to get my sh*t together. I'm like, you know what, I got to do something because no one else is going to do it for me. I opened this car yard, Executive Auto Group mechanical repairs and car brokerage based in south Geelong. I wanted to get into something where I could control myself and manage it over the phone. On my bad days, I can still manage to do some work.

I never had children. No one else in my family has MS. Just me.

I had symptoms years before I was diagnosed in 2010. I had a L'hermittes sign, which meant that every time I looked down, I got an electric shock down my spine. Every time I moved, it would happen. I brushed it off that it was just a pinched nerve. How wrong was I?

Because of all the medications I have been on, my weight skyrocketed. In 2022 I decided to have weight loss surgery. It helped with my mind and also my MS. I don't eat much nowadays, mostly in small quantities, but I make sure I have enough protein and eat healthy food.

When I was diagnosed, I decided to start disease-modifying therapy and started on Aubagio. This daily pill has major side effects like hair loss, something I didn't have to worry about being bald, but that played around with my kidneys and liver. So, they swapped me to Ocrevus, an infusion twice a year, which I'm still on. I know when I'm getting ready for my next round of infusions as I lag in energy and my symptoms flare. Since being diagnosed, I've had about four rounds of steroids to help with the relapses. I now have to wear glasses for distance as my eyesight is affected. Recently, I've had a couple of falls in public, which is very embarrassing. One particular time I fell while walking along the street, some lovely people stopped their cars and helped me get back up. My right foot has a mind of its own, and it just disappears, and down I go.

I am one of the lucky ones who doesn't mind having an MRI. I tend to fall asleep in them. To the surprise of others, I haven't had a lumbar puncture. It's important that you find a counsellor that you can connect to. I've struggled to find one, but I am blessed to have amazing family support. We are not a big family; I have one sister, and we are there for each other. I can sit there and talk if I'm having a bad day. I have attended MS peer support groups, but I personally didn't enjoy them.

My passion in life is my music. It's what keeps me going. I've been in a band since I was the age of 16. We play in a pub band called Double Vision, where we do covers, an ironic name considering

the blind spot in my eye. I play in a country band as well, called Bellarine Country Music Group. We play most Friday nights at the local recreation centre. It's a bit like karaoke but with a live band, as the audience can get up and sing with the band. I used to play a lot more, but my fatigue and legs have meant I've had to back off a bit from doing it five nights a week. Sometimes I have to ring up the guys and tell them I can't go to rehearsals as my anxiety is so bad and my legs won't work properly. I have to listen to what my body is doing. I still feel useless when it happens.

I'm the type of guy that, if I'm down and out and having a sh*t time, I want to be left alone. My sister will ring me every morning to see how I am. My friends have all offered that I can contact them anytime I need help. Often, I sit it out and do what I need to do to get my head in the right place. If I need to speak to someone, I'll call my sister or niece, and we'll chat. My sister will bring her children around as a distraction.

My day now all depends on how I wake up and feel. In my workplace, I've got a room upstairs, with a couch, television and all that kind of stuff. So, if I'm here and I'm not feeling too good, I'll just put the door down, go upstairs, and chill. I definitely can't do what I used to do physically, so I control myself and have a look and see what I need to do. I'll assess how I feel, and I'll plod along and do what I got to do. That's why I take a lot longer to do things well. The way I have my business set up, I don't have to listen to anyone telling me oh, you're too slow or you're this or you're that. I can work at my pace. When customers purchase a car from me, I tell them I'll have it ready in three or four days. If you're not happy with that, I'm so sorry, go somewhere else, it is what it is. It's like, you know, this is just the path for me. It's just to keep my head going.

I am of Italian background. The second I left school, my parents told me to get out of bed and look for a job! I was brought up to work hard. They were like you're not staying in bed; you're not getting on the dole; you're not doing anything like that. You're getting up, you're looking for a job, and you're working. So, I've been like that all my life. I'm the type of guy that hasn't had 20 jobs in my working life. I've had three jobs, my last one being at the prison. I was there for 12 years, and I thought I would be until my retirement. What I have found hard was not being able to do what I used to do. I was a hard worker. I was that person who people would call on if they needed something fixed. I was a jack of all trades and a master of none.

MS slowed me down, and I fell into that rut where I stopped working. I didn't want to believe it. I kept forcing myself, and by forcing myself, I ended up in hospital having a relapse. My neurologist then said to me, "It's like Don, you got to listen to your body." Because I still had in my head, no pain, no gain, no pain, no gain. He said to me, "You got to get that out of your head." But, you know, it's not like you're going into a gym where you know you've gone there for the first time, and you're hurt. And then you keep going, and you get better and better and better and better. And you keep lifting more weights. He goes, *it's different with you. You've got to listen to your body. And when your body tells you, okay, relax, you have got to do it.* So that was the biggest thing for me to learn to do that.

When I stopped working and all that kind of sh*t, where it just stuffed my mind up, it was more that I was sitting around not doing anything, which made me more depressed. You were thinking about the MS, then that part of my fiancé leaving me was too much, and my mental health suffered. Everything just happened at once.

Around the same time, I had to get my wrist fused because I had an old injury from riding my skateboard when I was a child. It had played up when everything else was crashing around me. I had three operations on my wrist. I was at a point where it was like, for f**k's sake, is anything else going to happen? It was a very bad patch, but with help and support, I pushed through it all. Getting out of the house and going to work gave me a boost that has helped me a lot. It keeps you focused and keeps your head off all the other rubbish.

When my infusion time is near, I'm always down as I head towards it. I'm a bit flat. That's how I am at the moment. I think I've got it coming up in three weeks. So, I've just died off a bit.

I get the infusion of Ocrevus, and then about five days after that, I come up and feel a lot better for the next five months, then repeat it all again. I hope I don't get any relapses in between, but I sure feel when I'm coming to the end of the cycle and need that pick-me-up juice. It's an indication that I'm getting to the end of the cycle.

I still love to travel and go away on my own. It's great because I take my time, and there's no rush for anything. When I go away, it's not that I go away to go sightseeing, and every day is hectic with tours and stuff like that, I'll plan it. I'll go there by myself and spend a couple of days just chilling by the pool, drinking. Then I might go do something the following day, depending on how I feel, and I find that very relaxing for me as well. It gives me a really good rest, and my brain shuts off. I won't let the MS slow me down or stop me from doing anything. I'm stubborn, and I'll keep travelling for as long as I can.

I have recently started seeing someone special, nothing too serious. It was very hard to put myself out there again due to the fear of rejection when they found out about the MS. It's a scary subject to bring up with someone new in your life. I often think that when the sh*t goes down, will they really understand? If you invest your emotions and time, you will get slaughtered again. It's like, f**k, is it worth it? I chose at first not to mention the MS when we were chatting online. We went on our first date to get a feel for things and see if there would be a second date. And then, on the second date, I told her. She said, *oh, that's all right, that's fine. That's okay, as long as you get treatment and it's getting looked after.* I have found it better to talk about it all to them as they can become inquisitive, asking questions. You talk about the questions because you don't want them to go on Dr Google and be scared of what they read. Then she's got her option of what she wants to do.

Some words of advice to someone newly diagnosed would be to contact MS Connect; they were a saviour for me. Don't Google anything but listen to your neurologist. Find other people who also have MS and ask lots of questions, but remember, no two people are the same. Please don't do what I did to start with and be too embarrassed and afraid to ask for help. It's a sign of strength, not weakness. I always helped everyone else, but now I let people help me. Plenty of my friends are always asking if I need help, but I do try to attempt to do most things myself. Then I realise I should have asked for help at the start.

I still have a great life filled with loving family and friends. My favourite love is my music.

Watch the VLOG/Podcast of Don on YouTube

ABOUT DON

Don Campanile, at age 50, found himself facing an unexpected life with MS. Initially experiencing optic neuritis, he was later diagnosed with relapsing-remitting multiple sclerosis (RRMS) after MRI scans revealed six lesions. Despite the challenges, Don remains resilient and determined to live life to the fullest. He is passionate about music and plays in two bands, Double Vision and Bellarine Country Music Group.

Don runs his own car brokerage business called Executive Auto Group based in Geelong. This gives him the flexibility needed to manage his disabilities and fulfills his love of cars. He values family support and emphasizes the importance of seeking help and staying positive when dealing with MS.

Check out Don's business here on Facebook:
https://www.facebook.com/Executive.Auto.Group.Pty.Ltd

7

Angharad Candlin

BUGGER BUGGER SHIT

I was about seven when the phone rang one day. My mum was around somewhere, and my dad was away with work, so I answered the phone. It was my dad's secretary, Anne, who asked to speak to Mum. We lived in a big house, so I yelled for Mum to come to the phone. She didn't answer me, so I told Anne I couldn't find her. Anne told me she had an important message for me to give to Mum. She told me that Dad had missed his flight. She asked me to repeat it and to make sure I told Mum as soon as I could. I promised her I would, but I have to admit, I thought she was making a big deal out of Dad missing his flight. I hung up the phone and promptly went off to play and forgot all about it. A couple of hours later, I wandered back into the kitchen where Mum, my toddler brother and my big sister were. Mum was on the phone, looking really worried. She was quiet and listening and then said, bugger. She listened some more and said bugger again. Then she looked even more worried and scared and then said shit. She hung up the phone. My sister and I asked her what the matter was, and she told us that the plane Dad had been on had crashed. It slowly dawned on me I had completely forgotten to give Mum the message from Anne, so I burst out and said, "Oh no, he wasn't on the plane. Anne rang and told me to tell you that he had missed his flight, but I forgot." Silence. Relief. Then my brother broke the silence by saying "bugger bugger shit" loudly and as clearly as a bell. He was pleased with himself that he had managed to put together a three-word sentence for the first time.

That was the day bugger bugger shit came into being. Bugger bugger shit is reserved in my family for the really bad things. It can't be just average bad. It has to be really bad. A few years later, my mum was diagnosed with MS. That was a bugger bugger shit moment. My older sister was diagnosed with malignant melanoma just before she turned 18. That was a bugger bugger shit moment. Many years later, my younger sister's husband was diagnosed with a terminal brain tumour. Another bugger bugger shit moment. A few years later, my dad was told the prostate cancer he had developed had become terminal. Bugger bugger shit.

It was a reasonably typical northern hemisphere autumn day in 1990, except I was at St George's Hospital in Tooting, London, sitting in a neurologist's office who was telling me that, in his opinion, following a battery of tests that I had had a few weeks earlier, I had MS. I needed to have a lumbar puncture to be 100% sure of the diagnosis, but he thought it would be inevitable. He further explained that a lumbar puncture isn't particularly pleasant and that a new machine had been developed called an MRI. This magical invention would be able to diagnose MS by doing a scan similar to a CAT scan, but a little bit noisier. Unfortunately, the National Health Service only had a few machines available in the United Kingdom at the time. Given that he knew I was about to migrate to Australia, he suggested it would be much easier to have one in Sydney when I arrived. I asked him what my future was going to look like, and he suggested it would be pretty normal, but I would probably find myself needing a wheelchair when I reached my 50s. Bugger bugger shit.

I was 23 years old and sitting in the hospital with my grandmother.

My parents had migrated to Australia a few years before, so Grandma came to the appointment with me. My grandmother was not well known for her subtlety, either then or as she got older, but at that moment, she was everything I needed. She was practical and no-nonsense. She offered no sympathy or worried glances, but she did say she thought I should enjoy myself while I was young, give up my job as a marketing executive with Newsweek International, get a job that wouldn't give me too much stress, not worry about having children and get on with life for as long as I could.

I, of course, did none of those things.

Unlike many people, I wasn't blindsided by the diagnosis. I had lived with MS since I was about nine years old because my mum had it. One of the most significant memories of my childhood is sitting in the car with my siblings as my mum and dad went into endless doctors' offices in search of an explanation for her weird neurological symptoms. She never got a diagnosis from these doctors. It was about 1978, and no one was willing to diagnose a young mum with four children with what they thought was a life sentence of an untreatable, debilitating and degenerative neurological disease. It was my mum's cousin *Uncle Jed*, a GP, who, in the end, gave her the diagnosis every other doctor had been too paternalistic and weak to provide. My mum, a nurse, midwife and health visitor, thumbed her nose at those small-minded doctors and worked full time, getting her undergraduate degree, her master's degree and eventually her Doctor of Philosophy at the same time as raising four children while her husband travelled endlessly for his work. My mum has outlived my dad but is now in a nursing home, coming towards the end of her life with MS-related dementia. But no one could say she lived her life in the slow lane because of her MS.

No one could say I have either.

I arrived in Sydney on Christmas Eve, 1990. Following the Christmas festivities, I made an appointment for an MRI at Royal

North Shore Hospital in January 1991. I can still remember with a cold sweat that first MRI. Having since had a lumbar puncture, quite frankly, I would have taken one of those any day than lying in that insanely noisy coffin. Following the MRI, I had my appointment with the neurologist. I expected it to be fairly straightforward, but no. The neurologist said there was no evidence of demyelination, that my symptoms were most likely caused by *boyfriend trouble*, and that I should seek counselling with a psychiatrist. I was 23; I was in shock, and I was furious. But I was polite and respectful and went on my way with my tail between my legs, thinking I was a crazy hypochondriac whose weird neuropathy was all in her head.

I was also bemused. My first dramatic symptom happened in July 1987. My parents had just migrated to Sydney, and I had joined them for a holiday, as I had just finished the first year of my psychology and business studies degree in London. We were in

Paddington in Sydney, having lunch with a colleague of my dad, who was welcoming us to Sydney. As he went out to the kitchen to bring in the starters, the fingers on my right hand started to go numb. I told Mum quietly what was happening, but then our host came back into the room with the food, so I didn't say anything more. As he went out to take the plates and bring in the main course, I told Mum that my whole hand was now numb. Following the main course, he went out again, and I whispered my arm was numb up to my elbow. After the coffee had been drunk and we said our goodbyes, my entire right arm was numb. The only way I can describe it was that it felt like a cold leg of lamb was hanging off my shoulder where my arm was meant to be. The symptoms lasted for weeks as I dropped and smashed almost everything I had picked up with my right hand. It reminded me that when I was 16; I had lifted a glass jar of sugar and couldn't work out how high the bench top was and smashed it as I rammed it accidentally into the side of the bench. It was a pretty dramatic incident as I sliced my hand and needed to go to the emergency department. We all put it down to me being clumsy, which was a reasonably common occurrence. Now, of course, I think that was when the demyelination started to grumble away.

I am unfortunate enough to have Psoriatic Arthritis along with MS. Apparently, the two go together quite often. I've also had a myriad of other conditions, and along the way, I have met some pretty awful doctors. In the last 15 years, I've fortunately met some phenomenal doctors. My story is about paternalism and sexism within a country that is rife with it in pretty much every avenue. It's a call out to all of us who may be in positions of power over vulnerable people. Most of all, though, it's for the medics and the would-be doctors. In 1978, my educated mum was treated like an imbecile because doctors wouldn't diagnose her. In 1991, I was treated like an imbecile; apparently, nothing had changed. It was 2018 before I finally got a formal diagnosis. I have missed out on years of disease-modifying therapies because doctors thought they knew more than their patients, refused to listen to their patients and silenced their patients. It stops with me.

A handful of doctors, however, who listened to their patients, took me seriously, diagnosed me and treated me.

"You know I call you my famous patient". "No, I didn't know that", I replied to one of my lovely doctors. Without looking at his notes, my interventional radiologist, Eisen, reeled off my complex medical history, including the 10 years of chronic lower back and pelvic pain, which all other doctors had passed off as psoriatic arthritis or endometriosis, essentially telling me to put up with it rather than explore it further. I'd only seen him in his rooms once before and then in the theatre as he fixed one of my pelvic veins. I was impressed. He told me he had presented me—anonymously— at Grand Rounds and a conference. He now tells me he uses my story as a teaching tool on how NOT to do medicine. About listening to and respecting your patients.

A few years later, I was back in his offices to see one of my other favourite doctors, Bevan. As I came out of Bevan's office into the waiting room, Eisen bumped into me. He looked worried and delighted at the same time. He was deeply concerned there was

something wrong. I reassured him I was fine and needed Bevan's medical opinion. He looked at me suspiciously until his colleague reassured him I had just come in for a chat and a catch-up. Satisfied, he gave me a big hug and asked me to come into his room because he wanted to show me something. Curiously, I followed him in. He showed me multiple posters and hundreds of brochures about pelvic congestion syndrome. The condition Bevan had diagnosed, and he had treated. He pointed to everything and said, "This is because of you". I looked a bit taken aback as he went on, "I decided after treating you and using you as a case study to train other doctors I was not going to allow another woman to be treated like you were. So, we created all of this information for patients, for doctors' surgery waiting rooms, for doctors, nurses, clinics, to be distributed everywhere". Eisen and Bevan are two of my amazing doctors. I have referred countless friends and other people to them. I am 100% confident that patients will be listened to by these doctors. All doctors should strive to emulate them.

I still hadn't been diagnosed with MS at this point. That joy was still to come. I had asked my GP for a new rheumatology referral and managed to get in to see Lynn, one of Sydney's leading professors of rheumatology. The first time I saw Lynn, she spent two hours examining me. She confirmed the psoriatic arthritis but also said I had hyper mobile joints, was a breach birth, had congenital left hip dysplasia, and as a result, my left leg was much shorter than my right. I was impressed. None of that had been in the referral, and she was correct on all counts. I thought this was the specialist for me, and I have been with her ever since.

In 2016, I complained to her of consistent numb toes over a period of months. She sent me for an MRI on a much-improved machine. The results indicated a hot spot in my cervical spine at C2/3. She wasn't worried, my GP wasn't worried, and neither was my physio, so I wasn't worried either. She just said we should repeat the MRI in 12 months. The numb toes continued into 2017, and true to her word, she organised a referral for a follow-up MRI. As I was walking out of her room, she called me back and amended the referral from a cervical spine to a full spine and full brain MRI.

I duly got into the noisy coffin again for nearly an hour and went off to see Lynn with the results a week later. There it was in black and white. Probable MS lesion at C2/3 and multiple lesions in my brain. As a bonus, they also found a meningioma, a type of benign tumour of the meninges, the gloopy cling-wrap-like covering of the brain. I wasn't thrown by the MS diagnosis, but I was a bit surprised by the meningioma. With hindsight, if ever there was a way to downplay an MS diagnosis, simultaneously having a brain tumour diagnosis, is it. Bugger bugger shit, indeed.

Fortunately, I'm a psychologist, so I understand the brain and know cognitively that if you are going to have a brain tumour, a meningioma is the one to have. Suddenly meningiomas were everywhere—on *24 Hours in Emergency* that night on television, on that week's episode of *Grey's Anatomy* and on some other random television shows— which was unsettling.

She referred me to John, yet another brilliant doctor I have in my camp. At my first appointment, he asked me to give him my history of symptoms. I said it spans a really long time, and I have no idea what are just normal things and what are abnormal things. He said give me everything, and I'll work it out. It took a long time. It turns out they were all MS symptoms. A quietly spoken man, he was horrified when I told him about my 1991 appointment, and I could tell he was outraged. He told me that my 1987 symptoms correspond exactly with quite a large area of old demyelination in my brain. It was always there. The magical 1991 MRI just wasn't developed enough to pick it up. John organised for me to have several other tests, including a lumbar puncture, and they all confirmed the MRI and the MS diagnosis.

I've officially had MS for five years, but I've actually had it for about 40 years. I've missed at least 20 years of treatment. For all the medics reading this, let that sink in. You don't want to be that doctor. You also don't want to be one of the doctors who was too insipid to diagnose my mum. Be an Eisen, be a Bevan, be a Lynn, be a John. I use their first names purposefully. First of all, of course, to protect their full identity. Second, and just as importantly, when I use their first names, we are equal. They are not more important than me. They are not more intelligent than me. They are differently qualified than me, but I am the expert in my health, not them. When I use their first names, just as they use my first name, we become partners working together. Not expert and novice. Not doctor and patient. Partners managing a couple of horrible conditions.

I've had frequent MRIs every three months since 2018 to monitor the development of the MS and the meningioma. In my December 2019 appointment, my neurologist was pleased to report that my MS and meningioma continued to be stable. But I had developed a significant disc rupture at C5/6, which had forced all the spinal fluid out of that disc space, explaining the increase in neurological symptoms I had been getting. He called his *neurosurgeon mate*, Yanni, and chatted with him over the phone while I was with him. I saw Yanni four days later. He looked at my scans again, examined me, and told me I needed to have surgery. I suggested January, given it was two weeks before Christmas and January's much quieter at work. Yanni looked at me as if I was slightly mad. He said, "Let me put it this way, I am booking into April, but you can't wait that long. We're doing it on Monday."

While Yanni was completing my anterior cervical discectomy and fusion (ACDF), he discovered I had, as he put it, "a big chunk of bone" where it shouldn't be. He said I had ossification of the posterior longitudinal ligament (OPLL), which he had removed. At my post-op check, I asked Yanni how long it would take for the bruising on my spinal cord to heal. He looked at me and simply said, "it doesn't."

In September 2020, I had a particularly nasty flare of psoriatic arthritis. I went to bed one Friday evening, reasonably ok and woke up on Saturday morning feeling like every bone in my body was broken. I haven't fully recovered since. Every time we get to the end of the road of available drug therapies, another one seems to get approved, but I feel like we're walking a tightrope. I'm on a daily drug cocktail, and I've found steroid

injections in general, but in my head specifically, have helped the ongoing neuropathy better than any of the prescription medications available.

So, in 2023, where do I find myself? Towards the end of 2022, I applied for my income protection and total and permanent disability insurance. I am so fatigued that I can work or have a life, not both. Having worked without a break for over 30 years, I now choose to have a life. I finished working permanently in the middle of March. I am a participant in the NDIS and have had much-needed support funded, including Ruby, my *personal mobility device—an Omeo*. It has opened the doors to freedom and independence. It is my passport to continue to live my life big and independently. I believe it is also one of the keys to keeping my neurological system functioning well.

I will continue to use my voice and advocate for better and more respectful treatment of patients, particularly women, by the medical establishment. I will continue to advocate for better support and accessibility to the community for people with disabilities and chronic medical conditions.

I've had MS for about 40 years now, give or take.

Bugger bugger shit? I think not.

ABOUT ANGHARAD

Angharad is in her 50s and despite having MS for about 40 years, was only formally diagnosed 5 years ago in 2018. She is however no stranger to MS as her mother was diagnosed with it during Angharad's childhood. Angharad was born in the US and raised in the north of England but is Welsh through and through. She migrated to Australia to join her family when she was 23 and continues to live in Sydney.

Angharad is a Registered Psychologist and Board Authorised Supervisor. She worked in the community sector for over 30 years and was an Adjunct Supervisor with Macquarie University's Masters of Professional Psychology for many years. Angharad is the lead author of two externally evaluated and internationally recognised parenting programs; Keeping Kids in Mind and My Kids and Me (which won an award for Most Innovative New Program). She is currently working on a book examining the impact of grief and loss.

Angharad is regularly requested to speak to the media and at conferences and events. Whilst she speaks about complex and challenging issues, she is down-to-earth and has a wicked sense of humour. Angharad rails against injustice and is a fierce advocate particularly around issues relating to parenting, trauma, disability, child protection and domestic violence. She is accurately described as compassionate, caring and sparky.

Angharad made the decision to medically retire from permanent work in early 2023 due to the dual impact of MS and Psoriatic Arthritis. Typically though, she sees this as an opportunity not a disappointment. She is about to finally embark on her PhD, continues to mentor, support and train practitioners and is planning on travelling wherever her brand new Omeo - her personal mobility device - takes her, starting with Europe. She is always available to speak at events; where she loves nothing more than sharing her passion for building a resilient community in whatever way is possible. Angharad can be reached via LinkedIn https://www.linkedin.com/in/angharad-candlin-056222171/

Watch the VLOG/Podcast of Angharad on YouTube

8

Nina Crumpton

PHOENIX RISING

Life wasn't always as good as it is today.

I grew up with my mother in a housing commission home in Bellambi, New South Wales (NSW). It was a three-bedroom grey-brick house with a yard that had a huge weeping willow tree in it, and in spring, the yellow flowers were dazzling like sprays of sunshine. I so badly wanted a dog, but pets can be expensive and living on the sole parent pension did not really allow for such luxuries, so the answer was always no, despite my pleading. Bellambi is a socio-economically disadvantaged area, and living there meant that people often had low expectations of their future prospects in life. That can become a self-fulfilling prophecy because when you don't have someone to believe in you, you often don't believe in yourself. The housing estate was situated on prime beachfront land, and I spent much of my childhood at the beach with unparalleled freedom. In Grade 3, I had a friend called Daniel. He was full of life, and as we lived close to each other, we would often play after school. One day, I saw the police at his home. His mother had died from an overdose. I never saw Daniel again after that day. I missed him. Many years later, as an adult, I heard that he, too, had died in unfortunate circumstances.

My father and brother were completely absent from my life. My mother was all I had in this world. Iris had grown up in a home filled with alcoholism, domestic violence, poverty and mental illness, and that trauma shaped her adult life. She did the best she could, considering the circumstances. Without any family support or assistance from support services, she was set up for failure. She was often violent and cruel towards me as a child, so school and books became my escape. Her mood swings were unpredictable and savage. I recall coming home from school one day to find that she had destroyed all of my baby and school photos with no rationale. Our dining table and chairs had been smashed up and thrown out onto the kerbside, so we only had milk crates to sit on and a tea chest. Most of my clothes and books had been torn up and thrown into the bin, and I was powerless to do anything. She would remain awake for hours into the night, smoking and screaming obscenities while I sat alone on my bed in the dark, often fearing for my safety. This sort of episode would occur many times in my childhood. Through it, I learned how to remain detached from material possessions. I was a skinny child. Food was never plentiful. There were often times when I would have all the food removed from me except stale bread and water for a week or longer.

People may find that hard to believe and wonder how it can be that teachers, neighbours or child protection services did not discover this. I lived in fear that it would be discovered and that I would have to enter *the system*. So, as much as possible, I masked and hid my daily reality.

Around the age of 12, my mother inherited a house from my maternal grandmother, and we moved to a white, middle class and affluent suburb. It seemed like everyone had two functional parents who both held down jobs, drove nice cars, and took annual holidays. It was going to be harder to hide in plain sight. Living in that suburb caused my mother's mental health to deteriorate further. I was mercilessly bullied at the local high school, not just because we didn't own a car. It was because I wasn't able to shower every day as Mum was terrified she wasn't going to be able to afford the water bill. My mother and I would regularly raid the op-shop donation bins and help ourselves to donations of clothing. Poverty wraps *her* arms around you and holds you in a tight embrace. I had never celebrated Christmas, birthdays, or went on a *family* holiday. Being different meant I was actively excluded from many aspects of a normal teenage life. My mother never went to parent teacher nights, but I loved her regardless, and despite her shortcomings, I would not be who I am without her. She taught me that mental illness does not discriminate and about the inoculating power of the community against many of the social issues we grapple with today. She taught me to be self-reliant, resourceful and non-judgemental.

By the age of 16, the mask I had held up to my face for so many years was slipping. I was not attending school, and I had lost hope and direction. It had become increasingly unsafe for me to live at home. So late one night, I took a taxi with all of my measly belongings stuffed into two giant striped shopping bags and arrived at the Illawarra Hotel, Wollongong. For the next two years, this place became my home. Upstairs above the pub were two floors of rooms for rent. I paid $90 per week for a room, and my neighbours were truly the underclass in society—sex workers, people with substance use issues, the homeless and parolees. The manager, Paul, was kind enough to lend me a CD player, and I would blast Michael Jackson LOUD! Paul would often warn me on whom to avoid and how to keep safe, so in this environment, I began to further develop my survival skills. I can recall one particular incident where I was approached by one of the long-term residents to go to the doctor on her behalf. She was an older woman with a long history of addiction. When I queried why, she explained that I was to procure a certain opioid painkiller so that she could *cut a speedball* and would then share the spoils with me. I declined this offer because I knew that if I opened the door to addiction, I would have no family who would care enough to pull me out.

I was alone. I had nobody, and yet I knew I was somebody.

A few weeks later, the pub dance floor downstairs was heaving. It was so loud upstairs in my room that the floor was vibrating, and sleeping was almost impossible. It was about 3:00 am, and I was woken by a loud, forceful knock at my door. "Hey, it's David from the bar. There is a problem with the power. I just need to come in and check something." I went into fight, flight or fawn mode and dropped to the floor. I was crippled with fear, but I crawled forward to try to look under the heavy wooden door. It was a very old door, and the gap was big enough that I could see a number of male members of a football team loitering in the hallway. I got up and started to panic. Do I try to jam the bed up against the door? Do I take my chances and jump out of the two-storey window? Do I find a weapon and try to fight if they get in?

The knocking turned into a thumping, which escalated to kicking the door. The door stayed strong, and eventually, they returned downstairs to the bar. I ran out of the room, went down a rear fire exit into the alley below, and walked the streets until I felt safe to return at sunrise. I have often thought about that moment and how lucky I was to be able to navigate out of the situation unscathed.

It is very difficult to break the cycle of generational poverty and family dysfunction. It is even harder when you have no real family support or role models.

The next few years were hard, yet they made me even more resilient to adversity. I bounced around from various precarious housing situations, and due to unstable employment, I often found myself lining up for food parcels and clothing. I was always lonely and hungry and could see no easy way out. Despite this, I maintained the commitment I made to myself to continue supporting my mother. So, every Sunday, I would always catch the train or bus to visit her. I enjoyed sitting to have a cup of Tetley tea with her in a chipped tin blue mug.

The years passed in a blur. I became a mature-age student at the University of Wollongong to study primary education. Even though I gained entrance on my merit, I never quite felt like I belonged there. I was finally creating the life of my dreams, yet it was slipping through my fingers, and I didn't know why. During a lecture one day, I began laughing hysterically and had to escape to the bathroom. I remember stuffing my clothing into my mouth to muffle the sound, but I couldn't stop, and there was nothing that was amusing. I visited a doctor, and they said it was *stress*, but I felt something was wrong. My right leg began giving way as I walked, and I would fall. I was struggling with my studies. Memory issues and chronic fatigue became so debilitating that I visited my doctor, who suggested I see a geriatrician to rule out early onset dementia. This all came to a head one day when I woke up, my speech was slurred, and my right side was weakened dramatically.

I was admitted to hospital and was told they were looking at either a brain tumour or MS.

I was diagnosed with MS in January 2013. To get the diagnosis of MS was a relief in one way. Though I immediately knew that the life I had been working so hard to achieve was gone, and I was going to have to be adaptable to this new season of life. I had no choice but to withdraw from the university and come to terms with my new normal. I was f**k*ng angry that I had climbed the ladder, so to speak, but now I was sliding down fast. By no means was it easy, but a childhood of adversity has made me an adult who is able to cope with change, resilient and good at problem-solving. I joined the Spinal Cord Injury Association of Australia peer support group and learned how to live a good disabled life. Many of the old blokes in that group had experienced their injuries in the prime of their lives, so their knowledge was invaluable to me.

I tackled the problems I had head on. I applied for an accessible home with the NSW Department of Housing. I now live in a wheelchair accessible home by the sea in Wollongong with my dogs Dante and Delta, a cat named Tommy, and a flock of chickens called The Ladeez! I applied for a Go for Gold Scholarship from MS NSW and bought a mobility scooter that looked like a Harley-Davidson, which gave me many fun-filled adventures.

With the right treatment, my condition stabilised, and I was able to return to study, completing a Diploma in Community Services and Counselling. I facilitated the MS peer support group in Wollongong, which I still attend to this day, and I have met and made many wonderful friends there. By serendipity, I met a woman who worked for MS, Susan Tame, who suggested I apply for a position working with MS as an NDIS Engagement Officer. My role was to support people living with MS to access the scheme and to attend their NDIS planning meetings with them as a source of advocacy and support.

I had been following with great anticipation the rollout of the NDIS, and I was firmly convinced that it would give me my life back. I attended every possible political rally I could, and I watched with glee Julia Gillard speaking of it on television.

In 2016, my life changed when I became an NDIS participant. I finally had the support I needed to return to work, to have support in the home with activities of daily living and to receive amazing, much needed assistive technology. I had support to access the community and to go on respite breaks. I found it easy to accept and embrace the support that was put in place for my disability because, up to this point, I had felt unsupported for much of my life.

I continued working in the NDIS space as a Support Coordinator with MS. For the next two years, I worked in the Specialist Disability Accommodation housing space. I was passionate about my work, and it was a privilege to come alongside people who were experiencing significant challenges and work with them to achieve their goals. It was very challenging to remain in the workforce due to the need to take time off when MS relapses occur. Every time a relapse occurred, I would have to rebuild my functional capacity, and fatigue remained my most debilitating symptom. I had a stretcher bed in my office and would take a nap after lunch and then have to work late to make up the time. I felt I had to work twice as hard as my non-disabled colleagues to be taken half as seriously. Workplaces are often inaccessible, and as an ambulant wheelchair user, it was exhausting to balance the need to request reasonable accommodations at work so I could do my job and the desire to fit in. But blending in is difficult when you are rolling through life on a 180kg power wheelchair!

I was diagnosed with bipolar 1 in 2020 after experiencing an episode of mania after the death of my mother. MS is associated with a higher prevalence of mood and psychiatric disorders, and I was not entirely surprised at the diagnosis. It explained to me why I had experienced difficulties with mood, relationships and stability all of my life, and yet I held hope that a diagnosis would lead to treatment and support.

I had taken a respite break at a hotel on the beach after witnessing her passing through palliative care, and I had difficulty sleeping. I was very agitated and spent three days wide awake, unable to sleep. The front of the apartment had windows that overlooked the sea, and I felt the ocean *calling* me. It became harder and harder to resist. I thought how easy it would be to slip into the deep water and disappear. I played loud music to drown out the calling of the ocean and kept the curtains shut so I couldn't see it. I was binge eating and pacing around the grounds of the hotel with a burning sense of anger and rage.

A few days later, my mood changed, and a depressive wave consumed me. I was exhausted, and now I was sleeping for most of the day and night. I did not shower or eat, and my emotional effect was flat. I would put a load of washing on and sit in the dark, watching it spin through cycles for hours.

I made a doctor's appointment, and he diagnosed me and started me on medication. I now see a psychiatrist at the Mood Disorders Clinic, St Leonards Sydney, and a psychologist who specialises in bipolar. I am open to all about having this disease because mental illness runs in my family across generations, and I refuse to accept the shame and stigma that society tries to impose on me. I did not ask to have bipolar, but that is my reality, and I accept it fully now and work with the limitations it imposes on me.

It takes a lot of work to manage having both a psychosocial disability and a physical disability. I live a strictly structured lifestyle to mitigate the mood symptoms, for example, regulation of the sleep-wake cycle, medication, exercise, light therapy and mood monitoring. I have to be very self-aware to avoid placing myself in situations that could trigger an episode, like stressful situations or taking on too many commitments. There are times I feel lonely and left out because I cannot participate in society in the same way a neurotypical can. Because of NDIS, I have the support that I need to manage bipolar and still live a full life. I also attend the

Wollongong bipolar support group and have met many wonderful neurodivergent individuals whose stories and time shared together are a source of motivation and strength.

In 2022, I experienced a bout of foreign accent syndrome following an MS exacerbation which is a rare symptom of MS. It is a medical condition in which patients develop speech patterns that are perceived as a foreign accent that differs from their native accent and not acquired in the perceived accent's place of origin. I woke up one day with a Russian accent. For weeks, this symptom remained. At first, it was a novelty, but then it was distressing as I became aware that it was a sign of possible further deterioration. I was very angry and avoided going out in public or talking to anyone, as I would have to explain what was happening to me. With time and intensive speech therapy, my speech improved, but it highlighted to me again how quickly things can change living with this unpredictable disease.

In 2023, I have now become an NDIS registered provider! The Hand Up Space provides support coordination and psychosocial recovery coaching to the NDIS participants. Using my lived experience with a dual diagnosis and my experience as an NDIS participant, I see a community in which every person with a disability lives the extraordinary life of their dreams. There are many days in which I pinch myself and wonder how I got here. I wake up every day and am driven to work alongside other people with disabilities to advocate for them to ensure they receive the outcomes they deserve. I have been fortunate enough to have been mentored and supported by some truly authentic people. I want to see many more people with disability showing up and being represented in the disability sector. It angers me when I hear statistics about the low employment rates of people with disability and that the number one reason why people with MS leave the workforce is fatigue. When people with disabilities are excluded from the workforce, the gift of our talents is lost, and we are often living in poverty as a result.

From the boardroom to the breakroom, we belong!

In the last 10 years since my diagnosis, I have faced many challenges. I have gone from being able to run along the beach with my dogs to using a stick, then a walker and now a power chair, yet I am the happiest I have been in my life. I have found a purpose and meaning to my life, and I know who I am. I try to live every day in the moment and to be grateful for all I have. With a degenerative disease like MS, the future is uncertain, but that is the same for all of us. Nobody is guaranteed a life without disease, disability, or frailty. While we imagine ourselves to be invincible, we are only human, after all. I live with the fear that another MS relapse will happen and destabilise my life, but I use meditation to stay in the present. Being diagnosed with MS and bipolar 1 did not end my life … it is a new beginning, and I can't wait to see what comes next!

Watch the VLOG/Podcast of Nina on YouTube

ABOUT NINA

Nina Crumpton's life journey has been one of immense resilience and determination. Growing up in a challenging environment, she faced poverty, family dysfunction and loneliness. Despite the odds stacked against her, she pursued education and dreamt of a better life. However, her life took a new turn when she was diagnosed with Multiple Sclerosis (MS) and later with Bipolar 1 Disorder.

With great courage, Nina embraced her new reality, adapting to her disabilities and using her experiences to support others. Becoming an NDIS participant provided her with much-needed assistance and support, allowing her to return to work and regain some stability in her life.

Her journey has been filled with ups and downs, including experiencing rare symptoms like foreign accent syndrome. Through it all, she has learned to live in the moment, finding gratitude and purpose in her life. Today she works passionately to advocate for people with disabilities and ensure they receive the support and opportunities they deserve.

Despite the uncertainties of living with a degenerative disease, Nina faces the future with hope and anticipation, knowing that each day is a new beginning filled with possibilities. Her story is a testament to the strength of the human spirit and the power of resilience.

YouTube: https://www.youtube.com/@ItsaWheelyGoodLifeCrumpton

9

Liliana Cuba

THE PASSENGER

All my work, my life, everything I do is about survival, not just bare, awful, plodding survival, but survival with grace and faith. While one may encounter many defeats, one must never be defeated. -Maya Angelou

My name is Liliana. I am originally from Lima, Peru. I grew up in the north of Peru, hours away from the Equator, then the South and, eventually moved with my family to the capital, Lima. Different circumstances brought me here to Australia. Initially I lived in Melbourne, but I've called Sydney home since 1996.

Although I did ballet, contemporary dance and trained in theatre I have always been very clumsy, I was the last of my friends that learned how to tie shoelaces as a child and always had problems coordinating my hands, if that can be attributed to MS I have no idea but I am happy to blame MS for it! I grew up in the north of Peru, hours away from the Equator, then the South and, eventually moved with my family to the capital, Lima.

The diagnosis of MS came as a surprise, I broke my ankle in 2015 in a very stupid fall (getting down of a bus) on ANZAC day 2015, somehow, I managed to break and dislocated it and ended with a metal rod and pins inserted. At the time I was having feeling of numbness on both my hands which I attributed to stress due to work.

I was diagnosed with MS in June 2016; I had also been diagnosed with breast cancer at the end of 2015 and had a unilateral mastectomy and reconstruction by June 2016 so all in all 2016 was not the greatest year.

What brought my diagnosis was that my injury did not improve and my mobility was getting worst even though I was walking (with crutches) and doing the physio exercises; it was my GP who referred me to the Brain Mind Research Institute (BMRI) and the rest, as they say, is history: diagnosed with MS but was told that I didn't fit either RRMS or PPMS.

I was started on Tysabri straight away, been on this medication since 2016 and there are no new lesions and the ones that I had (whom my first neuro described as a chain of Christmas lights in the MRI) remain inactive, but I do wish I had been diagnosed earlier.

In retrospect the symptoms were there and had been there for a long time, but I always had an explanation and rationale for them like stress, clumsiness, etc.

At the time that I received the diagnosis I had secured an amazing full time job and decided to disclose my diagnosis as I was pretty new (diagnoses within my probation period) and I was lucky enough that I have been able to keep my job and became permanent, at times it hasn't been smooth sailing specially with fatigue and the occasional brain fog but working from home since the pandemic started has helped me a lot to control it and allows me to be more productive.

However, working from home has had a downside, I have lost my ability to walk longer distances before the pandemic I was able to walk from the train station in Green Square or from a bus stop about 2 kms. away and there is no way I can do that now, and a recent trip to work has shown me how much walking capacity I have lost which has been quite upsetting.

MS is my reluctant companion, I am stuck with it and might as well accept it, this does not mean I am fond of it, but we have reached a kind of uneasy truce. The hardest part has been accepting the loss of mobility and brain fog, I love walking and my partner, and I had ideas and plans of going for long walks, bush walking and trekking now that, finally, I wasn't working weekends.

After my recent trip to work I must add the loss of further independence and capacity to walk to my list of activities/things I am grieving for.

The brain fog bothers me a lot, I hate forgetting things especially at work and my biggest fear is developing Alzheimer's; my biggest episode of brain fog I had was when I was sitting for a Pharmacology exam in 2013, I loved the subject and was doing quite well until that exam when I could only write my name and left as I could not remember anything.

It took me a visit to the ER after falling flat on my face (no broken bones, yay to me) to accept that I needed a walking stick; I was walking from the train station to work with my walking stick neatly folded and stored inside my backpack when somehow, I fell flat on my face, 2 passers-by helped me and called an ambulance.

I did learn my lesson though and started using a walking stick, reluctantly in the beginning but eventually I had to accept my need for walking aids and understand that that is what they are: aids and not a judgment on my physical or mental abilities.

I still have the original walking stick although it had been replaced by different ones, the latest a Canadian crutch that helps with the pressure on my right wrist. I also have a walker for home which I use when I am too tired, or my left leg decides to do anything but support me. My original walking stick was nicknamed "the passenger" and sometimes I feel this nickname also applies to MS although maybe "back seat driver" would be a more appropriate description.

I have a bit of and love/hate relationship with assistive technology, I have recently been fitted with a TurboMed which is the latest orthotic mobility aid which I admit it looks like a torture device and is not compatible with fashion! It goes outside my leg so there is no way to hide it.

I have these expectations that my walking distance will improve. Previous experiences with other types of AFOs have shown this not to be the case so then I start feeling bereft and disillusioned as I miss my physical independence; having said that I will be ordering a walker soon which has me again in 2 frames of mind: I do not want to rely on mobility aids but if I want to be able to go to exhibitions, walk some accessible tracks then I might have to learn to accept the fact that I need them which now I am learning to accept the fact that mobility aids will have a very important role to play in my day-to-day life at the same time I feel I am not there yet, but I said the same when I started using a walking stick, for some reason I had this idea that it will be a temporary measure only…little did I know!

Acceptance of my limitations has been the hardest part of MS, I travelled Europe by myself and travelled and walked in my own country as much as I could so walking has been part of who I am, same with dancing, my last class was a week before my daughter was born but I like dancing for the joy of it and sitting down and waving my arms is not the same!

I am not sure how I would have coped if diagnosed in Peru, we don't have the amazing healthcare system we have here in Australia and those who can afford it rely on the private health system. People with disabilities were invisible when I was growing up as the structure to support them was not there.

My family has been supportive as much as they can considered that they are all live in Peru, same with my children (now adults), I think that for my kids the diagnosis explained many things: why was I always tired and the short temper.

I feel that the diagnosis has also strengthened my relationship with Carl (my partner) who had to deal with a diagnosis of breast cancer followed by MS and is now, to a point, my carer. It has not been an easy road for him, but he remains solid in his support and encouragement.

Because I wasn't given a choice (no one is) I've decided to deal with this disease as best as I can, for me that means continue working full time to keep my mind active, take photographs, travel and continue walking. I don't want to allow MS to take over and limit me so I would say my attitude is to raise to the challenge…and adapt it to my condition.

Before you think I am Miss Positivity I do get frustrated, I used to have a great memory and as you can see was very active physically. The diagnosis of MS has provided me with some answers and also with more questions and one of them is if MS will progress and what the outcome will be; I get scared of needing a wheelchair and this is because I remember my grandmother (after what we thought It was a neurological episode) burst into tears when she was put on one, it was heartbreaking seeing her so broken and the image remains with me.

I know now that using a wheelchair won't stop me, I now find myself looking at wheelchair and trying to find a modern looking one that would allow me to take public transport and roam the streets when the time to sue one comes.

It took a while to accept my limitations, I learned the hard way to rely on mobility aids after that fall with my walking stick safely folded and tucked inside my backpack. I do still struggle with my limitations, and I can be very boring reminding people that I trained to be a dancer and was that once upon a time control of my body instead of my body making decisions for me.

I am the family trailblazer, as far as I know nobody else in my family has MS. Funnily enough my ex-husband's aunt had MS so I do worry about either of my children being diagnosed.

The pros of being diagnosed late is that I have travelled, danced, performed, had children and took risks including some stupid ones like diving into the sea headfirst from a pier.

The con of a late diagnosis is that the damage done has happened and progression has already taken place before anything can be done to reduce or minimise it

The challenges of MS are many, not only physical but also emotional. I grieve for the able-bodied person I was once upon a time and for what I could have achieved, as you all know MS was always present but not in an obvious manner, so it was easy to make an excuse for a missed dance step, forgetting something even though I just read about it, a lost word, etc. As I mentioned before, MS is a constant companion, sort of travelling along next to me even if I would rather travel alone.

I also grieve for not having been the mother my kids deserve.

I am also fearful at times of the future; I do understand that MS is not a death sentence (I am a cancer survivor after all) but it is a very challenging and capricious disease; my biggest fear is the loss of cognition and memory as I think I can deal with the physical side

of the disease but the fear of losing my brain function frightens me the most.

I don't think there is enough representation of minorities with MS hence my interest in this project. When I was diagnosed my first thought was that I am a mixed bag genetically speaking, lived close to the equator and cooked myself to a crisp every summer as a teen so how come I am diagnosed with this disease? This brings us to my thought that more education needs to be provided so the general public understands that MS is not a "one size fits all" disease (but which disease is?) and what might have worked for your great aunt once removed is not necessary going to work for somebody else!

The idea of losing independence is part of my fears, I want to make decisions about treatment, mobility aids, and work. I don't want MS to make those decisions for me, but I am slowly making my peace with this and crossing bridges as I need to.

I want to keep on working as long as possible not only because of the financial independence working allows me but also because of the way it keeps my brain engaged, it is challenging and there are days when I feel that I cannot keep it up but there are also days when I feel everything is going well.

I hope none of my kids or future grandchildren are affected by MS, I also hope that treatments keep improving so early diagnosis and treatment helps maintaining quality of life for all those who are or will be diagnosed with MS.

Personally, I don't describe myself as an MS warrior as I feel this term implies choice. I am willing to fight the disease but more of a sense of perversity because no one has a choice. I don't see myself as brave but just another human being trying to do their best with a not very good set of cards dealt. This is a personal point of view, so I hope I don't offend others. Although after the invisible scars form MS, and the massive one from the mastectomy my body is, indeed, a battlefield. Not using the term warrior to describe myself is a personal decision and by no means is meant to pass judgement on others. Maybe I can describe myself as the "MS (reluctant) warrior" who'd rather be an observer.

I see MS as a challenge and some days I am not up to it and wish it would go away and then I feel guilty (did I mentioned I am a lapsed Catholic?) when I think that I've survived breast cancer and also that the MS diagnosis came just in time to stop further progression (my neuro comment was that I've should have been on a wheelchair long time ago), a friend described once as perverse so I will use that perversity to raise to the challenge that MS is and adapt to it as best as I can as it is obvious I might not be able to bargain with it or outsmart it.

I keep active as much as possible by walking (as much as my legs will allow me to), seeing a physio and doing Pilates but I am the first to admit that I am not as flexible as I used to be, this had thought me not to compare myself especially to able bodied people!

Photography has helped immensely, I was exhibiting in my country of origin before coming to Australia but never been sure if I was good enough or not, I am past that now. My only disappointment is that I am not good with an SLR so most of my photos are taken with my phone, but one must adapt and raise to the challenge as much as possible.

Photography has always been very important in my life since I learnt how to use a camera, I like looking at things and finding something interesting and sometimes I have surprised myself by finding something else in the photograph better than what I was aiming for; it is a creative outlet which allows me to somehow be as my sight is not affected by MS there is a sense of freedom and achievement when somebody likes one of my photos.

I see photography as a dialogue, however, once the image is out there it is up to the viewer to find its own meaning and interpretations based on their own experiences.

I like photographing landscapes, urban decay, reflections and have developed a fascination with planes taking off or flying as it is impressive plus there is that sense of freedom and wonder and there are extremely graceful It those moments when they are floating on air just after take-off.

Am I scared of the future...a bit but then it will be foolish not to, as I said before the only weapon, I have left is resilience, raise to the challenge and adapt as MS won't play nice.

I respect the choices other people with MS have made, after all we are not given much choice so being able to make informed decisions re: treatment, mobility aids, etc. is very important.

I do have an issue with misinformation and snake oil treatments that might do more harm than good.

I decided to follow up my neuro's recommendation to start treatment with Tysabri, from my point of view there was not much to lose but I must admit that it was scary, especially when reading the possible side effects, I have heard of the treatments people can get in Russia and Mexico but I'll wait for more information to be available and for it to become available in Australia. My decision in starting treatment was based on the need to stop the progression of the disease which apparently happened very fast, hence my MS not fitting in either category: RRMS or PPMS, I am a bit of both.

I don't want pity, if you see me walking in an unstable manner do not feel sorry for me but offer your arm and help me cross the street, I'll learn from you, but you'll also learn from me.

Ask questions, they are welcome and don't assume that because you know one person with MS you know them all.

Look at me as an equal (a physically challenged one but same as you), life is hard for most of us and some carry visible signs of our battles and some don't, in my case you can see the external signs but not the internal ones (trauma, loss); we are all in the same boat trying to get to safe shore even if the boat leaks at times.

And to my fellow MS'ers: be kind to yourself avoid comparisons to anybody else, I have fallen at the times in that trap and brings nothing but sadness and anger. We might never climb that mountain but hey, there are also stunning views from below.

Watch the VLOG/Podcast of Liliana on YouTube

ABOUT LILIANA

Liliana was born in Lima, Peru. She has been living in Australia since 1994 and was diagnosed with MS in 2016. She enjoys photography, collecting beach glass, reading, and listening to music- especially Nick Cave and The Pogues. Liliana has two children and lives with her partner Carl, and two cats in Sydney. In her previous incarnations, Liliana has been a graphic designer, photographer, barmaid, sales assistant, mature-age student and Spanish interpreter in Australia.

Liliana completed a degree in nursing, which eventually led her to her current job, which is challenging and rewarding at the same time. Best of all it keeps her mind active and makes her feel useful and productive.

Apart from photography – see in Liliana's chapter – Liliana enjoys music very much. She has two songs that she calls her MS songs, Chumbawamba's "I get knocked down" and Blur's "Song No2" Please don't start talking to her about Nick Cave because it's likely she won't stop!

10

Colleen Daniels

ONE SATURDAY MORNING

41, divorced, alone and raising three children.
I was content.
I had a secure job and terrific workmates. My children were doing well at school, and apart from silly squabbles between themselves, they were good children.

I was healthy, and my children were healthy. There was no reason to think that would ever change.
My parents, uncles and aunts were all ageing well; even the ancestors seemed to have been a tough, healthy lot.
Life was good.

Maybe I should have known something wasn't right.
I see it now.
It all started after a full day at work, and the children were fed, washed and tucked in bed. I would sit on the lounge to relax in front of the television and be asleep before the first commercial.
Out of nowhere, that started happening every day.
I wasn't tired, and my eyes weren't feeling heavy.
It was exhausting raising children and holding down a job. It was.
But I would sleep without intending to at all.
I know now that other things weren't right either, like unusual sensations.

When I sat on my vinyl-covered office chair, which should have felt cold but was always warm, it was as if someone else had been sitting there. I was the one that opened the office every day. I was the only one there, and that chair always felt warm when I sat on it first thing in the morning. It was spooking me. I would tippy-toe around the office, checking no one else was there. So why did it feel warm?

There were also pins and needles in my fingers that wouldn't go away after a good shake of my hands—it was strange.

When food and drinks started losing their taste, I was convinced it was some new cost-saving idea of all the food companies. I figured they were not putting in as much sugar, salt, or flavouring, as nothing tasted quite the way it should.

I brushed all of it off—weird, annoying things but nothing that I thought was serious or medical.

Until one Saturday morning

It was July 1997. I'd woken up, wiggled myself to the edge of the bed, stood up—and I wasn't me.

Well, my legs weren't mine.

I was trying to walk, and my legs weren't responding, not properly. Something, maybe my hips or knees, was vaguely helping, but my legs were definitely not paying attention.

Feeling unsafe and unsure of my feet, I carefully made my way to the bathroom, holding on to furniture and leaning on the walls as I went. It didn't make sense, feeling so weak and strange, just like that. Thinking I must have been overdoing things, I quietly went through the rest of the day, stayed indoors and took it easy that weekend. The weakness faded away little by little.

I took the Monday off work to rest some more and, with a slight limp, returned to work on the Tuesday.

Before the week was over, I was walking again. There was no limp, no sign of any weakness.
I figured whatever I had, it had got better and was gone.

A few weeks later, I was shuffling my feet; it was the only way I could walk.
That was when I asked Dad to take me to the doctor. I would not have been able to get there on my own.

A neurologist appointment soon followed. Pins were stuck in my legs. The neurologist asked, "Tell me, is this sharp or blunt?"
Those pins felt blunt to my legs but not to my hands—pins being poked in my hands hurt and made me flinch; ouch! But not my legs. It should have hurt everywhere. What on earth was going on?
I didn't think it was anything serious, just strange and intriguing. Aren't I funny?
Something unique about me—haha.
Next, there was an MRI. They saw one spot on my brain, a spot they called a *lesion*. I had one.
I soon learned that spots on the brain are also known as sclerosis, the Greek word for scars.
The doctor mentioned the possibility of Multiple Sclerosis (MS).
They said one scar certainly didn't add up to anything being *multiple*, but possibly MS.
I decided they were wrong; they had to be.
I don't get sick; nobody in my family had anything like that.
Again, the weakness faded, and I returned to my usual day-to-day life.
To my mind, they were wrong to even consider MS.

Around three months later, I was limping and avoiding stairs.
I was referred to a second neurologist and learned that two scars were now showing on my MRI. The neurologist said, "I'd say, with your symptoms and this MRI, that you are in the early stage of Multiple Sclerosis."
I asked, "What does that mean?" and in reply heard something like, "It's a lifelong progressive disease of the central nervous system."
It sounded a bit serious.
When I pressed for more information, I was told I had RRMS

and that symptoms vary, with no two people having the same symptoms, although medications would help.
That sounded a bit better.
I was given pamphlets on three available medications to *read through* and choose one.
I read each pamphlet and then decided not to take any medication.

Months passed and I educated myself more about MS. I was walking without any problems and was firmly in denial even though I'd learned some of my symptoms were common to MS. I reasoned that everybody sometimes had pins and needles and the odd twitch or twang.

At my next neurologist appointment, I felt it was time to find out what it all meant and what I needed to do—just in case they were right, I still was not convinced.
We talked about medication, and I said I would think more about it. I was stalling; why start medication if nothing was wrong?
Several weeks after that visit, I was still feeling fine, walking and working, but numb from my neck to my knees.
I had to accept it. Numbness was a common MS symptom and being numb all over was not okay.

They had been right all along.
The diagnosis was official; I had MS.
I cried in those first few months, often on my own, and sometimes at work, I had to nip outside for a cry. I had no idea what I was supposed to do or what lay ahead, but facing an unknown, unpredictable future was frightening. My young children needed their mother. I had to keep going, work and look after them, and I didn't know if I would be able to do any of it, or how long it would be before I couldn't continue.
But people don't always become disabled with MS.
I had read that, and it helped me to know.

I decided to tell my boss about my diagnosis as he had shown concern. I wasn't telling anyone else. He was a good boss, a wonderful guide, and a born teacher. He soon introduced me to his friend, who had MS for eight years and was about to get married

a second time. With an executive-type position, she seemed to be living very well with her MS. She confirmed that MS symptoms come and go and said, "Colleen, do what you dream."
I didn't need any persuasion. I think I was blessed that day. What a wonderful example I had been gifted.
I felt fine again, and I knew not everyone ended up disabled.

My dream had always been to travel to England. Brought up on fairy tales of princesses, princes, castles, and lush green country paths, I was going to England— that kitchen I had been saving for could wait.

Mum and Dad were concerned about my health, but as long as I stayed in touch, they were happy to help. They were also delighted to look after their granddaughters for a couple of weeks.

I prepared as well as I could, knowing nothing about what my future held but feeling quite able, and perhaps bravely, confident. My neurologist cheered me on but gave me a prescription to fill so I would have medication with me if needed. I think it may have been a steroid, but luckily, I didn't need it, whatever it was.

I walked around every city and tourist attraction easily. I had no episodes of MS during the weeks I travelled, via Disneyland, no less, and to England—and finished it all carrying a definite case of the *travel bug*.

From there on, my attitude became, *MS, I can handle you!*

At my next neurologist visit, I decided to try some medication to slow the progression of MS.
It really did seem wise.
I tried a few, but unfortunately, I had nasty reactions to some and unwelcome sluggishness brought on by others.
I didn't feel well when using the recommended medications, so I stopped trying after a couple of years.
Many people do well on medication; I wasn't one of them.
I was still okay, only noticing the odd thing now and then. Nothing anyone could see, just mild episodes of things like disturbed vision, numbness or pins and needles, and those things didn't keep me from doing anything.

I felt well as the next few years passed by. I knew I didn't want my children to wait until their 40s as I had done before travelling and experiencing other cultures. Another dream was building, to take my three girls *around the world*. In 2007, the girls chose Ireland, Greece and England as their *must-see*, and we set off for seven weeks. On that trip, I opted out of one walk—a steep, rocky walk on Nea Kameni Island in Greece. It was the one time we were away that I thought I might not be able to manage. It had been a long day; I was nearly 50 and not the only tourist who sat and waited while the younger ones walked on. Everything was fine.

I sometimes thought about other people living relatively normal lives with MS. I assumed I was probably one of them.
I had always been lucky.

Perhaps I had a guardian angel

No longer in the bloom of youth, at 52 years of age and wearing a lovely shade of MS, I accepted a marriage proposal by an—obviously—brave and daring gentleman.
Before then, I had firmly decided that I would live my life alone.

Fate, however, had determined there was one man who would sway me from my choice of a single life, and despite some decent attempts not to, I had met him. On our first actual date, I told him I had MS. He answered, "Everyone's got something."
I asked him to read up about MS, feeling certain that would be that, while at the same time, I was surprised to find myself thinking, *what a shame I'll never see him again.*
It turned out he was brave enough to persist despite knowing my future health was uncertain.
We married that same year, and as I write, 14 years later, still going strong.

Fifteen years

The day I was diagnosed with MS, the neurologist told me it was a progressive disease, where it would be around 15 years before progression might show. There was also no way of predicting the course or extent of any person's journey with MS, as it was notoriously different for every person.

Five years after marrying, I started noticing there were limits to how far I could walk and needed to rest often. My sense of balance had become a problem. When going down the stairs in the office, I would joke as I reached for the handrail, saying "Don't mind the old lady coming through." People would laugh and say, "You're not old", while moving aside all the same. I would laugh with them, mumbling as I went down the stairs, *haha, getting old, get out of my way, haha*, and holding that handrail all the way.

My RRMS had changed to SPMS. It had been a little over 15 years since the initial diagnosis.

By 2017, I had lived with MS for 20 years. Walking was difficult; I had a weak left leg and an obvious limp, and my sense of balance had nearly disappeared. I needed to use a walker if I went out anywhere.

A year earlier, I had seen an online video about HSCT treating MS, with claims of success. I ignored it, assuming it was unsubstantiated, until stumbling across more information about it in the news. I

searched online and found it wasn't available in Australia, except under clinical trial conditions. Curious, I searched some more and found the trial registration details. I enquired but didn't meet the criteria.

In my situation, HSCT could only be accessed overseas.

After searching extensively online and asking questions, I made a huge decision. I was going to have the procedure in Moscow, Russia.

My husband did not want me to go overseas alone. He researched HSCT and said he was coming with me if I was sure I wanted to do this.

HSCT involved chemotherapy, so there'd be nausea, hair loss and probably worse. It wouldn't be easy, but I felt it could be my last chance. I was determined to try everything.

To Moscow

On 15 July 2017, nervous yet hopeful, we boarded flight EY451 from Sydney, heading for Abu Dhabi en route to Moscow.

We were surrounded and farewelled at the airport by our children, and our grandchildren who all smothered us with loving wishes. Later, it shocked us to discover that we could have been taking our last breaths.

Arriving in Moscow, news reports were saying there had been a terrorist plot to bring down our plane.

We were unbelievably fortunate that airport security had been alert in their job and the Australian Federal Police were called in after an explosive device was found in passenger luggage. A disaster had been averted; we knew we were lucky to be alive.

At the time, I remembered how as a child I believed I had a guardian angel, and whimsically thought *that little girl might have been right*.

To hospital

On arrival at the hospital in Moscow, we met the doctors, staff, and nurses. Not all of them spoke English; many knew enough to communicate, and translators were put to good use. I felt extremely safe in this very foreign country.

The day after arrival, I was admitted to the hospital. After rigorous testing of every part and function of my body over the first few days, I was declared fit to undergo the procedure.

Two days later, the doctors began my treatment with injections to prepare my stem cells for removal. This confined me to bed for around five hours while two million stem cells per kilo of my body weight were removed.

Four days of chemotherapy followed, and they returned my stem cells two days later.

Isolation came next, with no visitors allowed, as the chemotherapy had wiped out my immune system. This was the whole point of the treatment; to grow a new immune system, free of the memory of MS.

All things considered

Everything had been going great, and I felt terrific, considering I'd just had chemotherapy.

Until Day 10 of isolation, when I woke up barely able to move.

I felt too weak to wash myself and asked for help. My request caused a hullabaloo with the nurses taking my blood pressure and temperature, talking quickly between themselves. I thought they were overreacting. In fact, I was a bit annoyed by the nurse fussing over me, saying I had a temperature.

I wasn't worried; I was sure I would be okay.

My memory of anything after the nurses buzzing around me is hazy. I recall being told I was being moved to intensive care and thinking it wasn't necessary, even when I was struggling to breathe.

I was sure I'd be fine if they gave me paracetamol or something.

I wasn't fine at all.

The initial thought was that I had pneumonia. It was soon

discovered that it was fungal pneumonia, which had a 90-95% mortality rate for those with a compromised immune system. I had a 5-10% chance of survival.

Bad things happen to *other* people

We hear about bad things happening to other people all the time. Yet there I was. My lungs had collapsed, and I'd been revived after cardiac arrest. I was in intensive care, surviving on life support. The bad stuff truly was happening to me—to *us*.

Beginning to improve

After 18 days of round-the-clock care, lung scans and blood tests showed that I was recovering. I was discharged from intensive care and returned to my original hospital room.

We thought things were looking up.

That was until we realised we'd overstayed our visas and had unintentionally broken Russian law.

What followed was a battle of innocence to navigate a foreign criminal process on top of a life-changing medical situation. With assistance from the Russian hospital hematology team, steadfast family support and my husband's incredible efforts, we returned safely home to Australia.

On arrival in Sydney, we headed straight to the hospital. I spent another month seeing doctors, nurses, and physiotherapists before I was considered able and fit enough to return to my home.

Over and done

Going in with an EDSS of 6.5 to a score of 3 is a good outcome.
I cannot and do not claim to be cured because I am not. There is that disability score of 3 to remind me. I still baulk at stairs, watch where I put my feet, and wish for increased stamina. Other symptoms of MS, like heat intolerance, ugh, remain. There is obvious improvement in my mobility which has been acknowledged by my medical practitioners and certainly welcomed by me.

Chances and choices

Looking back, I see that by either my choice or that of MS, I have discovered a courage and determination that, without MS, would never have surfaced.

I have purpose now and am content again, still.

Mission – I have one

As anyone who has been given a second chance might understand, there beats within me a strong need to give back.

The world needs a cure for MS.

Further research *will* find it.

Today, people living with MS meet many who have no concept of what MS is. When we speak of it, we are asked, *what is that?*

Such a lack of awareness does not help when raising funds for MS research. If the public does not know the plight of those with MS, if they do not know there is no cure, there can be no urge to help or donate towards research.

I am driven, to be a part of the cure for MS by building awareness and supporting research. I hope everyone reading this book will take steps toward helping at any and every opportunity.

For all the people yet to be diagnosed, their families, and those beginning their MS journey—wherever they are and whatever symptoms they are dealing with. I say keep hope and know you are not alone. Research is happening somewhere, every night and every day, getting ever closer to finding the cure we need. More research and collaboration will find that cure. Thank you for helping our cause by buying this book.

Colleen

ABOUT COLLEEN

Determined to help others living with Multiple Sclerosis, Colleen leads an MS support group who have inspired and supported her focus on raising awareness of the disease. Awarded community recognition by a local MP after organising her first MS event, Colleen's determination continues to be evident in the effort, time, commitment and initiative she shows by bringing about local community events to assist those living with MS, as well as to build awareness and raise funds for research. Colleen has been invited to speak at various community groups meetings and is gratified when people speak with her afterwards to hear that they have learned of, or learned more about MS. Raised in Sydney's western suburbs, going straight from school to work after learning shorthand and typing, Colleen worked through secretarial to executive assistant roles - and now enjoys retirement on the NSW Central Coast where she and her husband enjoy fishing, time with friends, and visits to and from their family and growing number of adorable grandchildren.

Watch the VLOG/Podcast of Colleen on YouTube

11

Laura Di Iulio

NOT IN YOUR LIFETIME

I was fifteen years old and full of hopes and dreams. I lived my life with the knowledge that I must, I can, and I will achieve whatever I want. I was a popular girl at school, always with the *ingroup* and going to whatever party was happening at the time. I loved being who I was. Being close to my family gave me a feeling of safety and carefreeness. I was truly happy... and then came the worldshattering diagnosis. But first, let me give you the backstory.

My mother and her siblings migrated from Italy to Melbourne in the late 1950s to find a better life and opportunities to prosper. I was raised speaking Italian as my first language. Our house was brimming with constant life and activity. My two older sisters, my two uncles, my nonna and nonno and I all lived happily in one house in Hawthorn, Melbourne. This was before my grandparents purchased the house right next door and moved there with my two uncles. They cut a gate into the fence to allow access, making it feel like one giant house. I can't express how happy this time was—there was always family, food, laughter, food and more food and even more laughter! It was such a joyous time; people from next door and down the street used to drop by for Italian coffee, eat and have fun. This was happening while a prominent person was missing... my biological father. I loathe to call him a father, as he was mostly absent in my upbringing and caused fear and loathing in the household. All three of us girls were scared of him, and I remember hiding from him a lot. It wasn't just a fear for us as children, but we were also scared for our mum, who used to cop the brunt of his anger and shouting and throwing things. When he wasn't around, things were happy and blissful.

Then one day, the absentee father announced that we were moving. Things happened all so quickly. I remember not wanting to move and everything getting packed up all rushed, and the next thing I knew, we were in Burwood, Melbourne. But it was the same old story, just in a different house. He was there, but then he wasn't. He used to turn up in extravagant cars and expensive jewellery, which puzzled us as we didn't seem to have a lot of money. There was a period where he was gone for some time, and it turned out he was in jail. Oh boy, what a situation! The end of it, as I remember, was him telling me to tell my mum, "I'm going", before packing his belongings into his flashy car and leaving for good. I remember Mum coming home from work on the tram—she didn't drive—arms full of groceries and food for the family and telling her the news that he had left us. It turns out he had been having affairs, among other things, and left my mum and us girls for a different life. So that was that.

We had to sell the house and find somewhere new; it was around this time when Mum met Nick. We were in the middle of putting hard rubbish out on the street, and Mum had his name as a contact to collect these household items as he used to sell stuff at weekend markets. Now, let me tell you about Nick. Nick was a gruff Italian man from the same region of Italy as Mum. He also had recently separated from his wife after her infidelities. One thing led to another, and he and Mum kind of fell into a relationship. Yeah, I know, it sounds funny, but he needed someone to care for him, as did Mum. It's hard to explain, but I'm sure you get the picture. Nick had two daughters similar in age to us, who were very unwelcoming and downright nasty despite the fact that our side of the family was trying to get along. Nick's two daughters lived with their mother and, for reasons beyond anyone's comprehension, were also mean to Nick. My mum and Nick soon married in a small ceremony, and we were now living in Camberwell, Melbourne. Life was good again, as I was so happy to get out of that house in Burwood. My nonna, uncle and all of us girls lived so happily in Camberwell; unfortunately, my nonno passed a few years earlier.

By this point, I was fifteen and enjoying high school. Things were finally looking great, and we were content; life was good. But something was a bit off. At first, my right arm felt dead, and I struggled to use it. We went to the hospital, and I remember a swarm of medical students gathering around me, all talking among themselves, and the head doctor asked them what their thoughts were. I remember this was the first time I ever heard the term multiple sclerosis. From that point, they started testing for neurological diseases. They wanted to eliminate any doubt that it was something else—welcome to the world of blood tests and MRIs! Then came the day I got the information I didn't want, and my world changed forever. After my initial MS attack, I recovered, and life somewhat returned to normal. I remember thinking *these doctors must be wrong; there's nothing wrong with me.* I was trying to live life as best as possible, getting great grades at school and passing my higher school certificate and being accepted into the University of Melbourne, where I was studying for a Diploma of Education and a Bachelor of Arts. I was doing my best, studying and working at the same time to save money. I suffered a major setback when I lost vision in my right eye—the dreaded optical neuritis! Oh man, not good! This preceded many other attacks. At one point, I had an attack on my lower face and lost my ability to control my lips, and my speech was greatly affected.

I remember constantly being in and out of the hospital and having injections of prednisolone IV infusions. Remember, this was back before any decent breakthroughs or medications existed. I was determined to graduate from university at all costs and battled through these exacerbations when our world came crashing down. My uncle died—it was so traumatic as it wasn't natural causes but suicide. My poor old nonna, mum, Eric, my other uncle, and us girls were stricken with grief. How could this happen? Why? Too many questions remained unanswered, and life was never the same. I had to push all this down as I graduated from university. I remember wearing my graduation gown and mortarboard and being excited and relieved to achieve this feat despite everything that was going on. As I went to walk up the stairs to collect my certificate, my legs felt like jelly, and I barely had control of where I put my feet. I thought I was about to fall in front of everybody and take the most epic dive of all time! But I made it through to the cheers of my friends and family. I still remember that feeling of pure elation, a feeling I will never forget.

After graduation, I began my career as a teacher, going around different suburbs of Melbourne and living my best life despite the condition. I'm choosing to leave this part of my personal life less detailed as I met, married, and divorced a man who never deserved me. He had the nastiest mother, whom I remember very clearly, once said directly to my face, "You are a bad apple infecting the rest of the bunch". What the actual f**k? How dare she? He was the one who violated our marriage vows, and she had the audacity to scold me. These words pierced my soul like a silver bullet and filled me with a rage I never knew! I remember I wanted her to get sick, I wanted *him* to get sick, and I wanted her daughter to get sick. I wanted them all to get sick so they could understand what I was going through. To hell with them. I sold our house in Box Hill South and bought my very own place in Forest Hill, Melbourne.

Ah, Forest Hill, I so adored that place! It was pure freedom! At this point in the MS journey, I needed more regular help as the disease progressed. I was still working, driving, and living my best life. Then that fateful day came when my nonna passed. I was so close with Nonna that I couldn't bear the thought of losing her, not now, not when I needed her the most. The news had upset me so much that I couldn't function and missed her funeral. Even typing this makes me so sad; I loved her beyond words. She was an angel on earth and the most placid, intelligent, and beautiful soul imaginable. Things were different then, but I still had to go on, and on I did. I was enjoying my townhouse, nights out with my friends, doing brunch around beautiful cafes of Melbourne and living next door to one of the biggest trippers of all time, Fausto. He was a secondgeneration Italian like me, and coincidentally, his mum was also from Abruzzo, the same region as my mum. His mum even worked in the same factory in Richmond as my mum—talk about a small world! He was a good neighbour looking out for me and ensuring things were safe.

Despite the fluctuating condition of the MS, I was enjoying life and having fun. My friends were dating different guys, and I remember them saying to me, "You have to get back out there. No one is going to just turn up at your door," but someone did, in a nice red convertible!

Enter Anthony. He used to come and help where I needed extra support, but we mainly went out for brunch and clothes shopping. He was fit and strong, and I remember he used to bring his guitar and sing sometimes as we were into some of the same music. He was in some bands playing big shows supporting bands like *Jet*, *Spiderbait* and heaps of others; I thought he was a pretty cool guy. He had just broken up with his girlfriend, so the timing was perfect! We spent lots of time together, splitting time between his place in St Kilda and mine in Forest Hill. Life was amazing again.

At the time, I was autoinjecting beta interferon to help control the MS exacerbations. A few years earlier, I had a stint in the hospital as I kept injecting the same area and developed a massive infection... whoops! In 2004, I was told about a device that could help manage the spasticity in my legs with the use of Baclofen. This was an intrathecal Baclofen pump that would later be placed into my abdomen and spine and slowly drip feed Baclofen to help my balance, walking and movements. Interestingly enough, I think it stopped exacerbations, as I haven't had one since its implant.

I was spending more time with neurologists trying to manage my symptoms, as my walking had deteriorated more by now, and I was using two forearm crutches. I remember asking my neurologist if there would ever be a cure so I can walk normally again, and the reply has always stuck with me and etched into my mind. The reply was *Laura, not in your lifetime*. Oh, my shattered heart! That was not what I wanted to hear. That is not what anyone in my situation would want to hear. I refuse to believe *not in your lifetime;* nope, no way! A lot can happen in a lifetime, and I remain hopeful.

In the current day, I have two beautiful teenage children whom I adore more with each day. They are my world. My current level of MS is secondary progressive and has been for nearly 20 years. In 2013, I suffered a major fall that tore my left meniscus in my knee and cruelly robbed me of my ability to walk assisted. I now have fulltime use of a manual wheelchair.

I refuse to allow the condition to defeat me. I call it *the* condition because it's not *my* condition. I want to distance myself from it and remain in control of myself as much as I can.

Postpandemic, I keep my daily schedules moderately busy. For the past few months, I have absolutely loved getting back into creative arts, particularly painting. I love my Monday afternoon sessions at Juzt Art with Justine and Jo. I have been working on a display project for our gym which I recently completed, and I am now working on some new projects to give to my family. During the painting sessions, we have a blast, cranking some good tunes and enjoying a coffee and a laugh. By the end, I have progressed further on whatever project I'm getting stuck into. I have always appreciated art and love to be inspired by the world around me, and having the opportunity for an outlet in these art sessions has been completely therapeutic and boosts my happiness each week. Most of all, the classes give me the opportunity to be something I haven't been for a very long time.

Outside of art, I love to cook, but at this stage, my kitchen remains rather inaccessible, which is a huge frustration for me. The NDIS doesn't seem to like to modify kitchens for whatever reason, so I'm limited in what I can achieve and suffer burns more than I care to admit, but it doesn't stop me from trying. I can't tell you how much I f**king hate depending on people to do things when I know how to do it myself! It's never the same result! But I digress. From making fresh gnocchi with the children to making passata and lots in between, I love to create healthy fresh meals for my family; it's very important to me. My nonna passed down her love and knowledge of cooking to my mum and me, and I wish to do the same for my children. They are very good little chefs for their age, and I'd like to think that I'm responsible for that! Plus, nothing tastes better than homemade and with the shocking prices of everything these days, it's even more important to spend time in the kitchen having fun making healthy, enjoyable meals. My

partner is a great help as he loves to cook. Also, my support team are fantastic cooks, so there are no shortages of great meals or handy meals we freeze ahead of time that are available to us when we need to grab a quick meal or share one with family or friends. Ultimately, I WILL get a modified kitchen suitable for my needs... come hell or high water, I will get my kitchen!

NEW GYM TAKES AWAY BARRIERS TO WORKING OUT

HARRISON TIPPET

WHEN Laura Di Iulio and Tony Rankin felt frustrated by what they felt was a lack of wheelchair accessible gyms in Geelong, they decided to open their own.

The Geelong couple will this month officially open their ultra-accessible Grovedale gym DASH, which stands for Disability, Ageing and Specialised Health.

Ms Di Iulio said the idea came to the couple when her regular gym closed at the start of the Covid-19 pandemic in early 2020, leaving her unable to complete a crucial part of her treatment for multiple sclerosis.

"We wanted to start a gym because we didn't have access to go to a gym that was specifically able to cope with disability," she said.

The new Lewalan St gym includes accessible exercise and rehabilitation equipment such as an ergo machine and functional trainer.

Laura's partner Tony said it was important that everyone, no matter their age or ability, felt like they belonged at DASH.

"Some gyms can be intimidating and loud," he said. "We are open to everyone and to people who feel they're not comfortable in a standard gym."

For more information visit dashgx.com.au

When time permits, we occasionally trek down to Melbourne to visit Mum and spend time with family. I miss living in Melbourne, as it has everything I could ever need, and my friends are all based there. Although Geelong is only an hour away from Melbourne, with the hectic levels of daytoday life, sometimes it feels like hours away! Occasionally my pals will venture out this way, and we'll hit up some of the amazing wineries and eateries. We are spoiled here, with so many great places to eat and drink these days. It's a mission to get out and try them all—providing they have mobility access, of course!

For now, though, my focus is on raising our children and what great little humans they are. Allegra, our daughter, is now sixteen and independent and freespirited as ever but raised with values and respect. Our son, Valentino, fourteen, is equally amazing and full of that youthful energy I wish I could bottle! They are my world, and even though they are independent and doing mostly everything for themselves, I still try to do all I can. It's a difficult transition from having children who seem to need you at all times of the day to now having teenagers who can do everything on their own and no longer need mum's support. I am really proud of how they've grown and how respectful and understanding they are of the world around them; they are my everything.

I plan on becoming more involved in our allabilities gym as the business grows. There are lots of great things always happening there, and I enjoy my personal training sessions immensely. After my recent stint in the hospital—I finally got Covid for the first time—and losing my strength and conditioning, it reminds me of how crucial weekly resistance training is as I lost so much of my ability midway through 2023. Even as I write this, I'm still regaining that lost strength. Our gym is like a second home. Our children go in at night for their training sessions and love their results. But also, when I go, it's not only a place to focus on building my abilities but also a social outlet where I enjoy great friendships with many people from diverse backgrounds and where I can share my stories and enjoy their stories.

We all have a special story to tell. Every day is an opportunity to learn something new and enjoy the people and world around us. After leaving my teaching job to focus on raising our children, I'm enjoying the prospect of having a new purpose to my days and further developing my abilities and helping others do the same. Thanks for reading my story, and may your lives be filled with happiness, success, and an abundance of great health.

Watch the VLOG/Podcast of Laura on YouTube

ABOUT LAURA

Laura is the owner of an all abilities gym called Dash Gym & Wellbeing, is a former secondary/ESL and Italian teacher, artist, cook and supermum to 2 incredible kids!

She has lived with Multiple Sclerosis for 39 years in its current stage of secondary progressive. Laura refuses to allow the condition to dictate the terms of her life and through support of family and professional/allied health supports, she achieves whatever she sets her mind to!

Laura is from Melbourne, currently living in Geelong, and from an incredibly vibrant and energetic Italian family who are located throughout the Melbourne suburbs.

Website: **https://www.dashgw.com.au**

Facebook: **https://www.facebook.com/DashGymWellbeing**

12

Kim Eagle

MY LIFE AROUND MY MS DIAGNOSIS

Hi, I'm Kim—Kim Eagle.

I'd been known as Kim Kee in marriage.

I originally moved to Highton while I was a child in 1991 with my parents. This came after Dad's two businesses had to close permanently in Echuca, and we had to sell up and move. Both of my big brothers were in Echuca and Melbourne, and my sister was still in Echuca.

Then I moved on to Ocean Grove for a few years with my parents.

I attended school in Belmont at Oberon High and then at Queenscliff High, Queenscliff campus. Following finishing Grade 6 at Echuca Central 208 where I feel lucky to have attended my entire primary schooling. Next going to years 7 and 8 in Echuca at Saint Joseph's.

I moved to the Geelong, Victoria, area from Echuca in 1991.

Sadly, my big sister, Shez—Sheryl Eagle, RIP—had stayed on living in Echuca. Shez was killed in a car accident before she could move nearer to us. She was announced dead in the hospital, with her six-year-old son—the eldest of my nephews—staying there in hospital for many days after.

A year later my dad was killed playing golf near Geelong. He suffered a heart attack. My dad—Ivor Eagle, RIP—had no heart issues known before this.

I think he actually died of a broken heart for all that went wrong and because his eldest daughter died. He was a good dad and a good man.

I was a child grieving the other changes in my life, such as puppy love, boyfriends, getting bullied, moving and being new, girlfriends stealing my boyfriends, jobs, and general growing-up stuff. It was probably not the easiest childhood, and I know it.

Is childhood or growing up ever really easy?

There is only so much I can say in several thousand words or less, but in a nutshell, there is all this.

Since the early 80s, throughout the 90s, and after 1991 onwards, I had had definite attacks, possibly of less obvious, invisible and silent symptoms—especially fatigue—of multiple sclerosis. During that time, I experienced a massive loss of my vision, though very short-term, before having an MRI in the summer of 2007 and being referred to see an ophthalmologist in early 2008. Through all of this, my son Blaze, an only child for me to this point, was born—and that's another story. The blindness I experienced was while he was only a few months old.

My neurologist in Geelong told me that the results of my specialist ophthalmology eye test showed it likely to be because of MS, as my MRI showed ample permanent, irreversible lesions in my brain.

To treat the temporary blindness I experienced in both eyes, one worse than the other, I was prescribed a short-term oral treatment. The MRI report satisfied their diagnosis of MS, the probable cause of my blindness.

My definite diagnosis of MS came on my 30th birthday. I was already struggling with post-natal depression and general health problems. As usual, it seemed like a sense of grief overload!

I was told these results, and getting some answers was good, but

I was really scared to take Copaxone. This auto-inject daily needle treatment was so damaging, with the cricket ball-sized stinging and bruising, that I had to change to different medicine after about a month.

Because I was a needle wimp, my actual diagnosis was recorded as being in early April 2008. This was because I delayed starting the injections due to my needle phobia, and the thought of injecting myself was traumatic.

I can never actually maliciously self-harm by cutting or stabbing, even if I have ever wanted to. I only took the medication if someone else injected me! My child's dad got the honour and took some pleasure in the role too! We got along mostly then.

He called it jabbyjabby, which, yes, made us laugh and made it a little more tolerable. Comedy can help!

I had not heard of or listened to very much in those recent years before my diagnosis of MS! It just was not being heard or seen in my world. I'm not sure why, but I just heard or noticed so little about it then. No idea why. Having heard of it hardly at all since the late 80s, of which I'd enjoyed raising funds and reading books—nerd me—for the MS Readathon. I even raised the most money the very first year my country primary school participated in it.

There were no prizes until the following years, lol, which made people easily outdo me. Therefore, now I can laugh when I look back. I pushed my limits for no prize and am glad I did. It's about giving to give, not to receive sometimes, but it should be more often than in this world.

At that stage, there were no cures.

Guess what?

There are still no cures for MS.

With NO cure for MS, the treatments for our symptoms can have a lot of side effects, for example, cold and flu symptoms, liver and kidney issues, fatigue and many more.

Most are manageable for many people with MS.

There are ample treatments available for some symptoms at various stages of MS, and different things work better for different people.

I was diagnosed as having relapsing-remitting MS (RRMS). I still experience symptoms in that RRMS grouping daily, as it doesn't reverse.

But I have not progressed to be any worse. But I am not exactly better or cured. The previous damage of MS is irreversible.

To be blunt, when getting referrals and MRIs to find out about my MS, due to having my head in the sand grieving a big move and other life issues, I thought of MS as a death sentence.

I was not up to date with research, treatments, therapies, and the times regarding multiple sclerosis. So little did I know it was not a death sentence these days. Not anymore. But there is no cure. It is by no means fun having MS.

Having a new baby while having MS was no easy feat. Having a super significant attack like optic neuritis led to my MS diagnosis. I think I'd suffered for a long time before having a very challenging pregnancy, along with post-natal anxiety and depression, which made life tricky for yonks afterwards.

It was massively challenging and still can be that challenging most days—almost always.

Thinking about how beautiful my baby son is and knowing how essential his needs and development are, being a mum or carer is easier with vision. I love seeing him grow literally and reach milestones visually. To witness or aid him in reaching his milestones and developing skills was something I thought I'd have to struggle with. I know and maybe took for granted these senses and felt a little fear not knowing if my vision loss may be short-term or long-term was scary too.

The idea of wheelchairs had worried me, but not because of anything other than the fear I face of having vulnerability or dependency on others.

Also, at that time, while I was a new Mum and had blindness due to MS—optic neuritis—we were living in a really run-down dive of a house that should have been already demolished, and I love character homes! This house was past that by far.

I was trying to make the best of practically nothing.

This lily pad was in the suburb of Geelong, named North Geelong, and even had an outdoor laundry and toilet! It was functional, yes, but yuck! It was horrible. But it was home at that time. It was the only place I had to call home or go home to. It was a really hard time.

Even patches of the floor in that house were so unstable I wondered if we or our cats would fall through sometimes, but we didn't. It was actually really horrible. But as humans, we have ups and downs, and things can get better, and most often, they will, and they do.

My first Christmas and summer as a mum was in 2007-2008. I had a wonderful surprise from an MS nurse in the Neuroscience Department. They were a fellow person who'd raised a family and ran a business, incredibly having MS themselves. They wrote me an inspiring Christmas card anonymously. These things can actually mean a real lot! And these things can inspire and help if you want better outcomes yourself. So can better finances, kindness, honesty, integrity and respect.

The struggle is real.

At that stage, I tried to step back into work in a kinder assistant role. It was a hot Australian summer pretty typically, and this old house had no fans, air-con or cooling installed.

It was a private rental property, and I was purely grateful and lucky for MS Plus, formerly MS Connect. MS Australia and others financially aided me with a portable air con, but unfortunately, pedestal fans were more effective.

I tried an unsuccessful return to work. My flexibility and core fitness were probably at their worst ever.

Most people with MS relate to many of the symptoms of multiple sclerosis, including some or all of the following, but not exclusive to heat or cold intolerance and chronic fatigue.

For example, I did not feel I did well at all, most regularly.

My legs, unusually in my case and somewhat severely and functionally, played up, and I ceased paid employment. I also needed to walk to and from our harsh Aussie summer. This job lasted less than two weeks, I think.

I did a volunteer phone job once weekly, where I checked in on isolated and elderly clients through the Geelong Red Cross. It was not telemarketing, not sales, and not marketing, either. It was named the Red Cross Telecross, though it was more like the emergency beeper device, only a personalised and super quick call allowing the client time to answer. I held this role for approximately three years.

We were living further North in Geelong in Corio, Rosewall, where things were better in some ways for us at that time.

It was a much better house than North Geelong structurally. Even if the suburb has a bad name from many, it has a reputation but was affordable.

I was not personally ever hurt by living in that area as such, and sh*t happens anywhere and everywhere. A spicier area is sometimes because of the socio-economic proportioning, maybe.

Blaze—my son is my purpose in life, really.

Regardless of anything, my love and my children always will be. Ideally reunited wether alienated or together my son is the best creation I have collaborated in making and one of my favourite people Blaze, my only child, was about two when we moved there. We were living there a good three or four years before we got to move back to my favourite side of Geelong, the southern suburbs, and Grovedale. I LOVE this side of town best!

I often face ridicule, criticism, and doubt for continuing to live and learn through life, mature-aged, outside the typical age groups and general boundaries! I frequently find myself ridiculed or copping others' assumptions for having MS, for example, because someone knows one or three people who have MS. They think we are all identical and that they are qualified to assume anything and everything based on what they think they know!

Sorry if saying this hurts feelings or egos! It happens to me.

I am shy, and I am most definitely not neurotypical, so ridicule, doubt and criticism can heighten my anxieties. I try to stay strong and focused and not melt down much! I know I am strong, and I know I am capable of being focused.

I am built differently, and I am unusual, and this girl can. Really. This girl can. Can what? We'll see and hear!

I love dancing, including pole, barre, adult classical, ballroom, and more. Almost any dance, realistically, and I may love some straight-down-the-line subjective things like general math, types of science, English and sport. I am passionately creative in expression and music. I love playing, listening, appreciating, creating, making, and writing music. I love music from most genres as far as I know, and possibly more. My love and affinity with sound, music and movement and my love for sport and fitness is to infinity and beyond!

I enjoy target rifle shooting, learning and playing badminton and joining in wheelchair basketball whenever I can.

I am writing a lot of poetry and songs. I have become a songwriter, a singer, and a multi-instrumentalist. I have several works in progress.

Same as I love love. And I love my family, which I make. I love my child and my pets. And I love my lover.

But I am very much a loner, with or without company. Sometimes I prefer company, but I so often love my own space and my personal space. I know I have moments, though; in those, I can be quite demanding!

I am continually growing to love writing again. Songwriting, writing poetry and stories, playing music as I had since childhood and, of course, dancing still, too. I'm really just very Kreative—creative.

I really love everything creative. I like all-around most things, really.

Fond of creating art too! I can be somewhat the home chef and a foodie. I totally love to cook, mostly homemade cooking, homemade meals or basic baking. I am comfortable in kitchens. I like food and nutrition and have studied it. I like flavour! And I also think presentation can factor in better taste! Strange, but sometimes true.

Admiring or checking out some art is fun sometimes, too—for example, visual or fine arts. Justine Martin helped me remember my love for art! She is a very deserving and awarded artist and business savant! Amazing human, that one. We go through a lot, and we can both understand that too. It's not always easy, usually not at all easy.

I've always tried to be too independent. Maybe some of us have that in common too? I only know I am for sure.

I received a birthday gift voucher several years ago now. I wanted to spend my music lesson gift voucher whole and not top it up with my own dollars, so I chose singing lessons because I love most of all instruments and music. I was so shy I generally only chit-chatted through that whole lesson and my next and, for a while, struggled to not be too shy to even do voice training exercises and or warm up or anything, even at all!

So, knowing that I was intensely shy, I switched and started some beginner piano lessons instead, but I have continued to sing.

I had some guitar lessons, too, and then there was a pandemic thrown into the mix as a challenge to me and everyone else, too, for once, haha. Cop that—jokes.

And I am playing and learning the violin too. And drums! Love hitting them.

YouTube is fun regarding music, and mucking around is fun. There are even apps I find look worth getting which relate.

I scored a drum kit free, too. Thank you, Facebook marketplace, generous persons. I recently found out I can drum and want to drum more, and I love drumming. I love being a multi-instrumentalist, singer and sing more. I love being a musician now.

I bought myself a looper. I need to learn to be more self-sufficient with my songwriting.

Music can be therapeutic, and that can count for my purpose and benefit as much as it can be therapeutic, fun and or even enjoyment to and for others. Different things work for different people.

Other creative stuff, even fine arts and photography. Plus, I think food creativity and nutrition, food knowledge and all-around sports, movement, fitness, dance, math and numbers, all language, letters, research and science go together in perfect harmony. I think, therefore, I am. That's right! I am Mofos!

So, to explain better: that I am fussy is my little reference to the Aries star's theme things. Yes, I am an Aries. I take that stuff lightly. Good for a giggle.

I am looking forward to always learning as much as I want and can learn as always.

I am looking forward to performing better and performing in general and, most importantly, developing myself as much as ever in any and every way I can.

I think there are always things to learn, and there is no end to improvement as a human. Self-goals. Self-improvement. I practice the theory Yogi, not only Yoga.

I want to push my barriers. I want to succeed, and I love having the space and time to not feel watched, judged, or anxious. I continue to learn and develop in what I do unless it is specifically time for that—examinations, for example.

I would love to continue to do the plenitude of things I enjoy and never stagnate or snub learning.

I'd love to achieve greatness in all my interests and to become renowned for this greatness.

I would further like to better any talent I have and showcase my creations on my home ground nationally, internally, universally and planetarily!

With abundant thanks to my MS treating team at Neuroscience and MS Australia—MS Plus—and NDIS, as well as science, research and teams promoting education and awareness, I am fairly stable with my RRMS. Though I consistently have to battle my existing damage head-on, that being my invisible symptoms that are irreversible, I thankfully have not had recent new-coming symptomatic attacks to deal with.

Also add MASSIVE APPRECIATION AND THANK YOU to Justine of JUZT art, Resilience Mindset and Morpheus Publishing and to the various providers contracting for us with MS through the NDIS that have their hearts in right places with sense of decent humanity and professionalism, good ethical treatment and demonstrating integrity.

Watch the VLOG/Podcast of Kim on YouTube

ABOUT KIM

Kim Eagle's childhood was marked by a struggle to accept her given name, Kimberly, as she preferred the simpler moniker of "Yil girl." Growing up as an Australian country kid, she was a shy yet affectionate child, earning the endearing family nickname of "Kimberly Koala". Throughout her life, comedy has held a special place in her heart, bringing joy and laughter to her days.

Despite facing persistent fatigue over the years, it wasn't until 2007, after successfully giving birth to her son Blaze, that Kim received the life-changing diagnosis of Multiple Sclerosis.

Blaze, a beautiful and handsome child, became the center of Kim's universe, instilling her life with purpose and unconditional love.

Kim is known for her strong work ethic, approaching every task with determination and dedication. Her diverse range of interests includes music, art, sports, fitness, nutrition, writing, and cooking, all of which add excitement and fulfillment to her life.

Supported by an incredible network of friends from her hometown in Country Victoria and a loving partner, Kim finds solace and encouragement in their presence. She is currently engrossed in various writing projects, aiming to publish her work in the near future. Additionally, Kim strives to maintain her strength and fitness, embracing a healthy lifestyle.

As a true foodie, Kim delights in exploring the culinary world and actively participates in shooting, dancing, playing sports, and more. Additionally, she frequently contemplates study options, seeking to expand her knowledge and skills.

In the face of challenges, Kim Eagle's life journey exemplifies resilience, determination, and an unwavering love for her son Blaze. By pursuing her passions and with a supportive network by her side, she continues to inspire those around her with her positive outlook on life.

13

Jayne England

MS...

I didn't know anything about multiple sclerosis, but I associated it with people being in a wheelchair.

When I was in primary school, I took part in the MS Readathon a couple of times and raised money for people living with a disease called MS.

Other than that, my knowledge was very limited.

I had a great childhood.

I spent my first years living on a farm in central Tasmania with my parents and two of my brothers. We moved to a seaside town called Carlton River in southeast Tasmania when I was in grade 3. When I was in grade 6, my parents built their forever home on 55 acres, just outside of a town called Sorell, 20 minutes southeast of Hobart.

I was fit and healthy. I loved playing basketball and spending my spare time with friends. I was never really very academic. I finished school at the end of year 10, studied to get my advanced diploma in beauty therapy, and worked in the beauty industry for many years.

When I was 18, I started seeing a guy called Scott. I had known

Scott and his family since our family had moved to Carlton River, and Scott was good mates with my older brother. After dating for two years, in 2002, we moved to the Gold Coast.

Our son Josh was born in 2004, Scott and I were married in 2006, and our family became complete in 2007 when our daughter Kayla was born.

Shortly after Kayla's birth, we purchased a block of land in Tasmania, moved home and built our family home in Dodges Ferry. It is a beautiful seaside community not far from my family and close to the beach—heaven!

It took a while for me to re-acclimatise and settle back in Tasmania, but we were close to our family, and it was the perfect place for our children to grow up. Looking back now, I know I was where I was supposed to be because little did I know I would soon need my family's support more than ever.

Life was great—until it wasn't.

One morning in November 2009, I woke up with pain in my left hip. Over the next week, the pain progressed down my leg. Then slowly up my torso and down my left arm. I thought I had put my back out, so I made an appointment to see my chiropractor. When I arrived to see him, I explained my symptoms, and he straight away phoned my doctor. He explained to me that he thought it to be something more serious, possibly a series of mini-strokes or even multiple sclerosis.

Ok, this could be serious, but nothing was confirmed.

My doctor straight away sent me for a CT scan. Afterwards, while waiting for the scans—back then, you would take them with you—a lady came into the waiting room and sat beside me. She told me that there was something showing in my brain, but they couldn't read the scan properly. I could tell by her facial expression that this was getting serious.

I was then sent to the Hobart Private Hospital for another CT scan, but this time with contrast so they could read the scan better.

They rushed the results through, and by the time I got back to my doctor, she had them. My chiropractor was right. There were lesions in my brain, she couldn't be certain, but it looked like it was MS.

That morning I had gone to have a back adjustment, and by late afternoon I knew my life and my family's lives were about to change, and not for the better.

I could have gone straight to the emergency department, but I wanted to be at home with my babies and try to digest everything that was happening to me. I left the doctor's surgery with a plan to see neurology the following day.

When I woke up the following morning, the left side of my body was totally paralysed from my neck down.

I arrived at neurology at the Royal Hobart Hospital and was seen immediately. I remember the neurologist poking my arm multiple times with a pin; I couldn't feel anything.

They admitted me to a ward, and I waited for an MRI, and thankfully I didn't have to wait long. Then at 5:00 pm on Friday, 13 November 2009, only 26 hours after seeing my doctor, I was officially diagnosed with relapsing-remitting multiple sclerosis. I was told they didn't need to run any more tests because of my severe symptoms, and my MRI lit up like a Christmas tree with all of my brain lesions. They didn't want me to leave the hospital because they were concerned that if I didn't receive steroids, I might not be able to walk at all the following day.

So, I stayed in the hospital until Monday and was given three days of intravenous steroids. At this time, my only concern was for my children. I knew nothing about MS and was concerned they would be given the same diagnosis one day.

I was given a crash course in MS. I was told what could happen and what I might experience, but also that no two cases of MS were the same. Don't go home and Google MS because there is a lot of misinformation on the Internet.

I left the hospital, and I went into denial.

In my mind, my doctors, my specialists, everyone; they had to have gotten it wrong.

I waited for a phone call that would confirm this.

Every time I received a call from an unknown number, I had a moment of hope. At that moment, I imagined they would tell me they had made a mistake and, in fact, I didn't have MS at all.

That phone call never came. My doctors were right. I had multiple sclerosis, and there was nothing my family or I could do to change it.

I had to accept my new diagnosis, try to process everything, and hopefully, with time, accept it.

Even after steroids, I could hardly walk. I had no strength or coordination in my arm, so cutting up a good steak was certainly out of the question unless someone cut it up for me. You can imagine how useless it made me feel.

I felt totally out of control of my body—a body that had served me well for the previous 28 years.

It took me a good three months to overcome that relapse.

In January 2010, I started medication; at first, a drug called Copaxone. For 14 months, I self-injected daily. Something which

was incredibly difficult for me to do as I have a needle phobia.

Then, after 14 months of my dreaded daily injections and my health continuing to deteriorate, I had a routine MRI scan. The results showed that I had more lesions in my brain and new lesions on my cervical vertebrae.

When I saw my specialists, there was a sense of urgency for me to change medications. This was absolutely terrifying for my husband and me at the time.

New medications meant new possible side effects that, at the time, I couldn't even bring myself to tell my family about.

However, I had to trust my doctors that they knew what they were doing.

In March 2011, I started on a medication called Tysabri.

For around six years, I would go to ambulatory care at the Royal Hobart Hospital for my monthly infusion. I had some minor side effects that would last for around 24 hours post-infusion, but they were manageable.

The amazing staff at ambulatory care organised, with the permission of my neurologist, for a medi-port to be implanted into my chest because my veins weren't easily accessible. I would have a lot of anxiety leading up to my infusion. The port has direct access to my veins, which makes it much easier for my infusions and blood tests.

When I was on Tysabri, my MS stayed in remission, but I relapsed and once again had new lesions.

I chose to start a new infusion called Lemtrada. I had two yearly doses of this treatment, but I continued to deteriorate.

My neurologist obtained permission for me to have a third Lemtrada infusion. Unfortunately, this was also unsuccessful. I had failed yet another MS medication and suffered my first major spinal relapse.

This was absolutely heartbreaking. Nothing was helping, and I was still getting worse!

I was offered to go on another MS treatment or the opportunity to have a stem cell transplant right here in Hobart!

This was huge and absolutely terrifying.

However, within five minutes of talking to my neurologist and husband, I decided that I would have a stem cell transplant.

Thankfully, I had already researched this treatment over the years, so I had a pretty good idea of the process.

I had surgery to have another medi-port inserted—this time on the right side of my chest. This port had the capability of the blood being removed on one side and then being reintroduced on the other side. The doctors needed this to remove my stem cells later during this treatment.

At the beginning of September 2021, I had a strong dose of chemotherapy. This was so strong that I started losing my hair within a week. Because of my new port, I was unable to shower, so I would awkwardly have a bath, all while trying to keep my port dry.

A week later, I started daily injections to stimulate stem cell growth in my bone marrow. During this process, your bones expand. I was told this would be painful, but the more pain I experienced, the more stem cells I produced.

Within a few days, I was in a world of pain, but for the first time in my MS journey, I was actually happy to be in pain.

My stem cells were intravenously harvested on 20 September, and I was told that I had produced a record number of cells—no wonder I was in so much pain.

My stem cells were frozen, and I waited for a hospital admission date for the next part of my treatment.

One night, I asked my daughter, Kayla, if she could wash my hair. Within minutes, I heard her breathing increase, and I knew my long blond hair was falling out in her hands. I knew to expect this and was mentally prepared for it. We knew it would happen, but my daughter was 14 at the time, which was incredibly confronting for her.

The following evening Kayla had a friend stay over, and together they shaved my head. I was given a number of different hairstyles, and having Kayla's friend with us made this process a lot less emotional. There were still tears but a lot of laughs!

I was then admitted to the hospital on 13 October and started six days of chemotherapy. The chemotherapy removed my current immune system.

Thankfully, I only experienced a little nausea and loss of appetite. My MS symptoms flared up during this time, and I experienced severe nerve pain in my arms and legs. I was told that this may happen during treatment.

During my third day of chemotherapy, we got the news that southern Tasmania was about to go into Covid lockdown. A man had escaped quarantine and put Tassie into a three-day lockdown.

Thankfully, we found out before the public announcement, and Scott was able to pick Josh and Kayla up from school early and come in for a visit. I was so grateful that I got to see them because the hospital went into a nine-day lockdown.

This was devastating but thank goodness for modern technology. FaceTime allowed me to see my family virtually.

I was also lucky to have a lovely roommate, and we kept one another entertained.

On 18 October, I had my last day of chemotherapy. They moved me into a single room in preparation for my stem cell reintroduction. I was excited, exhausted, and so nervous!

On 19 October, I had my stem cell transplant.

We were still in lockdown, so unfortunately, Scott couldn't be with me. Luckily a close friend was finishing her nursing degree and happened to have a placement in my ward. I felt so blessed that she was there and was able to hold my hand throughout this experience.

The transplant went really well, and I had no side effects.

A few days later, I had two antibody infusions; unfortunately, I did react to these. I experienced severe temperature spikes—fevers and chills, and a horrific-looking rash that covered my torso and gave me intense pain.

I became septic, my temperature reached 40.7 degrees, my heart rate went crazy, my blood pressure was extremely high, and my oxygen levels dropped. I lost consciousness.

When I came to, it was terrifying. The room was full of nurses and doctors, the emergency response team, and I was hooked up to a lot of medical equipment. The nurses called Scott into the hospital. There were lots of tears, but he was able to stay with me until my vitals stabilised.

I was rushed to surgery to remove my port, as they thought I might have an infection.

I had to have intravenous steroids and antibiotics to help with and prevent more side effects and infections. I also needed two bags of platelets and two blood transfusions to keep my levels normal.

What an experience!

I had an incredible medical team and was well looked after—before, during and after my treatment.

I was discharged from the hospital on 1 November, and for the first couple of weeks, I slept and had little energy.

Blood tests showed that the stem cells were multiplying, and my immune system was slowly recovering.

I was told that my mobility could be affected and that there were instances when some patients walked into the hospital before treatment and left in a wheelchair.

Thankfully, I walked out of the hospital. However, for a few months after I returned home, I did have mobility issues. I had lost a lot of strength and could only stand for around five to ten minutes at a time before my muscles would cramp, and I would struggle to walk.

Recovery was slow, and at times I wondered if I had made the right decision to have a stem cell transplant.

Even though I was well educated in the treatment process,

nothing could have mentally prepared me for it. It was like being on a rollercoaster ride—so many highs and lows. It has certainly affected my mental health, but I am in the process of healing.

Here are some of the MS symptoms I have experienced living with multiple sclerosis.

Every morning I would wake up tired. I felt like I hadn't slept.

I've suffered bad insomnia; there have been days and weeks I hardly slept.

The exhaustion is like no other. I can't even explain it—days when I struggled to get out of bed.

I have suffered from debilitating headaches, which hasn't been easy when I have family, a business and a household to run.

Nerve pain. I felt like my limbs were on fire.

The dreaded MS Hug—it feels like tight contractions around your chest, and I have ended up in the hospital from this, thinking I was having a heart attack!

At times, I have had bowel and bladder issues.

I have dealt with vertigo, paralysis, memory loss, anxiety and, at times, depression.

These are only a small number of symptoms that I and other people living with MS live with on a daily basis.

You are unable to see the majority of our symptoms. That is why they call MS an invisible disease.

Fast forward to November 2022, 13 months after my stem cell transplant and 13 years of living with MS.

My sister Karen and I, along with a group of people we had never met—and now consider friends—completed a four-day MS Mount Kosciusko fundraising trek. We collectively raised over $27,000 for MS research!

I climbed Mount Kosciusko! It was amazing, so emotional and such a huge achievement. An incredible four days with my sister that we will never forget. Something that I would not have been able to physically do prior to my transplant, and I did it pretty much pain-free.

I am now 21 months post-transplant.

I hardly have to take any pain medication.

I have had two MRIs—one of those was only a month ago.

My MS is stable, and I have no new MS lesions.

This is something that I could never have imagined two years ago.

I'm not naïve enough to think that my MS will be stable forever. But right now, I feel positive and so incredibly blessed that I was given the opportunity to have a stem cell transplant.

I still have difficult days and MS symptoms, but they are manageable. The stem cell transplant doesn't heal the damage that existed prior to my treatment.

I have an incredible MS community around me and amazing friends, which is so important for anyone living with MS.

I have the most amazing supportive family, and I know they

would give everything they have to take my MS away.

Scott is my rock. My husband and my best friend. I am so lucky to have him, his support and unconditional love—regardless of what my future holds.

Josh and Kayla are now 19 and 16 and can't remember me from before my diagnosis. They have grown up with it. I could not have hoped for more patient, caring, and loving children with so much empathy.

I am truly blessed and can't wait to see what the future holds.

I hope to one day write and publish my entire journey.

Watch the VLOG/Podcast of Jayne on YouTube

ABOUT JAYNE

Jayne is a self-employed businesswoman, married and a busy mother of two teenagers.

She trained and worked in the beauty industry for many years.

Jayne was diagnosed with relapsing remitting MS in November 2009. She was 27 years of age at the time of her diagnosis, her children were aged just four and 18 months old at the time.

Since her diagnosis, Jayne has held roles with Multiple Sclerosis (MS) in Tasmania, been involved with the Tasmanian MS Community Engagement Council, including roles as Chair and Deputy Chair. She is a member of the consumer and community reference committee for the MS Research Flagship at the Menzies Institute for Medical Research. Jayne is an active fundraiser and advocate for those living with MS.

Jayne has also tried and failed many MS disease modifying medications - and most recently undergone a Stem Cell Transplant with fantastic results.

14

Penelope Gemmell

VALUABLE LIFE LESSONS I HAVE LEARNED FROM MS

Have you ever rounded up chickens using a wheelie walker? I have. Hint—do not try it in bare feet! While not one of the goals I had set for myself as a young adult, it is an achievement I'm quite proud of these days. MS has taught me to notice and celebrate achievements and to grab opportunities, no matter their size. I'm not sure how the chooks feel about the wheelie walker, but they are still laying, and I'm safer than I once was.

Twenty-three years ago, I could never have imagined that I would be using a wheelie walker and a wheelchair or have chickens. Twenty-two years ago, I was diagnosed with RRMS. I was devastated. I still remember sitting in my car in a gloomy shopping centre car park after the MRI. All I could see in my head was a wheelchair and ads for the MS Readathon. I was numb from shock. I don't remember leaving that car park, but I must have. That date is forever etched in my mind. It happened to be the day before 9/11.

I was alive. I was not burning in a mangled passenger plane. I was not crushed and dying under one of the tallest buildings in the world. I was not trapped by fire and phoning loved ones to say goodbye while waiting for the building to collapse.

I was too shocked to be able to process anything about MS. It felt like I was in a cold and grey pea soup fog and couldn't take a breath. It was like walking through wet, sticky mud wearing cheap gumboots. Little did I know that this news was simply the beginning of what I now call my mid-life crisis. Nor did I know I would become very familiar with that feeling of walking through mud.

Six months later, my mother died after a battle with ovarian cancer. I regret telling her about my diagnosis before she passed away. Why on earth did I tell her? She did not need to hear that when she was so close to leaving us. My father had passed 12 years before.

Six weeks later, my husband died in a motorbike accident. I ended up as an in-patient in the local psychiatric ward. I suspect I was under a self-harm watch. I don't remember much of my time there, but I do remember hearing the emergency helicopter landing at the hospital. As strange as it might seem, it was a reassuring sound. The sound of the whirring helicopter blades reminded me that life for billions of people was still going on, both the good and the bad sides. My life had simply changed.

MS taught me I still needed to grieve for all I had lost: my sense of self, my mother, my husband, and the reality of never having children. I had endometriosis, and we had spent the nineties in the IVF program. When my husband died, we were on the overseas adoption bureaucratic paper trail. With an MS diagnosis and a dead husband, that was the end of that.

MS has taught me that the grieving process is necessary to heal and move forward. MS has taught me that while my heart might have broken, it would heal, but with a scar or two on it.

My life plan was to fall in love, marry and have two, maybe three, children, and, like the fairy tales, live happily ever after. Well, that didn't happen! MS taught me that fairy tales don't always come true. The life plan was not panning out as expected. I had no life plan left, no new goals. What was the point of having goals when they were just ripped away? I lurched from one crisis to the next.

MS reminded me I still had responsibilities and commitments. They revolved around my job, close friends, and faithful pets.

I had the best boss in the world. She supported me through those difficult months that turned into difficult years with kindness, patience and understanding.

MS taught me I had the best friends in the world. They went above and beyond to help me recover and get my life back on track. My friends helped me by looking after my loved dogs. While I was in hospital, they sent my dogs to another friend's boarding kennel. When I was well enough to bring my fur family home, this friend refused to let me pay for their food or board. He said, "… that's what friends do." A phrase I will never forget. Mal, thank you.

MS taught me to take one step at a time, even one breath at a time. It really does work in difficult times. My friends supported me by helping with the paperwork side of death. They organised a working bee at home. I remember we had to almost detach one friend surgically from his whipper snipper as he battled the weeds in my yard. I remember the look of horror on another friend's face when she opened my pantry. I knew I would never be able to repay the kindness I received at that time. I am now a big believer in the pay it forward theory. Maybe I could offer support to someone I hadn't met yet? Was that a new goal starting to form?

My remaining human family was worried about me, but they had their lives three thousand kilometres away. They kept in regular contact when they returned home after my husband's funeral. They even arranged an overseas holiday for me with them around the first anniversary of his death. They did this even though they were having major life challenges themselves, and those challenges are their stories to tell.

People asked me why I didn't return to Melbourne, but my life was no longer there. MS taught me my life was here in North Queensland. I had good friends, a job I loved, a little house, my fur family, and the North Queensland weather. The variable weather in Melbourne would be a nightmare.

Without those things that made up my home, I doubt I would be around to write my story now. Yes, I did consider that there was an easier way to deal with my overwhelming grief. I had the means, the plan, and the motivation. MS has taught me to ask for help. I asked my doctor for help and received it.

I had many sessions with my psychologist. She helped me to understand my grief regarding these life-changing events. MS taught me it was a constant in my life and was not going to go away. My psychologist called me resilient. I wonder, can resilience be considered a superpower?

I had the opportunity to do a yoga course. I did it and still practice now. I also learned about mindfulness and to listen and trust my body.

When I went public with my diagnosis, I learned there were two other staff members who also had MS. Apparently, everyone knows someone with MS. MS taught me to recognise when I could not work safely or as part of a team and take responsibility for it. That was something I could control. I struggled to keep up when we were transferring a patient; the team would slow down for me. I could no longer run for the resuscitation trolley. If there had been a fire, I would have had enough trouble getting myself down the fire escape stairs, let alone be capable of helping with the evacuation of patients. I was furniture walking around an intensive care bed space, which was not best practice for patients, other staff, and me. After two falls at work, I realised my colleagues were keeping an eye out for me. I was a distraction from their patients. I made the decision to retire. That way, I was in control of my life. It meant no one would need to take me aside to have a quiet word. In the aftermath of taking control of that decision, it occurred to me I had continued to work for thirteen years after my diagnosis. MS has taught me to recognise that achievement.

So, what now? Around this time, I was told I had progressed to SPMS. It was time to reinvent myself. MS taught me to think outside the box.

I tried face painting. My friends' children were keen to volunteer so I could practise with them. One day, my four-year-old friend Maddie and I decided to do some reverse face painting. That is where the person being painted also paints the painter's face. When our creative juices had been used up, Maddie's mum stepped onto the back veranda. Beth took one look at us, and the veranda groaned and returned inside. I had face paint up my nose and in my ears. Maddie needed a bath!

MS has taught me that some bright ideas are not so bright. The next idea was to grow some plants to sell at one of the local markets. There were little terracotta pots with seedlings on and in every spare space around my house. Then I realised I would have to get out of bed very early on a Sunday morning to set up my market stall. That Christmas, a lot of people found baby pot plants under their Christmas trees.

There were several other ideas, but the one that worked was to become a volunteer Justice of the Peace (JP) and join the JPs in the Community program. I'm one of those people you see sitting at a table at the local shopping centre, witnessing a variety of documents. I've been doing it for five years and love it. I feel I'm doing something useful for the community. I'm always learning and can offer a little help to grieving people doing battle with the paperwork related to death. Hopefully, I am helping people I haven't met before and paying it forward. It seems ironic that the shopping centre where I do my JP shifts is the one where that car park was and still is.

Meanwhile, I attended some of the MS support group lunches here in Townsville. I found these lunches to be a great resource and have made many friends through them. The first time I attended a support group meeting, it was overwhelming. All these people using wheelie walkers and wheelchairs. Was that what my future looked like? I stayed away for a few years and now have found the lunch- time gatherings friendly and informal. I recommend getting involved with a local support group, whether specifically for MS or not. MS has taught me that getting to know other neurologically challenged people is a great privilege. MS has taught me that while there were people doing it easier than me, there were also a lot of people doing it much tougher.

Somehow, I found myself the Services Management Advisory Committee (SMAC) representative for Townsville to MS Queensland. I did have to explain to some people that the acronym SMAC had nothing to do with the Fifty Shades of Grey book that had just arrived in bookshops. It made life interesting when chatting to people about the role.

Almost everything I know about the National Disability Insurance Scheme (NDIS) grew from MS Queensland's education

sessions. Something I will always be grateful for.

I was also attending various rehab centres and learning about MS from a rehabilitation perspective. I was having contact with allied health professionals such as physios, occupational therapists and exercise physiologists. They and MS have taught me so much. For instance, how to get up after a fall—invaluable information. The importance of moving, even if it is just a tiny little bit. It turns out yoga was one of the best things I could be doing to help manage MS for both the body and mind. A phrase I learned through yoga was to stop and listen to the silence. I still do this—listen to the silence. Maybe try it one day. One of my goals is still to be able to sit in lotus when I'm, umm ... much older.

MS has taught me that goals must be specific, achievable, and timely. For instance, I have always wanted to go on a cruise to Antarctica, but the cost is astronomical and not achievable for me. MS has taught me to accept that but to dig a little deeper. I have discovered that you can do a flyover of Antarctica which is achievable for me.

MS has taught me to trust my intuition and grab opportunities as they float by. If you are reading this, you will know I grabbed the opportunity Justine offered for me to tell my story. I can now include being a published author among my other achievements.

In my pre-mid-life crisis life, I used to teach and compete in dog obedience and agility. I loved it, but in the post-mid-life crisis fallout, I had to stop. Just last night, I had the opportunity to visit the old training grounds, so I grabbed it and realised I still love that part of the dog world. While there, I discovered I could take up the opportunity to attend, with my dog, a canine disc—frisbee—workshop. For me, throwing a frisbee from a wheelchair is achievable, just so long as my dog decides to bring it back! We'll work on that.

I had the opportunity to learn Auslan—Australian Sign Language—and met a few members of the Deaf community. They are another inspiring group of people.

MS has taught me to clarify and refresh my life goals. Among the frisbee throwing and volunteer JP achievements, I also want to stay in my home for as long as I safely can. I want to keep learning new things. I want to keep looking after my chooks, my dog and my cat. I want to keep attending physio and exercise physiology sessions and yoga classes. I want to potter about my garden. I want to keep moving. I don't want to have any more falls and deal with broken bones. I want to stay well, both physically and emotionally. Exercise plays a big role in that. I have found when feeling miserable, doing a simple exercise always makes me feel better. Getting those endorphins moving through the blood-stream is always a good thing. I wonder, is exercise related to the mythical elixir of life?

MS has taught me to persevere. I entered our local running festival three years in a row with my wheelie walker. I was consistent. I came last each time in the 2.5 km event. I would find myself going slower and slower and dragging my feet. It felt like I was walking with an ankle weight and swimming flipper on one foot through sticky mud. I was exhausted. Each time getting across that finish

line was the goal and another achievement for me. It would take a few days for my support worker and me to recover. The support worker would usually walk backwards over the last kilometre. She would have to lean on the front of my walker to stop it from flipping over as I was leaning on the handles so hard. I haven't told her I'm thinking about doing it again, but in the wheelchair.

MS taught me something else that I had control over—driving. When driving got to the point I had to use my right hand to lift my right leg off the accelerator to slow down, I knew it was time to consider my driving future seriously. Yes, my occupational therapist and I did consider getting my car modified so I could use hand controls. The exercise almost turned into one of those supposed reality television shows. That story could have its own chapter here. I don't know enough about sociology, but driving seems to represent independence in our culture. Being unable to drive does limit where I can go. I can't just pop out to have a cuppa with someone spontaneously. The thought of causing an accident that seriously injured or killed an innocent road user weighed heavily with me. I knew I could not live with that responsibility. I could not let my stubbornness and pride rule over other people's safety. I voluntarily surrendered my driver's licence. Something else I had control over. I did not want a judge or the police to make that decision for me. It was one of the hardest decisions I've ever made. Through the NDIS, I was able to arrange other transport options. Do I regret my decision? Not at all. Once done, I felt like a great weight had been physically lifted off my shoulders.

MS has taught me that purchasing products for that MS problem we don't like to mention in polite society from the supermarket is far less embarrassing than having a major accident in a very public place. Been there, done that, and don't plan to do it again.

MS has taught me to look at walking aids from a new perspective. Before I went from using a walking stick to using a wheelie walker, I thought using a walker was a sign that I was becoming more disabled. After three days on the walker, I realised I was less likely to fall, could walk further, could carry things, and had my own place to sit when there was a shortage of seats. I also discovered the wheelie walker subculture. Users will share discrete smiles. They will start up random conversations about the pros and cons of their

walkers and might even challenge you to a race.

When it came time to consider using a wheelchair, the same thoughts reappeared. After a lot of tears and two psychology appointments later, I started using a wheelchair when out and about, and guess what? I realised the same things all over again! This time MS taught me I could have days without that all-over fatigue. I can get things done in a reasonable amount of time. On the walker, it used to take me three weeks—that is what it felt like— to get down an aisle at Bunnings without distractions. In the chair, I can get down an aisle in three minutes with distractions. And I am safe. I have not had a significant fall and the resulting broken bones in the last six years. That is since I started using the walker. I feel more enabled rather than disabled. I also have a whole new appreciation for automatic doors.

I have MS. I have worked my way through the grieving process. I am not in denial. I have reached the acceptance stage of the grieving process, and I can breathe. Now that the fog has cleared, I can see the bright blue sky.

With a few modifications, wonderful support workers, and thinking outside the box—such as using a wheelchair in a running festival—I can do anything I really want to do.

Beth's mum and Maddie's grandmother said to me once, "Focus on the things you can do, not the ones you can't do", and that works for me.

ABOUT PENELOPE

Penel (aka Penelope) was diagnosed with RRMS 22 years ago. She has slowly, but surely, progressed to SPMS. Penel worked in the health care sector for approximately 30 years. Nine years ago, she made the difficult decision to retire. These days she is busier than ever with volunteer work, yoga, exercise sessions and learning new skills (not always related to MS) with the aim of staying happy, safe, and well. Penel sometimes wonders where she found time to work. She currently lives in North Queensland with a variety of animals, MS and the NDIS and is a strong believer in the 'use it, or lose it', theory.

Watch the VLOG/Podcast of Penelope on YouTube

15

Candice Graham

IT'S ALL OVER BEFORE IT BEGAN

There are some key points in your life where you take a deep breath, and you have a very clear thought to yourself, *right, this is it ... this is the beginning of the end.* I presumed that this was going to be the day I either die or find out that I have pushed myself so hard that my body had given way—and it was all for nothing. Not something you expect to happen when you are 25.

It was roughly 5:30 am on a Saturday morning. I woke up like someone had slapped me in the face, but I didn't think much of it at the time. I tell myself, *ah, I must have slept on my arm.* I take myself off to the bathroom to put warm water on my right hand, expecting to *wake it up*. I was still living with my parents, and their upstairs bathroom was designed to have a basin in the walkway before entering the toilet. I turned to put my right arm in the basin. I tried to lift it, but it felt like it weighed 20 kg. I look up in the mirror. The right side of my face has dropped. *Shit, I'm having a stroke!*

My life as I knew it was all downhill from there. I kept saying to the paramedic, "It's a good way to get out of work on a Saturday morning ..." It was the strangest thing. It was like I had two parts of myself. The first was fixated on the moment my father was tearing up and couldn't look at me, absolutely devastated after I stumbled into their bedroom moaning and slurring. The other part was completely numb—nothing. I couldn't think. I couldn't feel it.

Nothing

I kept getting asked by medical staff, "Are you in pain? Where does it hurt?" The weirdest thing was no; there was nothing. Every thought I had, and everything I said, was on a replay and repeat in my head. I don't think that even now, I have the right words to describe it. Was it a medical episode I was having, or was it shock? Too hard to tell. All I knew was that it was bloody awful, and I needed this to stop. I had my master's thesis to complete, and I had absolutely no time for this.

Following this was a life that I never thought I would have. My licence was taken away, and I was unable to even write my own name, brush my teeth or bring a spoon of cereal to my mouth. This is not what I had planned. This was not happening to me. Yet it was. And then I had the worst day—well, so far, anyway. One day, I had a problem at home. I did not feel well enough to study. I still couldn't use my right hand. I remember it was dark, lying in my parent's lounge in the living room. Everyone else was busy, and everyone else could drive. I had nothing.

I spoke to a friend to reach out to get support. They felt sad for me, and my friends were so good to me around that time. I wouldn't be around, I don't think, without the support of my friends from university. They invited me out to a house party to meet this guy. It was a kind of do-over party. That Saturday when it all went to shit, and that evening I was meant to go to this person's house party and meet him.

Tierell

Now this guy was described to me as *a male version of me*. I'm still not sure if that is a good thing or not. I think they were trying to be kind. I was never one to have a boyfriend. I always felt I wasn't attractive enough. I was always the fat girl that was the good friend to talk to, not the girl to pine over. Despite losing a tonne of weight, I still felt the same. I never felt good enough. I know that everyone usually says that, but I can't identify a time when I felt like I truly fit in. I felt awkward: too tall, too fat, too much, too noisy and too lazy.

I had nothing else to lose, so screw it, I went to the party. This person saw me for who I was that night—well, at least I think he did upon reflection. I didn't have to pretend with him. Hell, I thought I was going to die for the past two to three weeks, so why did I need to pretend to be funny or interesting? I was trying my hardest to be present and in the moment. He had pink hair and a goatee and tried to interest me in photos on his phone of a dress-up party he attended as a *naughty nun* with fishnet stockings! He was hilarious! He wasn't like anyone else I had ever met. He was charming, funny, intelligent, and interested in me. Why me?

I didn't have anything to offer in a relationship. I couldn't get my university course completed. I certainly doubted that I could finish my university course and get registered as a psychologist at that time. I didn't think I could even get my driver's licence back. But that night, we stayed up talking the entire night outside, sitting on a lounge under a pergola. Didn't sleep a wink. We talked, and talked, and talked some more. When his friends woke up in the morning, they said that Tierell had *never* not slept throughout the night—he was renowned for falling asleep as soon as he had a few drinks! Maybe this was turning into something.

Tierell and I have been together since. I never truly thought that it would happen to me.

Capacity

My capacity was different from there on in. I couldn't work full time, and I couldn't get my thesis done on time. Everything was delayed, which I did not feel comfortable with. I was eventually diagnosed with multiple sclerosis when I saw an outpatient neurologist who repeated all the tests. At this point, they saw about five to six more lesions. My scans looked like *Rorschach's* pictures. I started daily injections from then, which was quite overwhelming. I previously had a needle phobia, but I needed to overcome this quickly to prevent further relapses.

I eventually got my driver's licence back when they ruled out seizures. I would have these moments where I would lose my speech and couldn't function for several minutes. It was pretty scary when I had these spells. But to have seizures ruled out was such a relief. I didn't need any more complications.

It took quite some time to improve my stamina to return to full-time employment. I was sceptical that this was going to happen, but I was determined to not let MS rule my life. After we moved out together and got married, Tierell was flexible enough to agree to move several times to follow my career choices. I gained my endorsement in clinical psychology, which seemed to be my biggest achievement since I completed my master's program in educational and developmental psychology. A few weeks later, we found out I was pregnant! It looks like our celebrations were productive.

Nothing done in halves

Several scans were in, and we had the question asked during the scan, "And how many babies were you meant to be having?" The biggest shocking question I had asked of me thus far. I couldn't stop saying *holy shit* after the sonographer found two heartbeats and congratulated us on having twins. Tierell had to be quite assertive with me before exiting into the waiting room as he said, "You can't go out there like that. You'll scare the shit out of everyone. Hold it together until you get into the car, then lose your shit." Good advice, and with that, I did.

We didn't know we were having twins, obviously, until that day. We announced it to our families on Christmas Day via Christmas cards. It was wild—so much fun. The pregnancy was wild too. I remember never feeling the same once I found out that everything I did impacted not one, not two, but three people. Although it was tough, they were happy and healthy.

At 25 weeks, I needed to cease work overnight because of my cervix shortening. Those nine to 10 weeks were such a punishment. No work, not driving. Stuck at home on the lounge. Only left the house for appointments. I had the twins at 34 weeks plus six days. What an effort. The second twin was breach, but both were healthy at 2 kg and 2.1 kg. Two beautiful girls—Althea and Addison. I remember that from the get-go, they seemed different. Addison, the second twin, especially behaved differently from other babies in the neonatal intensive care unit and special care nursery—she yelled instead of crying. Althea was a very serious baby—nothing like I had ever seen before.

A year or so later, we wanted to try again. Despite my health, we found it easy to fall pregnant each time. We fell pregnant again, and under three years later, we delivered Frances—well, we all call her Frankie. And there's *Cranky Franky*—her alter ego when furious about getting her way. Happy and healthy as well at just over 3 kg. Having three children under four is no easy feat.

We very much underestimated how hard it would be. And the twins proved to be quite challenging the older they got. Althea continued to be very serious, easily overwhelmed and could speak in full sentences at a very young age. Addison, on the other hand, struggled with most things and could barely speak at four years of age. After several hearing tests, we found out that Addison was borderline deaf in both ears. She had her tonsils and adenoids removed and grommets inserted into both ears. It changed her behaviour slightly and improved the rate of her speech. However, she never caught up with her sister or her peers.

During the time after my pregnancy, my fatigue continued to worsen. My vision would deteriorate from time to time, my tremors would worsen, and my leg weakness would increase. My symptoms improved dramatically while pregnant, but I struggled significantly afterwards. Plus, the demands of having three little children and being the breadwinner didn't help. There were times when I could not lift my legs to get out of bed. There were times that I would lose my speech and couldn't think again. My neurologist hadn't re-prescribed me immunosuppressants, but I feel he doubted my disease progression. I have a bad habit of under-reporting symptoms during appointments. I found those appointments so overwhelming, and my mind would often go blank. My symptoms were so vague and highly changeable that it was increasingly difficult to report.

2019

I had a lot of stress occur in my family—details of which I would prefer not to put into writing. It was a parent's worst nightmare. I wailed for days. I still find it hard to talk about. Around this time, I noticed that my walking had changed. I tripped over regularly and fell when turning around. The worst of it was my right leg. I could no longer lift it at the knee. It felt like I had a prosthetic leg—becoming less and less a part of me every day. When people ask me what it feels like to have MS, I describe it like that. It feels, for me at least, like I have a prosthetic limb or like my skin is plastic. The other familiar feeling is the *MS tingles*. It feels like pins and needles, but it pulsates. I usually get it in my neck when I put my head down. Other times I experience it for days at a time throughout specific regions of my body—sometimes one side of my body or one specific limb.

Falling apart

I did the usual. I visited my physiotherapist and doctor—both professionals are very supportive of me and have been pivotal in my recovery and treatment. They both referred me to the local emergency department, where I was admitted and determined it was a relapse. No new lesions; however, they treated me with IV steroids. I found most tasks a significant challenge. I couldn't even stand up straight. I was working for myself at the time and was still the breadwinner. When I fell apart, my entire household fell apart. It is not fair to children who have a parent with a chronic illness. It affects them the most, and they are the least in control.

My symptoms continued. I was sent back to the emergency department, and because I didn't have new lesions and they knew I had stressors in life, I was treated very poorly. Even though it was the same hospital, I was managed by a different neurologist. And he was sceptical that I even had MS! What a f**king joke! I don't know how some people sleep at night. I respect that they have countless patients that they see in public hospitals each day. However, there was no need to treat me the way they did. That experience led me to spiral into depression. And what better timing to do this than when a pandemic hits. And how do I manage hardship, excessive anxiety and low mood? Work even harder. Yes, what a great plan. I focused on my career and wanted to gain a specialisation. However, the pandemic proved to be very challenging to provide group therapy in psychology. We managed to get through it, though.

I isolated myself from my friends. I couldn't bear to see people thinking that I was *going crazy*. I gained a lot of weight and struggled with acute back pain. Everything was hard. Everything was heavy. Everything was painful. My stamina was poor, and it felt like the world was on fire.

I was so embarrassed. I still tend to isolate myself from my old friends. I understand they are hurt by avoidance. I didn't mean to hurt them. I miss them, in fact. However, when you suffer from a chronic illness like MS and you hit a relapse as I did, the hurdle feels insurmountable. Your thoughts become distorted, and your mind becomes a train that is out of control.

Now

In order to recover, I needed to place self-care at the forefront of my mind and rely upon my family and friends for support. I sought the neurologist from the first admission, and he tested my muscles and nerves for conductivity and spasticity. He also recommended that I undergo a sleep study. All of this found that, indeed, I had optic neuritis and abnormal nerve conductivity on my hands, legs and feet—worst of all, my right leg. To have those test results come back may seem like bad news—but for me, it was validation.

I was referred to the MS Clinic at Liverpool Hospital, New South Wales. The neurologist there was fabulous! She validated my experience and apologised for how the medical industry had treated me. She discussed how some doctors become *obsessed with lesions* and that we need to listen to the patient's experience. The symptoms will tell you the story of what you can't see on an MRI. She prescribed a treatment plan and educated me on the relationship between body mass and inflammation. She was compassionate, empathic, wise, and considerate.

I digested her advice and decided to undergo bariatric surgery. I felt like if I didn't take this next step; it would not only affect my career but, most importantly, the quality of life for my family. In December 2022, I underwent a mini gastric bypass from a very knowledgeable and respectful surgeon. I have since lost over 40 kg and continue my path to recovery. Losing weight has not cured my MS, but it has improved my mobility in spades.

I also reconnected with my exercise physiologist—another professional essential to my recovery. I followed her to her new practice and haven't regretted it. She motivates and educates me on how MS affects my body, sensations and mobility. Although I continue to have difficulty walking because of weakness in my right hip, leg and foot, I am improving my ability to walk and step up steps. She keeps it real with me, and I am forever grateful.

If anyone reads this, who is diagnosed with MS, knows someone with MS, or is just curious—having MS is not a death sentence. In my darkest moments, I wished to have cancer or any other illness other than MS. I would think to myself, *at least you can cut out a cancer,* but I can't cut out my nervous system. There can be a temptation to say, well, others have it worse too. But who has it worse in an oncology ward? The breast cancer patient? The brain tumour patient? The child with leukaemia? None—no one gets out of chronic or acute illness better or worse than others. I now say that *everyone has a something, and this is my something*. I won't let it define me, nor will I deny myself accommodations to have quality of life. I am happy with the trajectory of my life. It is far from perfect, but heading in the direction that is best for a bad situation. I am focused on what is best for me and my family.

ABOUT CANDICE

Candice is married and has three children; twins aged 10, and a seven-year-old. Her hands are full with three girls, three dogs, and five cats. Not to mention 2 fish tanks.

Candice is a clinical psychologist and works in a private hospital, plus runs a successful private practice. She has been a Clinical Director there for five years and enjoys treating clients with complex trauma, personality disorders and chronic mental illness. Candice enjoys spending her free time cooking and baking for the family, being creative and listening to music. She always dreamt of publishing her writing, and now she has taken her first step. She is not going to let MS stop her!

Watch the VLOG/Podcast of Candice on YouTube

16

Robyn Hart

LOOKING THROUGH A DIFFERENT WINDOW

Starting at the beginning of my life when my Nan used to say *from the time you were born, you have got where you are from sheer guts and determination.*

In 1970, I was born 10 weeks premature. In those days, survival rates were very low for either the mother or baby. My mum sadly passed away the day after I was born.

My Nan used to put a pound of butter on her hand and say, *that's how big you were, and that's how much you weighed.*

I spent six months in a humidity crib, and my Nan fed me every half hour with an ounce bottle. I began to grow and became a healthy baby.

This was the beginning of my sheer guts and determination to survive.

My Nan raised, guided and nurtured me from the time I was born to the time she passed in my early 30s.

I've had many chapters in my life, but in this chapter, we are going to fast forward to 2016.

It was a beautiful, warm summer. I had just celebrated my

husband's 50th birthday, along with my 46th birthday, being born on the same day but different years. We were surrounded by friends and family; what a celebration, the party festivities went all weekend.

About a week later, it started, insanely excruciating painful migraines, the sort that I couldn't bear the light. I needed to huddle in a dark room, hot packs, cold packs, and rest when I could. Some over-the-counter medication took the edge off, but it was still lurking. The fogginess was not forgiving; the pain would go from lurking pain to intense, excruciating pain again. I'd had these before, but not as intense or for as long.

I initially thought, okay, you've pushed it, and you're stressed, working long hours. My passion was essentially one that meant I was a workaholic. Most people knew, for me, that it was rare to have time off, downtime or holidays.

After a couple of weeks of this, I decided to go and see a doctor. I'm not one to think I needed to see a doctor unless absolutely necessary, but this was a big thing for me.

I was prescribed some migraine medication, but this didn't seem to make much difference. In fact, it made me feel more nauseous.

Another two weeks followed, and I had to go back to see my doctor to explain that nothing had really changed.

With this, my doctor sent me off to have an MRI.

This was my first MRI, so I really didn't know what to expect. I'm one of those people who will generally give anything a go, having faith in the medical system.

I got to the clinic and walked into a large waiting area with lots of people in it. I remember thinking, geepuz, were all these people having MRIs? Being a newbie to this and relatively naïve to this part of the medical system, it wasn't until I checked in at reception that I found out the clinic was for various types of scans.

Was I nervous? Sure I was. I had no idea what was going on behind the closed doors. The hum of the people in the waiting room was a distraction, and no one seemed to be coming out upset, so I think I just thought, okay, this is a simple exercise.

After a short while, it was my turn to enter the doors into the seemingly unknown. I was greeted by kind and friendly nurses and radiologists who asked me to de-robe from my regular clothes into a hospital gown. I was the only one in the room, so your head does start wondering and spinning a bit in anticipation and probably slight anxiety.

Once in my flattering hospital gown, hospital booties and yes, the obligatory *butt* showing out of the back of my gown as I tried to twist my hands behind to close my modesty, I was kindly escorted into another waiting area. They asked me questions about any previous medical conditions, surgeries, or metal objects on or in my body; it was quite a list, but nothing that worried me. I guess I was more curious than anything by this stage.

As with any hospital, there is always a throng of unusual noises, medical staff going about their daily routines.

It was now my time to enter another room. As I entered, I remember seeing a large spaceship circle-looking machine with a bed. I'm sure I'd seen them on a television series but not really taken that much notice, like most things, until it's right in front of you. It was a cold but brightly lit room, and at the other end of the room was a tinted glass window.

I was placed on the bed that currently lay outside the cylindrical tunnel. It was explained to me they would give me earplugs because the machine can be quite loud. A frame with a mirror would be placed over my head so I could see the radiologists and hear them, and they could hear me. A round orb was placed in my hand so that I could press it if I needed help, and the bed would move into the tunnel, and I needed to lay as still as possible.

A warm blanket was placed over me, which in itself was quite comforting.

The bed started to glide into the tunnel, and I could hear lots of

noises through my earplugs. It is quite loud ... de de de de de ... daaah daaah daaah ... de de de de de .... For me, it was actually soothing white noise, and I could feel myself drifting off to sleep.

I can't remember how long it was, but for me, it wasn't a bad experience.

I headed home from there, as with any *test*, waiting in anticipation for the results to come through, still pondering my journey into the tunnel of intrigue.

A couple of days later, my doctor rang and suggested my husband and I come to see him; hmmm ... both of us, was this to be good news or bad—I really had no idea what to expect.

We entered our doctor's clinic—it was an old house renovated into a medical practice. It always gave it a comforting sense of walking into someone's home rather than a cold, dank medical clinic. It was our time to see the doctor. We sat down, and my doctor explained that the MRI had come back suggesting that I had MS and that they would need to refer me to a neurologist.

I'm not sure that it had really sunk in at that stage, and we just said *okay*.

So, I was referred to a neurologist.

I remember going home in the car and discussing that I remember a childhood friend's mum had MS, and someone in my husband's family had MS. Both people we knew were fine, and then they weren't, and their progression seemed quick.

I can't remember how long it was between seeing the doctor and the neurologist. But I remember I just wanted to know what on earth was going on and what did it mean for me.

The day came to see the neurologist.

We went into the rooms that were once again full of people waiting to see neurologists. I thought in my naivety again, did all these people have MS too.

The neurologist came to greet us in his room. It was a dimly lit room with plenty of screens. The office looked out over the city. It seemed quite fancy but not a personalised office.

The neurologist looked at my MRIs and then did some reflexes and other tests on different parts of my body. At that stage, I didn't know what they were doing or what it meant. The neurologist confirmed that it all suggested I had MS, but they wanted me to have what seemed to be a huge number of other tests to be done.

I left quite upset, confused, and concerned. Why did they need to do all of these other tests? What was wrong with me?

We sat at a cafe down the road to digest everything we had just been told.

It was extremely overwhelming, and I didn't feel comfortable with what the neurologist told me, and I decided I wanted a second opinion.

In my head, I kind of felt how could migraines mean this. I also had in my head my Nan's words from a young child to growing up was that if ever I was to get sick, I must have the top medical professionals see me. Not that a diagnosis of having MS was anything to do with my premature birth or the death of my mother, but most of my immediate family had passed away years ago. I had very little knowledge of family medical history, and at the time, sitting ... contemplating ... all these things go spinning around through your head.

I needed proof from more than my doctor and this neurologist. I needed another neurologist's opinion.

I asked a close friend whom I trusted if they knew of a neurologist high up in the system, and they did. Within a week, I was referred to another neurologist in a major hospital.

I walked into the office of the next neurologist to be greeted

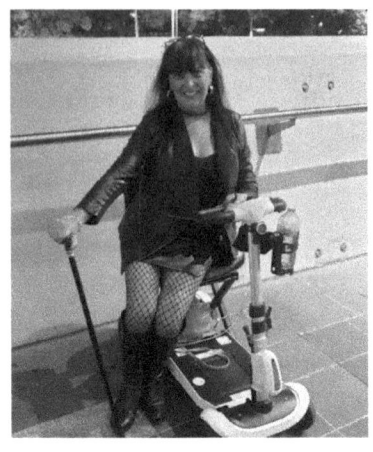

by an older gentleman with a kind face and one that seemed so caring. This room was full of accolades and certificates, models of the brain, and there, on the screen, was my MRI.

Somehow, this felt right. I felt like I would be in good hands.

We sat down and talked for about an hour. The neurologist performed tests on me in a kind, compassionate, and extremely professional way, explaining as they went along.

It was confirmed that I have MS. This was when the shock set in.

The neurologist discussed several medications that were available to reduce the risk of relapses and disease progression. It was decided I would use one drug for my migraines and another disease modifying drug (DMD) for my MS. Much was discussed over this hour, including that MS didn't mean my life was over, that we are so fortunate there are several DMDs available to treat MS and that I would find that there would need to be several lifestyle changes that needed to happen, including the possibility of my work-life balance, which there really was none at the time.

I walked away feeling like everything had been explained to me, that I was in good hands and had faith in this neurologist.

From there, the medication for my migraines helped. I presumed the DMDs were helping as I had no side effects or symptoms that would suggest anything was out of the normal.

By April of that year, I had deteriorated. I woke up and couldn't feel the right side of my body. My right leg didn't want to move, and my right hand was burning like it was on a hotplate. Pins and needles and fireworks were shooting up my right foot and leg, and it felt like someone had poured a truckload of concrete down into my leg. I couldn't walk properly.

I was taken to the hospital, where I saw my neurologist; I was having a relapse. Another what does this mean moment.

I was admitted to the neurology ward and put on a course of IV steroids for five days. Another set of full-body MRIs were done. Yes, another new experience. Most of us think being admitted to the hospital means something bad. I actually felt I was in the best place, with the best care, because I had no idea what was going on with my body.

The scary part was I hadn't really had any of these symptoms before. What did it all mean?

My neurologist checked in on me each day, and we discussed if the steroids were working. The nurses and physiotherapists worked with me to gain my strength and walking ability to leave the hospital.

Did the steroids work? For me, yes, they did, and no, I didn't get roid rage. I was just wide awake and extremely hungry.

My neurologist also decided that I would be placed on a different DMD that would be an infusion. This meant attending the hospital once a month for the infusion.

Physiotherapy continued once I left the hospital to regain my mobility. I also saw an occupational therapist and speech therapist at the same clinic as my physiotherapy.

I now remember pre-diagnosis times when I did have those symptoms, but I just put it down to the stress and long hours of my work.

Unfortunately, the next few years saw me average a relapse with hospital admission for steroids twice a year. This is even though most times my MRIs showed *no significant changes,* which is a term from neurologists I still don't understand. In my mind, it is black and white ... there are either changes or not. My body, brain and its functionality were certainly changing.

My cognitive function was, without a doubt, changing early on. I was having trouble word finding, not just the *oh damn, where did I leave my keys* brain fart. I would stop mid-sentence and not know what word I was looking for. I couldn't even try to charade the words; they just wouldn't come to me. Sometimes I couldn't even bring back the memory of what I was talking about. This led to me going to a neurophysiologist who performed a 3-hour testing session on me with various word and memory games. I was highly intrigued by this, as I wanted to find the answers to why my memory seemed to be failing me.

It was conclusive from the results that my cognition was impaired. To this day, I still have annual neurophsychological testing done as I still recognise cognitive challenges.

Along with my cognitive challenges, my regular relapses, my mobility challenges, and, most of all the undeniable fatigue led to the decision to stop working. All of this was not conducive to living a life of a workaholic, high stress, and long hours. I was devastated.

My life had seriously changed. I needed to build a new mindset. I needed to understand what was next.

There was and is still a huge feeling of grief and loss. I had lost what I thought was my purpose in life through work. I had lost friends, and I lost the body I thought I had control of. Along with this comes denial. Denial and loss of what was and what could be.

On Facebook, I found several forums for people with MS in Australia. It was great; I didn't feel so alone, and there were a couple of people who really helped me through a lot, and that life was still achievable.

A couple of years into my MS journey, a close friend with MS suggested we attend a local meeting about this thing called the NDIS; it was a great insight for both of us. I then started another journey with the wonderful team at MS Australia to be an NDIS participant. This was also confronting because you have to lay it all on the line, essentially about your current condition, your goals, and how you want to still live independently now and in the future. The confronting part, I think to this day, is that you never know what day-to-day is going to bring and how your condition will progress. But the team at MS Australia has always been there right beside me all the way, even today, to assist with that part. I can tell you, without MS Australia and the NDIS, I would definitely be a ball in the corner, more isolated and not able to live an independent life.

I must admit I'm still struggling with not working in the world and industry I love seven years on and still struggle with my purpose. I grew up in my industry from the time I was born and thought it gave me my purpose. I'm regularly alone due to personal situations. I also have support people who assist me with daily tasks that help me keep my independence and community participation.

I spend most of my time with medical and allied health people, psychologists, physiotherapists, hydrotherapists, exercise physiologists, monthly MS DMD infusions, and the list goes on, so it often seems like my diary is full of more medical appointments than a social life. But I realise now that without this team of health professionals maintaining my body, I would deteriorate more, and I know the importance of continuing all of these aspects.

My occupational therapist was incredible in helping change my mindset. I remember talking to them regularly, and they would say that I hadn't accepted my MS. We had several robust discussions with me, saying, *yes, I have*. We came to an agreement one day when I saw them and said, okay, I may not have accepted I have MS, but I acknowledge I have MS. We both agreed.

Three years after my first session, when I entered with my walker, they looked at me and said *now you have accepted you have MS*.

My MS psychologist was also amazing in helping me first and foremost in finding myself. I understand MS and its effect on me, my life and my personal relationships.

I did and do sometimes still feel isolated and alone, scared of what the future holds.

I now have a lot of accessories—mobility aids—and personal assistance. Yes, it was hard and confronting at first in many aspects, but I embrace them now and see them as an extension of me.

I have several fabulous *support workers* or *carers* who, each week, take me to appointments, get me out in the community, assist with home duties and much more. They really do support me and see me for my abilities. In this and many things, I am grateful for this country we live in and the NDIS support.

Never being one to be idle, I spend time on crafts, volunteering, charities and finding new opportunities. I'm still working on this. The pandemic and having two brain surgeries for aneurysms and another relapse during the pandemic didn't help in *getting my shit together*.

I think I had been fighting it for so long that I believed I would beat this disease. I came to the realisation that for me to be my best self with MS, I needed to actually fully accept it in all its ugliness, in all its forms, in all its good days and bad days. With the support and assistance from my amazing team of medical professionals, the MS community, support workers and those close to me who are willing to hold my hand as I walk this path.

What I now understand is that I AM STILL ME! I'm just looking through a different window. Some days are good days, and I can look out at the sunshine and think, I'm doing ok, and some days are meh, crappy days. With each new chapter in this journey, especially new symptoms or flares, my nan's words still ring true that sheer guts and determination still exist within me.

Watch the VLOG/Podcast of Robyn on YouTube

ABOUT ROBYN

Robyn Hart has led a full life with many achievements throughout her many overlapping careers and industries.

Robyn has been involved in the entertainment industry since she was born and founded her career over 35 years ago. Being heavily involved as a general manager and hands on technician of a renowned Australian company, Robyn's career covered all facets of the industry from theatre, concert, film, television, festivals, circus and performer flying, events, and opening and closing ceremonies within Australia and across the world.

Prior to her career in the entertainment industry, Robyn was an Award-winning florist, which she has now turned her skills back to as a hobby filling her days.

Robyn also founded other businesses in lifestyle, home and living, homewares, and interior design.

Robyn is a current board member and 2IC for Operation Angel, a humanitarian relief organisation that brings practical relief and self-sustaining assistance to individuals and families affected by natural disaster or large-scale human tragedy in Australia.

Robyn is passionate about mental health and wellbeing for crew in the entertainment industry and was also a board member for Entertainment Assist and Roadie for Roadies. Robyn supports many other charities and organisations including Crew Care, Support Act, Backpacks 4 Vic Kids, MS Australia and MS Research. Robyn's Philanthropy extends to other areas of giving back to groups, organisations and ventures within the entertainment industry

Robyn Lives in Victoria with her husband and 13-year-old Keeshound and now focuses on living her best life with MS.

17

Justine Martin

THERE IS NO SUCH WORD AS CAN'T

My story of MS started in 1980 when I was nine years old; we were living in Melbourne. My parents had recently separated, and my Mum Marian, who was 33 years old, became very ill with what the doctors first thought was a tumour in her brain and wanted to do exploratory brain surgery. My grandparents, who lived in Sydney, wouldn't allow this and flew her to Sydney to spend the next eight months in Sydney Hospital and a rehabilitation centre before she was well enough to come home and care for my brother Simon and me. The day she found out she had MS, my grandfather kicked the three of us out of the house. I guess it was his way of coping. It was the second time in my life that Simon and I had to live with our grandparents, the first being when Mum had breast cancer when she was 27 years old, and we were both three.

Through primary school, I partook in the MS Readathon. So desperately wanting a cure for my mum, I would pound the neighbourhood, getting as many sponsors as I could for so many cents for each book I was to read. In the end, I cheated on how many books I had read to raise as much money as I could to find that cure for my mum. I thought every year they would find her a cure. Forty years later, we still don't have that cure.

Mum, Simon, and I had some good years before her MS took hold of her. When her legs had become affected, she started using a walking stick, and people would ask if she had been in a car accident. My brother and I had developed some evil stares at people who would rudely stare at how Mum walked.

I became my mum's carer through my late teenage years, and we had a complete role reversal. Though in the years leading up to looking after Mum, I would help with the grocery shopping and cleaning. I had learned how to cook from the age of 10, so when Mum was too fatigued or sick to feed us, I knew how to. Very few people at school knew what I was living through. It was beyond hard. She was defiant in everything she did; she hated the world, her body and what was happening to her. Therefore, I took the full force of that anger for many years. She was worse than a toddler when I asked her to do something or even to help herself in her later years. Mum would have at least one major relapse a year, normally towards the end of summer, around my birthday. She would end up being flown via air ambulance to Sydney Hospital as we were living In Glen Innes, some eight hours north by road. Simon and I would have to look after ourselves for a day or two before a family member could drive up to look after us. Nowadays, this would never be allowed, and child services would be called. It had become our normality. We had no choice but to grow up fast.

As I entered my early 20s, my brother Simon enlisted in the Australian Army and lived all over the country. He would come home a few times a year to see Mum. She would pick up when he was home for those few days but fall back into her depression shortly afterwards. I found myself as a single mum to a six-month-old baby Zakariah, and it was my mum's full-time career. I had very little family and community support. It got to the point where I could no longer cope; I couldn't wipe three sh**ty bums anymore; I was heading for a breakdown at 22. The only support I got was an hour of cleaning a fortnight, and there were only certain parts of the home they were allowed to clean. After 14 years, my grandfather finally stepped up and had Mum admitted into full-time care.

At that time, disease-modifying therapies were being introduced to Australia. My Mum didn't qualify to take them, so her MS progressed rapidly from RRMS to SPMS, and she gradually lost her will to live. After seventeen years of living with her diagnosis, Mum was wheelchair-bound, had major cognitive impairment, had a tracheotomy, catharised and was peg fed straight into her stomach with a tube. In 1997, she passed away from complications related to MS at the age of 49. I had a seven-week-old daughter, Alexandra and Zakariah, now four. I felt so much guilt for putting Mum into the MS home in Lidcombe in Sydney for not being able to care properly for her in those final years; that time was robbed from all of us. The trauma over the years it caused is something I still carry to this day. My mum was the most courageous and strong-willed woman I have ever met.

Throughout our lives, Simon and I were always told that MS is not hereditary. However, nobody mentioned that there can be a genetic predisposition if specific environmental factors are present. Ignorant of this fact, I believed there was nothing to worry about and neglected my own health.

In my 20s and early 30s, I was morbidly obese and under tremendous stress because of a failing business and a troubled marriage. I took my health for granted and made poor lifestyle choices. However, in my 30s, I finally decided to take control of my weight and well-being. I embarked on a journey to shed 46 kilograms, watching what I ate, exercising daily and taking up the sports of tug of war and weightlifting, competing nationally and internationally. I packed up the children and moved to Perth in 2004 to start a new life with more choices.

I was working in the weight loss industry and had reached my dream job as a program director for Jenny Craig. I began to lose my vision. It was like someone had smeared Vaseline across my eyes, and the world was blurry; there was no set time or length this would happen for. I went to visit my doctor for another reason and happened to mention my bad vision problems. This had also happened to me some 10 years earlier, yet I had put it down to the eyeliner I was wearing. However, this time I wasn't wearing any!

Within 24 hours of seeing my doctor, I was sitting in a neurosurgeon's office, sh**ing myself. Two years earlier, I'd had an MRI because of a lump in my neck, and it showed a cyst behind my right eye. I had one specialist tell me it was nothing to worry about, so I didn't. In 2008, they misdiagnosed me with myofascial pain syndrome from that MRI. Yet here I was now, seeing a surgeon who cuts brains open! Something about this seemed like history was repeating itself!

The first thing I asked him was, do you think it's MS? He said no. He then sent me to an ophthalmologist to check how well my vision worked. It turns out that when my vision works; it is 20/20, and when it doesn't, it's just crap. He suggested I was having cluster headaches, yet I wasn't having any pain. I now know that it was optic neuritis. None of it made any sense. There is very little I can do when my vision impairment flares. I can't read, watch television, or do any hobbies. I can get very frustrated, and a lot of sleeping goes on.

I had a repeat MRI in the tunnel of terror in 2010, and they found several white glowing bits that shouldn't have been there. A week after these results, I was referred to a neurologist. I again asked if it was MS, as my mum had MS and two cousins through my mum's side of the family—a strong genetic link. My neurologist dismissed this and diagnosed it all as having to do with my migraines, as I have suffered from them since I was 15. I asked why now, all of a sudden, my vision had changed, yet I wasn't having any headaches or pain. There was no answer; it fell on deaf ears.

I was put on Topamax for three months for the migraines and

sent on my way. Frustrated more than ever that I wasn't being heard and merely dismissed. No one knows our body better than we do, so why don't medical professionals listen more to us?

Over the next three months, I deteriorated even more. I couldn't lift my left arm, would cry for no reason, and would break into laughter for no reason and often at inappropriate times. I now know this is called the *pseudobulbar affect*. I was trying to hold it together in a new job and trying to learn. I remember new things caused so much stress that my short-term memory was gone. Then more things were failing in my body. I had pins and needles on my top lip, and even more concerning was that I couldn't count anymore, read the time, use money or multitask, and all I wanted to do was sleep. I felt like I was being possessed. I was screaming on the inside, yet no one could hear my anguish on the outside.

I had a repeat MRI in March 2011, my third in a short period. This one showed even more white glowing spots. On 14 March at 8:30 am, I sat across from my neurologist with my girlfriend, Flik, when he mouthed the words, *you have MS*. The world as I knew it stopped in the blink of an eye. I went into shock and felt relief, anger and fear all at the same time. Not once did that neurologist ever apologise to me for calling it wrong for over six months. This still makes me angry!

How was I going to tell my family when I was in shock myself?

I went out and sat in the car and made some very hard phone calls. First, Kelly, my fiancé, was 1,400 km away working in the mines and couldn't come home for a week. He didn't take the news well, and I was so scared he would leave me.

Next were my grandparents, my mum's parents. My grandfather answered the phone, which brought back the memory of ringing them to tell them that their daughter had died. I was again ringing with bad news, and through my tears, I told him I was diagnosed with MS. He told me I had it wrong. I couldn't have it that the doctors had it all wrong. He put my nanna on the phone to explain to her. She was well aware of what I had been going through, and she had chosen to keep it from my grandfather at that stage. It was gut-wrenching to tell them I had the same incurable disease that their own daughter had and who died from complications. My nanna, over the years, carried a lot of guilt, blaming herself for me having MS. I would try to reassure her that I carried no hate or malice towards her; it was just something that happened. I had won the lottery, just the wrong type of lottery.

Next was my Aunty Lynny, who filled the void of my mum—another hard phone call to make. Lynny and Uncle Gra have been with me through thick and thin, and I'd be lost without their love and support.

The hardest phone call was to Zakariah, who had just enlisted in the Australian Army and was in basic training. I made contact with the Army Chaplin first, so Zak would have some support if he needed it. I didn't want him to find out and then feel he needed to quit the Army to come home to look after me. There were lots of tears, and I assured him I would be okay. History really was repeating itself.

I was to work from 1:00 pm to 9:00 pm that day and was a mess with flashbacks of Mum's journey with MS. How do you hold it together when your world has just crashed? When in the blink of an eye, the future you thought you would live was now tarnished forever.

I called into work on the way home at about 11:00 am to tell my manager face-to-face rather than on the phone. Through sobs, I told her my diagnosis. Her reply was to go home and put my big girl panties on, get into my business suit and come back to work at 1:00 pm till close!

So I did!

How I did, I'm really not sure. There was very little compassion. A week later, I was in the hospital, having a lumber puncture, then my first round of steroids, for a relapse that had lasted for many months and was getting worse.

Work was getting harder by the day; from the bouts of fatigue and cognitive damage, I struggled to get through each shift. MS had given me an acquired brain injury. Steroids often take weeks to fully kick in. I discovered I became the bi*ch from hell when I had them. No sleep, suicidal, huge mood swings and weight gain! I hate them! I was not a nice person to be around, and unfortunately, Alexandra and Kelly bore the brunt of all of it.

Four weeks later, my neurologist told me to stop working and take sick leave. The stress of work wasn't helping at all. Again, telling work didn't go very well. My manager told me that the big bosses in Melbourne wouldn't like me taking three months off on sick leave and that I was to quit. The next day I got a phone call, and the head office approved my sick leave. My guess was they were scared I would take it further if they made me quit or fired me.

I have been the child of someone who had MS, a carer of someone with MS, and now someone who has MS.

I started my first disease-modifying therapy. A daily injectable called Copaxone, and a tablet called Tegretol. For both medications, I had allergic reactions and had to stop both. I ended up with hives the size of bread-and-butter plates from the Copaxone. I clearly remember telling my neurologist what was happening. I couldn't wear jeans from the pain and the itch. He told me I would have to put up with it! Like hell I was! The Tegretol gave me high fevers in the 40s.

The MS was taking hold of my body and my mind. I slept for the next three months, missing medical appointments, catch ups with friends, and not picking up my daughter from school.

I was slipping into the deep, dark hole of depression. I didn't want to leave the house; it was my sanctuary and becoming my jail at the same time.

What was my purpose going to be for the rest of my life? What if I could no longer provide the basic needs of shelter, food, and clothing for my daughter? Kelly earned too much money for me to get Centrelink. We had just lost $60k overnight and had more medical expenses than ever. Each MRI cost $800, specialist bills, pharmacy bills, and the list went on. I had solely become reliant financially on another human being. I felt humiliated and such a burden to him and to society. We discussed breaking off our engagement, and I gave him a ticket to leave to end our relationship. He assured me he was in for the long hall, that he loved me, and wasn't going anywhere.

My neurologist also referred me to a psychologist, as he said a lot of it was in my mind. After three months of antidepressants and weekly psychologist visits, my psychologist said I wasn't the one with the problem. Clearly, my neurologist did, and that it was perfectly normal to feel the way I did, considering my family history of MS and what was happening to my body.

My left leg was affected, in constant spasms through my hip flexor. I had a L'hermittes sign, and every time I looked down, an electric shock would go from my neck to my feet and bounce back again. Then my bladder decided it too needed to be in on the action, and I would go to the toilet to pee and think I was finished, stand up and then wet myself. I would have to psych myself into having a shower, as when the water runs down my legs, it feels like razor blades slicing into them. The crunch came when I lost the ability to orgasm. I couldn't feel a thing there. I think my neurologist nearly fell off his chair at the next appointment I went to as I demanded he fix me and give me my orgasm back! I went back to the hospital for another round of steroids. Too many of us experience a loss of sensation sexually and don't speak up because of embarrassment. Speak up to your medical team and be heard!

It was then decided that my MS was aggressive and Copaxone wouldn't cut it, as I had another relapse. So, I started monthly infusions of Tysabri. This was the big gun of disease-modifying therapies. I had to have a blood test to see if I had a virus in my brain called the John Cunningham virus (JC). If I had the JC virus,

I would be at great risk of developing another incurable brain disease called progressive multifocal leukoencephalopathy (PML), which either leaves you in a vegetative state or kills you. My results came back as JC positive, not something I wanted to hear. They considered the first two years safe, with 26 infusions. Then, going into the third year, the odds increase in developing PML. I stayed on that medication for 37 rounds, well into the danger zone. Every month thinking, will I get PML? The stress was horrendous. All disease-modifying therapies come with a leaflet of fine print on the side effects and what could go wrong. Whoever reads what could happen? Certainly not me. It wasn't going to happen to me!

The only good thing that the neurologist suggested was that I find a hobby, as I was going to have a lot of time on my hands. I had always wanted to try painting and thought I would do it when I retired at about the age of 90! However, all I had now was time. I had a girlfriend who owned an art studio. I drove there every week for nearly three months and sat outside, struck with fear and crippling anxiety, too afraid to walk inside. Every week I would drive home, angry at myself, crying, and screaming out of frustration.

Why couldn't I just walk inside? Who was this person I would look into the mirror and see? I was becoming a shell of my former self and was losing control of my life. That black hole was getting deeper by the day, and I was struggling to hold on to myself. I cried a lot as I started through the process of grief.

One week I got really angry and thought to myself, *what is the worst that can happen?* Just do it, and I walked in through the art studio doors, and my life changed for the better!

I took to painting like a duck to water. Apparently, I'm pretty good.

The end of 2011 saw us moving from Perth to Geelong to be closer to my family. We didn't have anyone to look after Alexandra when Kelly was away working, and I was in and out of the hospital so much.

In April 2012, I entered my first art exhibition and sold my first painting for $300. It felt like $3 million to me as it was the first time in over 12 months that I'd actually earnt my own money as my partner was fully financially supporting my daughter and me. I had to ask to buy everything, including food. But selling that painting gave me something else. Purpose! I couldn't believe people were buying my art, hanging it on their walls and, more importantly, handing over their hard earnt cash for something I had created that made them smile.

I started entering lots of exhibitions and winning a lot of awards too against people of all abilities. My relationship with Kelly soon broke down. He declared that my having MS would affect his goals and dreams in life, so 20 months after being diagnosed, I was living on the other side of the country, away from all of my friends and back to being a single mum of a 15-year-old daughter and sitting in my self-pity.

Questioning why me? Why not me? What did I do so wrong to get so sick? I had the dream job and relationship, and we were

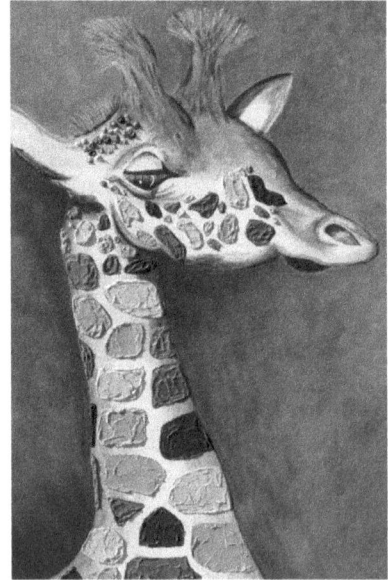

under contract for our dream home when it all crashed. All of it was actually a nightmare.

I sought counselling to cope and change my mindset. I knew I couldn't burden all of this on my daughter as my mother had done to me. We both were very scared of what the future would hold. With Kelly leaving, so did our means of financial survival. I swallowed my pride and asked for help. I had a child to feed and provide for. We had to live on food bank for four months until my disability pension came in. It was terrifying and humbling.

I wanted to give back to MS Australia and help educate what MS is, so I became an MS Ambassador, a role I did for nearly 10 years, leaving the role this year.

I started selling a lot more art, doing markets and making a name for myself. I have won over 40 art awards. Not bad for someone who was terrified of walking into the art studio. I went back to weightlifting and competing, keeping my body as fit as I could, and I love the endorphins that are released when picking up heavy things.

In 2013, I thought I had developed internal shakes in my chest, a bit like butterflies having a party. I was getting back on my feet when I was rushed to hospital with heart problems, a racing heart rate of 160 beats per minute instead of 65, known as atrial fibrillation. Not everything that goes wrong in our bodies is MS. Other things can happen too. We often forget this and tend to blame it all on MS.

After visiting a cardiologist and being put on beta-blockers that didn't work, I saw a cardiology surgeon six months later. This led me to have my first pulmonary vein ablation later that year. I was told that if it didn't come back in the first 12 weeks, I'd be good to go. It came back 11 weeks later with a vengeance at 217 beats a minute and threw in atrial tachycardia. It was an epic fail! I then had to have a second pulmonary vein ablation in February 2014. Each ablation never went smoothly, and I haemorrhaged after each surgery.

I kept questioning why it was happening to me, considering that these heart problems normally affect men in their late 60s or early 70s. No one could give me an answer why. At the same time this was happening, my liver levels were elevated. It was put down to the disease-modifying therapy drug.

I had to come off Tysabri, as the risk was too high to stay on it. My veins kept collapsing, and it was a terrible time for myself and the nurses each month trying to find veins and then having them collapse halfway through an infusion. I had a new neurologist in Victoria who was worth moving across the country for. We decided I should try Gilenya. After four months on it, I developed seven major infections, including shingles on my face. That was also an epic fail. The next drug that was recommended was Augabio; this drug scared the life out of me as it takes two years to naturally come out of your body. I held off taking it, and unfortunately, I developed a new lesion in my brain at that time. So, I ended up taking the drug. It's never an easy decision going on a disease-modifying therapy, as the side effects can be horrendous. This one caused a lot of hair loss and headaches.

The end of 2015 saw my heart play up for a third time. This time I was missing heartbeats. One in every five wouldn't beat, and the sixth beat would be very strong, sending a shock to my chest. Back to the cardiology surgeon and in for another ablation, this time on the front wall of my heart, and me wide awake for the four-hour operation. Afterwards, I felt like an elephant had sat on my chest. I developed pericarditis after it and was very ill for the next two months. Again, I questioned why this was happening, but no one could explain why.

I continued to weight train and changed my diet. 2016 came around, and I was competing at the Australian Masters Olympic Weightlifting Championships in Hobart, Tasmania. It was freezing cold in June, and my hands, ears, nose, neck, and feet were turning purple. I looked like a zombie. My children thought it was great;

Mum was turning into the *walking dead!* I brought home a few medals and was diagnosed on my return with livedo reticularis. The small blood vessels under the surface of my skin were clotting. This led me to be diagnosed with melanoma in September 2016 on my right leg when they were looking for lymphoma. I had to have a bone marrow biopsy, PET and CAT scans. I couldn't bend my fingers or toes. I thought the MS was doing that, too, but it wasn't.

I then had trouble breathing and had decreased lung capacity; I'd never smoked in my life. The results showed I had lymphoma, but my haematologist wasn't sure what type. Things never go as fast as what you see in the movies. A week later, I was diagnosed with mixed cryoglobulinemia IgM, which was causing so much inflammation around all my internal organs and choking them off.

I was dying.

Christmas 2016 was bleak, thinking it may be my last and waiting to see what type of lymphoma I had.

At the end of January 2017, I was diagnosed with chronic lymphocytic leukemia (CLL) and small lymphocytic lymphoma (SLL), stage 4. I had three primary cancers, two blood disorders

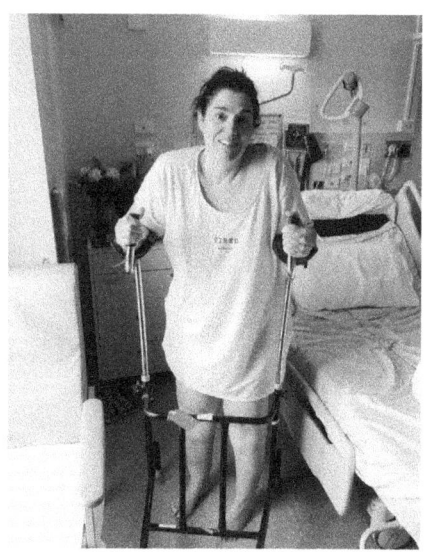
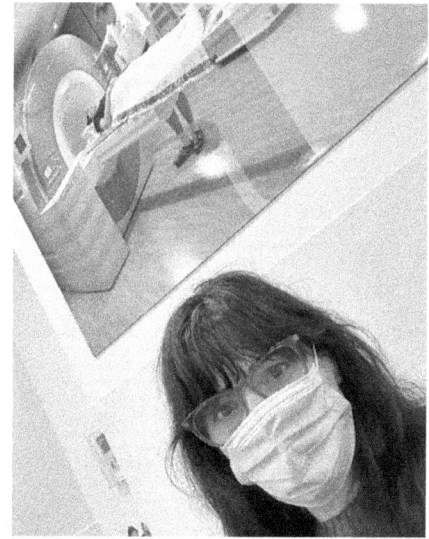

and MS, all at the same time. I couldn't start chemotherapy straight away as I had to take a chemical flush to rid my body of the Aubagio. That took three weeks of drinking a vile, salty, cloudy solution three times a day. Then we waited a few extra weeks just to be sure there was no trace left of Aubagio before I could start on bendamustine, a derivative of the mustard gas from World War One and Rituximab, an autoimmune suppressant.

Life was harder than hard. Nausea and hair loss. Weight gain from the steroids because I developed an allergy to chemotherapy. A chemical blister rash from head to toe and the purple road map rash of livedo and the Rituximab tripled my cryoglobulin and created another rash. I was a real mess physically. With each cycle of chemotherapy, I had to take large doses of steroids. This caused me to gain nearly 20 kilograms. How did I end up with three primary cancers and two separate blood conditions? Well, remember that fine print I forgot to read; it's all written there! Go figure!

I kept up my counselling and things that made me happy, like creating art. I had lost the ability to hold a paintbrush or pen. I discovered I could still finger paint and continued to sell my work. The day I found out I could have cancer was when I got the keys to the new house I had just bought. I had great plans to build a huge art studio to teach other disabled artists. I started to renovate my house while undergoing chemotherapy. It gave me something to look forward to and focus on rather than my ailing health.

I never used to listen to my body and would push myself too far. Okay, so I still tend to do this, but I am a lot more cautious. At the end of 2017, I had just finished chemotherapy. I woke up one morning, and my feet were on fire and shooting out what felt like bolts of lightning to the point where I couldn't walk from my bed to even the ensuite to go to the loo. I knew I was in trouble and called triple zero. I spent the next three weeks in the hospital waiting for the inflammation to reduce and learning to walk again. I was beyond terrified, and it was a real wake-up call to look after myself.

I went into remission in 2018 from the MS and the cancers. I went on to open JUZT Art wellness classes in 2019 for people with disabilities.

I often get asked if, given the time over, I would go on disease-modifying therapies again, and my answer is always YES. I saw what MS did to Mum and knew my journey would be different to hers, and would try all that was available to slow down the progression.

Everyone wanted to know my secret as to why I was so positive when experiencing so much adversity. I had to sit down with someone and work out what made me tick and how I developed such a positive mindset when facing death and disability. I choose to be positive. My business, Resilience Mindset, was born out of all this. I now help other people through online coaching, courses, consulting, books I've co-authored, and keynote talks around the world on resilience and my journey.

I'm known as the *queen of resilience.*

My story has become the survival guide for hundreds of thousands of people around the world.

Over the last 10 years, I have been in romantic relationships. I always disclose that I have MS before even meeting them face to face. If they run after that conversation, I've just saved myself time and energy getting ready for a date that was going to end badly. I have a one hundred per cent honest policy; it's not like I can hide it.

Having MS makes us more vulnerable as prey to narcissists; making them look better when caring for a disabled partner. There are some very evil people in this world. Because of a certain relationship, I had my tailbone broken, my arm broken, and the cartilage in my right wrist torn in half, resulting in surgery two years later, thanks to delays because of Covid. This man said he wanted to be with me despite all that was wrong with me. I used to think I would never be good enough for a man and made a lot of poor choices in men, then throw in there the mix of MS and low self-worth, and it was always going to head for disaster.

I took my responsibility of being in such a toxic relationship with so many red flags back into counselling to find out how I could change and become the person I had always wanted to be. I deserve to be loved and treated equally, despite what life has thrown at me.

My faith was restored in men last year when I met Deany, the most kind, loving and compassionate man I have ever met. He understood what life with me was going to be like living with MS and as a cancer survivor, yet he stuck around anyway. The Universe had other plans for the future we were planning, and I found him dead on the floor in August last year. I am still waiting on the coroner's report. Life is cruel. As I get out of bed every day, I remind myself that he died in that room, and I didn't. Deany was my biggest fan and support, and for me to sit in a corner and rock and cry, *oh why me*, wouldn't be serving anyone, let alone his memory. Life goes on despite how painful it can be. We do build resilience.

I made the decision with my medical team to be triple-vaxed and throwing in having Covid in February 2022, saw the CLL and SLL return. I was put on a wait-and-watch, something I'm not good at, as patience is not my forte. I am finally back in remission. I have a very low immune system and am constantly battling infections.

Prior to Covid, I was on IVIg therapy in the hospital every four weeks. This infusion comprises other people's antibodies from their blood to boost my immune system. When Covid happened, I was taught to give myself the injection at home in the subcutaneous fat layer, SCIg therapy; three needles into my tummy or leg. I do this every week at this stage with no end date. Although it doesn't stop

my infections, it reduces their severity. It allows me the freedom to go out in public, although I still have to be careful around anyone sick. I am not allowed at this stage to be on any more disease-modifying therapies because of my low immune system.

MS has brought many bad times into my life, but equally good things. The community I have around me nowadays have all come from me having MS. I reinvented myself for the better. I always had the job of helping people, but not on the scale that I now do. I look after my health better than I ever have, and I am more proactive in my health journey than I ever have been in the past.

I have weekly massages to help with the spasms in my legs and feet. My medical team consists of a neuro-physiotherapist, chiropractor, ophthalmologist, podiatrist, counsellor, haematologist, neurologist, massage therapist, acupuncturist, Bowen therapist and general practitioner. I have huge support from NDIS, and I couldn't do half the things in life if it weren't for them. I have learned that asking for help is a sign of strength, not weakness. I have support workers, friends and family who all help in their own ways.

I have MS symptoms that never go away—spasms, pain, pins and needles, and numbness affect my legs. My fatigue is managed with prescription CBD oil and scheduled rest. I eat a low histamine

diet as I developed mast cell activation syndrome from long Covid; it's now been discovered to be a symptom of MS. I have so many food intolerances that there isn't much left to eat or drink, but I'm still alive and happy.

My mum used to tell us when I was a child that there is no such word as can't, you need to find a way to do it.

Since March 2011, I have modified and adapted around my disabilities, around the MS. I am back working despite being told I'd never be able to work again. I've managed to live and love the most rewarding life, and there is still plenty yet to come!

Don't let anyone tell you that you can't because you know you can!

ABOUT JUSTINE

Justine Martin is the visionary behind this extraordinary anthology MS Book *"Whispers of Resilience; Our MS Stories"*. She is the Founder/CEO of the Justine Martin Corporation (JMC), a conglomerate comprising six successful businesses: Juzt art, Resilience Mindset, Van-Go Decals, Morpheus Publishing, Team Fingerprint, and Geelong Residential Cleaners.

An accomplished and award-winning artist, keynote speaker, resilience coach, author, and podcast host, Justine embarked on her entrepreneurial journey a decade ago with the establishment of Juzt art.

Despite facing significant health challenges, including a diagnosis of Multiple Sclerosis twelve years ago, as well as three heart surgeries and battling three primary cancers, Justine's unwavering spirit and resolve kept her focused on building her businesses. Doctors told her she would never work again, but she proved them wrong by crafting a purposeful and driven life.

Using her art as therapy, Justine's passion for painting grew, resulting in numerous awards and recognition. She channeled her own journey of resilience into the birth of Resilience Mindset, where she coaches, hosts a resilience podcast series, has co-authored a number of books and delivers inspirational keynotes on resilience.

Expanding her literary endeavors, Justine launched Morpheus Publishing in July 2022, facilitating her dream of writing and publishing resilience and self-help books, including her first children's book, "Same Same But Different." Additionally, Morpheus Publishing has proudly brought to life this book - the anthology "MS Book, Our Stories" a collaborative effort with 26 authors living with MS.

As a finalist in the 2023 Australian Small Business Champion Awards and continuously being recognised as a woman to watch, Justine's impact on her industries and the lives she touches remains an inspiration to all.

Justine's dedication and outstanding performance across her businesses have garnered national recognition with seven prestigious awards in 2021 and 2022. Her contributions to coaching and creativity were acknowledged at the national AusMumpreneur Awards and Roar Awards, among others. As a finalist in the Australian Small Business Champion Awards and continuously being recognized as a woman to watch, Justine's impact on her industries and the lives she touches remains an inspiration to all.

www.juztart.com.au
www.resiliencemindset.com.au
www.justinemartin.com.au
www.morpheuspublishing.com
https://linktr.ee/justinemartincorporation
Youtube: **https://www.youtube.com/@justinemartincorporation**
Email: **hello@justinemartin.com.au**
Phone: **+61 403 564 942**

Watch the VLOG/Podcast of Justine on YouTube

18

Stacey Metcalfe

INTERRUPTED

I dedicate the following chapter to my forever and always, the children of the corn and my family and friends who have always stuck by my side, despite me sometimes being a thorn in theirs. I may indeed be a walking contradiction and, at times, irrational, annoying, frustrating and handsome with a disturbingly dark and witty sense of humour, but for some reason, you're all still here. It honestly means the world to me.

I've spent the last few weeks thinking about how I could write this story and do it some form of justice. I'm a master at the art of procrastination. I will diligently obsess over anything else if I'm unsure how to move forward, or, being my own worst critic, I avidly avoid completing a task if I can't meet the nearimpossible standards of the overbearing voice in my head.

Trying to wrap my head around the idea that maybe my words could offer understanding, solace, or at least a smile to someone who is going through the lifealtering situation I endured at barely 22 years old when I had no one who could even begin to understand how I felt and what I was going through, is so incredibly surreal.

I had friends and family when my world was turned upside

down. Their attempts to comfort me felt awkward, uncomfortable, and even frustrating. I became a recluse and a prisoner to my thoughts and body for far longer than I'd like to admit. I didn't want pity; I had enough of my own to wallow in, and too often, people would try to relate or sympathise without realising how condescending it felt at times. I should start by emphasising that no two people's journey living with this *MonSter* are the same, just as we are all unique and ultimately different people from the various experiences that shaped us to become the vastly unique people we are today.

Your story and how MS affects you, or will, will be your own path to walk, but that does not mean you have to do it alone. It is unnerving how simple it is to close everyone out, especially under the guise of freeing them from a life they didn't sign up for when their future becomes uncertain. I'll be the first to tell you that this disease will eat away at more than your myelin if you let it. I had a vision of who I wanted to become and all the adventures I would take when suddenly, my body betrayed me.

Backtrack with me to August 2011. I woke up one morning while overhauling my life when I couldn't feel my foot. Over the next few days, that feeling slowly crept up, encompassing my entire left side from my shoulder down, taking all sensation and leaving a bonechilling cold and weakness in its wake. I didn't know what multiple sclerosis was, or much of anything, to be honest. I arrived at the emergency room with the conclusion that I'd had a stroke. The next few days were a revolving door of tests, scans and, at times, medical professionals who seemed just as confused as I was. It wouldn't have been more than a few days later when I found myself back in the emergency room at 2:00 am, scared and in pain. My MRI results were back by then, and my tears were falling fast and freely as the doctor struggled to find the words to explain what was happening to my body. I was in a haze, oblivious to my surroundings and strangely, for some reason, I was counting the tears as they hit my legs. My mind struggled to comprehend that I could see when a tear landed on my left thigh, but not once did I feel it. Briefly, words like paralysis and incurable would break through the haze as the doctor spoke, but try as I might, I couldn't focus. I didn't want this to be my reality, and at that moment, all I wanted was to be unconscious. I was so exhausted and frankly quite pi**ed off that my body could feel completely numb, yet ironically was causing me so much pain.

I could continue on and go into infinite detail over my first relapse, like the fact no one warned me you could lose bladder control and not even be aware until you're standing there wondering why the f**k there's a puddle of water on your lounge room floor. When reality hits you like a ton of bricks, you will probably get a vague response that it could be permanent or it might not be. Only time will tell.

There's no way to know for certain how MS will affect you or even when and to what extent. I could tell you how those closest might say things like they no longer were going to take their life for granted, making you feel you had wasted your life and all your goals and dreams now felt pointless. That is only true if you let it be or that when I mentioned half my body was numb, it was like someone had clean cut down my middle with laser precision; half of my vagina had no feeling, yet the other half was business as usual. These things were all too real, especially at the moment. But luckily, with time and significant amounts of highdose steroids, most of my side effects subsided.

I continued on and recovered from the majority of symptoms from my first relapse and had no other major relapses until late 2019. I had since begun a job in a nursing home as an *assistant in nursing* and now had three boisterous children in tow. We had suffered some devastating losses in the previous couple of years. That year hit hard with my daughter fracturing her head and my beloved Nanna passing away too soon. I took it all in my stride and buried myself in work, picking up as many shifts as I could and ignoring the telltale signs of an impending relapse.

One morning I couldn't ignore it as symptoms were beginning to have a significant effect, with my right side gradually becoming weaker. Every time I attempted to speak, my speech was worsening, with words coming out slurred and requiring an immense amount of concentration and slowing down to be able to pronounce basic words, which I'd never had issues with. I called in sick to work and wound up at Townsville Hospital, being admitted that night for IV steroids and observation. It was the first time my children were old enough to see what this monster was capable of and the first time my partner could see the extent and speed at which relapse can take over.

Day by day, my MS slowly broke me down piece by piece. I was so determined to go outside one night despite pure exhaustion for some fresh air and, to be honest, a cigarette. I began the arduous journey from the secondfloor neurology ward down to the smoking area out the front of the hospital. I must have looked like a right idiot as I used a combination of pushing my wheelchair for support and sitting in my wheelchair pushing myself along and stopping for extended periods to rest. I was messaging my partner during my brief intervals there and back. At some point on the way back, I had messaged him saying that I was maybe a mere 100 metres from my bed, and I was stopping for a breather. About half an hour later, my phone started ringing, and the other half rudely awoke me. He was wondering why I hadn't messaged him when I got back to bed, as promised. The only problem was that I'd fallen asleep hunched over in my wheelchair, probably just moments after I had texted him last. This is where the saying, *if you don't laugh, you will cry,* comes to mind. Thankfully, I've always been great at having a laugh at my own expense. I continued on and made it back to my bed, refusing a nurse who stopped to offer to push me back because I'll be damned if I was going to make it that far and give up on the

home streak. I'm sure they probably thought I was a stubborn fool during my fiveday vacation in the hospital, as I also refused any help for my showers. It may have taken an hour every time, and I barely got the job done while sitting on the shower floor, having just managed to wash the bare minimum, but was annoyingly determined to do so independently. On day four, I briefly escaped the hospital with my partner when we went outside for a *walk*. We drove to my motherinlaw's house to surprise the children before rushing back before my next set of observations with no one the wiser of our little escapade. Things had barely started to recover by day five, but I had completed my steroids. My symptoms were no longer worsening, so with a followup bombardment of allied health specialists scheduled for the next six weeks, I was finally sent home just in time for Christmas and my partner's birthday. Thankfully, my speech recovered over the next two weeks, but my strength took a bit longer to even come close to normal again. My little staycation away was a haunting reminder that I needed to learn to slow down and process grief and stress and not spread myself so thin.

Your venture will be different to mine, and as much as I want to indulge in every unique sensation, every devastating thought and every relapse from the beginning until now, I'd have missed the most important part. I let the uncertainty of having MS dictate my life for so many years between then and now. I never pursued so many goals and secondguessed absolutely everything. I held myself back because, in my eyes, what was the point of trying to accomplish anything if one day I could wake up and no longer walk or talk? I felt like damaged goods, a reduced to clear item on a supermarket shelf that had not expired but was definitely past its best before date. I stopped so many good things before they could even happen under the pretence that my health would take it all away at any rate. Funnily enough, that mindset robbed me of opportunities and years long before my MS had a chance to take it from me. I hesitated when it came to friendships and love. Thankfully, as much as I tried deterring my husband, convincing him that a life with me wasn't worth it, he is a persistent bugger and stuck around despite me ... or maybe to spite me, haha.

It has been over 10 years since we first met. Despite everything that could have broken us from then until now, we have four beautiful children. We are stronger than I could ever have imagined. Every disagreement, uncertainty, unexpected death, betrayal from loved ones, depression, doubt, homelessness, and several close calls resulting in surgeries and hospital stays only strengthened our bond. I'm writing all this while working through another relapse; this one has taken away strength again on my left side, just as it had the first time. I still have feelings for the most part; however, large portions from my hip down go through feeling intermittently ice cold or burning hot. Ironically, I don't have any real feeling or sensation in those patches, and my toes on both feet have remained consistently numb for the last few weeks. I also discovered that I have nearly entirely lost the ability to orgasm thanks to numbness consuming my left side.

With any luck, the recent course of steroids and the fourth different medication I'm currently receiving through a drip for the first time as I type this will make some difference. The first medication was difficult, involving a daily injection. I could handle the needles, but every day I would have a worse reaction to the medicine with welts and pain. I then went years with no medication until what was hailed a miracle for many came under the Pharmaceutical Benefits Scheme, in the shape of a tiny cytotoxic tablet taken for five days, followed by a brief hiatus for a few weeks and another fiveday course for two years. Unfortunately, it didn't work as intended, and my MS progressed and remained active. A brief pause to safely carry my youngest and recover and breastfeed her ensued, and after, I was able to start a new medicine. I began a monthly infusion this year; they say the third time is the charm. I guess that meant having a severe allergic reaction that stopped any chance of safely continuing.

I'm currently sitting in the hospital's oncology clinic, which doubles as an infusion centre, for the next few hours to receive what will hopefully be my final medication, and fingers crossed that it is a success. Despite what happens with my MS or any other life event the universe throws my way, I still intend to continue working. I will begin studying next month to become a nurse after accepting an offer from a university.

Eventually, I realised I might not know my future, but I never truly did. To begin with, what kind of role model would I be to my children or myself if I didn't at least try. Despite everything, I've got so damn much to be thankful for. I never could have envisioned how my life has developed and how much I've grown since then. If it weren't for having MS and the relapses I've endured, I wouldn't be the person I am today. Having gone through times when I had difficulty speaking and swallowing and needed to use a walker or a wheelchair allowed me to have a deeper understanding when assisting residents in the nursing home I worked for and in the disability support sector as a carer. My compassion and knowledge gained through those deficits have helped me to be a more empathetic carer and enabled me to relate to clients and residents, knowing the grief, anxiety and sadness that comes with the loss of function and motor skills.

It has not been easy, but just between you and me, the hardest blows I've taken had nothing to do with my health. I might have MS, but it no longer has me. If I could give you any advice, it would be don't change your life for something you have no control over. The world will continue to spin on its axis, regardless. My only regret is letting MS hold me back from life—studying, a career, and missed opportunities—for fear that I would let myself and others down when eventually my relapses stopped remitting.

Watch the VLOG/Podcast of Stacey on YouTube

ABOUT STACEY

Stacey Metcalfe's personal perspective is a powerful journey of resilience and self-discovery. Diagnosed with multiple sclerosis (MS) at a young age, she faced uncertainty and fear, but she refused to let the disease define her. Stacey navigated through numerous relapses and challenges, refusing to let MS dictate her life.

Stacey Metcalfe's remarkable journey of resilience and self-discovery unfolds as she faces the challenges of being diagnosed with multiple sclerosis (MS) at a young age. Confronting uncertainty and fear, she refused to let the disease define her, navigating through numerous relapses with determination. Stacey steadfastly refuses to let MS dictate her life!

Despite the setbacks, she found strength in her relationships, especially with her supportive partner and four beautiful children. Through the years, she battled depression, doubt and health struggles but persevered, eventually pursuing her dreams. Stacey became a carer, drawing from her own experiences to empathise with and support others.

Though she continues to face relapses and new medications, Stacey remains determined to move forward. She has learned not to let MS hold her back, embracing life's opportunities and pursuing her dreams of becoming a nurse.

Stacey's story is a testament to her resilience, strength and unwavering spirit, inspiring others to face their challenges with courage and hope.

19

Elizabeth Neal

MY VERSION OF EVENTS

When they asked me to write 3,000 words about my MS journey, two things came immediately to mind. First, I dislike the word journey, mostly because it suggests a certain amount of fun, which is so far from reality that it makes all journeys look like the worst thing ever. Second, I'm on a mission to get positivity into my life, and this story evokes mainly grief and a general sense of *what the hell happened to the life I was so excited about when this all began*. This is not a story about my MS journey, but instead a raw documentation of what has happened so far in as much detail as 3,000 words allow. But a warning, it has scenes that may distress some viewers. But if that's your thing, read on. Or if I have piqued your interest, this may be your thing too. Buckle up, and let's do this. After all, it's only one chapter.

    I have had MS since at least 1988 when I first noticed bizarre symptoms, which I now know were exacerbations. I was in the RAAF at the time. I was labelled a malingerer and treated with hostility, disbelief and bastardisation. I now refer to it as the worst three years of my life. After leaving the RAAF, I was sure that my health would improve. When it did not, I saw a real doctor who, in

1991, sent me to have an MRI—at Australia's first MRI machine at West-Mead Hospital in Sydney, New South Wales. I was diagnosed with MS three days later by my neurologist. My first reaction was, "Thank god I had begun to wonder if the RAAF doctors were correct and there really was something wrong with my mind!" My neurologist assured me, "Don't worry, they will have a cure in three years" Thirty-two years later, I'm still waiting.

Rewind several years from this, too, when my MS odyssey began on 19 November 1987 at 21, which was the first day of my three-year tenure in the RAAF. I was sure this would be the job I would do for the rest of my life. Yes, I thought I was set. The training was rigorous, and for reasons I didn't understand, no matter how hard I tried, I could not pass the physical requirements of the training and, most specifically, the 2.4 km run in under 12 minutes—the age requirement. I was training every night for what seemed like hours, and on top of that, I had to accomplish all other requirements, such as perfectly ironed uniforms, a spotless room and other ridiculous requirements, such as polishing all the silver plumbing in the ablutions block—that catered for 30 female personnel. I remember crawling into bed most nights at 2:00 am in order to get up at 4:00 am to get ready for fatty's parade—the fond name given to the extra training that had become mandatory for those who couldn't pass the physical requirements for the RAAF training.

Enter the curveball. Unbeknownst to me, I had a very rare muscle disorder which I was born with and not picked up at the entry medical. The rare disorder is McArdle's Syndrome—so named a syndrome because it is neither caught nor developed, but rather you are born with it. The logistics of a recessive gene disorder make it a one in a trillion chance of having. This would become the anomaly that would make diagnosis even more difficult, not to mention its impact on my life since I can remember.

McArdle's means that whenever I move, all I have is ten seconds of energy before my muscles start looking for fuel—or glycogen—which my body cannot retrieve. What happens then is extraordinary muscle cramping, an inability to keep going, and a need to rest for approximately two minutes before the next ten-second burst. Seriously, as a child, I thought I was the fattest, most useless person on the planet. If I thought that was bad, I could never have conceptualised how much more difficult life would become. And honestly, even at this point now, where MS has become a slippery slope, if I could choose between MS and McArdle's, I would choose MS in a heartbeat.

Finally, in my gaining unit, the more often I went to see the RAAF doctors, the more I was threatened with being charged with malingering—an indictable offence in the RAAF. Coming from training, I had assumed the worst was over. And yet I woke every morning feeling worse than the day before.

The bizarre kept coming at me as I battled with continual nausea, mainly due to what I now know as nystagmus in both eyes, each at differing degrees. In layperson's terms, it's a beating of the eyeball on the left more than the right, making the world appear spinning. Nothing in my gaze would remain still but instead darted about, creating an eternal dizziness to rival any roundabout ride in terms of, *oh my god, I can't even stand still*. It made trips to the pub a continual accusation of "Haven't you had enough to drink"? And "Maybe it's time to go home and sleep it off?" often said when it was still light out. These bizarre symptoms continued sporadically during my time in the RAAF and then into civilian life. Even to this day, 35 years later, throw alcohol into the mix, and you get the picture.

Every day is fraught with incessant and unrelenting fatigue. No matter how much sleep I have, there is no relief, along with continual headaches for which the RAAF doctors would prescribe Panadeine Forte.

The dizziness to this day continues, and with the dizziness comes the falls. In the RAAF, I was finally seen by a neurologist who asked me if my then boyfriend was hitting me because of all the bruising down my right side. I burst into tears over such an absurd suggestion, which he assumed was an admission. Instead, I told him I was sure I'd had a stroke, to which he patronisingly rolled his eyes and, with a smirk, said, "Oh really, do you?" He further asked, "What makes you think this?" I explained further that my whole right side had slumped, and I was having trouble walking, to which he responded with more eye rolling and smirking. I left the RAAF in tears several years later. When I got a copy of my medical documents under Freedom of Information, I noted I seemed to have a high-stress and irrational response to my symptoms and also noted *has had a psychosomatic illness in the past.*

But wait, there's more

After seeing the neurologist about what I thought was a stroke, I next saw him with the most painful dysplasia on my right forearm, where it was bizarrely itchy. When I scratched it, I screamed in pain. The only relief was to grab my arm and pinch it with my fingernails until it bled. Then, of course, it was self-harm for which I would require psychiatric intervention, which, interestingly, was never followed up on. This went on and on, until finally, almost at the end of my posting, the neurologist commented on my current symptoms as genuine and added, "Getting out of RAAF in November, no further action." Since then, I have been chasing answers as to why my treatment had been so appalling and had little or no compassion for what was surely obviously a serious illness.

And that was that, as far as the RAAF was concerned. Off I went into civilian life, and I recall sleeping for what seemed like months, finally running out of money. I had to return to work, and since my training was admin, it made sense this would be my starting point. I looked in the *positions vacant* section of my local newspaper, applied for the position of *medical receptionist* and, although untrained, got the position. I always had an exceptional memory that I knew would serve me well, but I had noticed this incredible memory was not as incredible as it once was and just assumed it was because I was older now. I had agreed to do the medical terminology course. I undertook it at 25 when we learned how to spell multiple sclerosis. The worst ah-ha moment of my life was when our teacher described the disease and its symptoms. I began to cry as I realised this was what I had had all along and the most awful realisation. *How the f**k did they miss this?* They gave me two sentences, and I figured out the RAAF had been three years and didn't even believe something was wrong. What followed was years of counselling! That was 30 years ago, and I am still angry and dismayed.

1991 was my year of diagnosis, at which time there was no treatment, only steroids to treat exacerbations which were effective, although the side effects were unbearable! And then came the interferons in 1996, which was an every-other-day subcutaneous injection and no auto inject available. It was a 17-minute process of injections that lasted six years until I decided the side effects and the trauma were no longer worth the *anecdotal evidence of reducing exacerbations by up to 33 per cent.*

When people learn I was diagnosed in 1991, they seem to think *I'm doing pretty well*, and I think to myself, *gosh, I'd hate to see what bad looks like*. Yes, this seems like the perfect comedy line, and I'll address this later.

On the days when I want to stay in bed, I realise it's the MS talking. It's time to push through, and I keep reminding myself, *either way, I'm going to be exhausted, so I may as well keep going*. And this applies to absolutely everything.

If I track back to the beginning, MS was always visible as I struggled with the simplest things, like stairs without rails and a noticeable limp since the first exacerbation. My right side had begun to decline, and the very noticeable, incessant need to urinate so often was preposterously ludicrous. While this seems like too many words to describe, anyone with MS who has this symptom will agree. There should be more adjectives to describe this unwelcome fact that invades our lives.

I could keep going, but really this has become just data entry, and the brief said to keep it upbeat and positive with some light at the end of the tunnel.

While working on my upbeat closing paragraph that will inspire and fill everyone who has MS with hope, I went for a routine appointment with my doctor, who got angry with me. With a raised voice, the doctor said, "You can't afford to do this." I had missed a neurologist appointment, and I pointed out I only missed one because I was at a funeral; I wasn't out clubbing. "You have a progressive disease," her voice raised even further as she told me, "You have to commit to your appointments so you can manage your disease." I felt as if she was telling me *life is not about the journey, it is about the destination,* and the destination doesn't look good. I must be fully prepared for it.

Then back to reality. "How many falls did you have this week"? "Only two was my reply", as quite honestly, I am tired of the pain of broken ribs. And, of course, to me, every fall will be my last because I'll definitely be more careful from now on. Then there's that terrible moment when you know exactly what's about to happen as you catch your foot on that piece of pavement a micro millimetre higher than the rest. You feel the tipping point of your centre of gravity as you hurtle towards the ground, and at that moment, looking around for something to grab and cursing yourself again, "Why didn't I bring my support worker with me today?" As soon as you hit the ground, you assess the situation. "Can I get up?" "Did anyone see?" Most importantly, "Did anyone get this on film?" Because frankly, it's about time someone put this on YouTube so I could go viral and finally make some serious money doing what

I have become so damn good at.

And with less than 500 words left, here are the good bits! Well, mostly good. My first marriage was in 1992, and until the divorce—five years later—it was a good experience as my then husband was a musical director, and life was hectic and fun. Although diagnosed, I almost managed to keep up with this life. And in 2000, I met and fell in love with the father of my three amazing children, who have luckily inherited my sense of humour, which will serve them well in life.

I have completed two university degrees, one in journalism and political science and the other in health sciences. So, when I ask, "What are scientists doing? Why haven't they come up with a cure?" being a scientist, I have to put myself in that category, too, and realise it's not as simple as that. I Have created a garden in my tiny rental that astonishes anyone who visits. For me, it's my happy place, where I sit with my plastic wine glass and enjoy a nice white.

My health science degree has helped me realise the importance of exercise in making sure I remain fit and able to remain upright and walking. However, doctors and friends alike have been very encouraging when it comes to getting a wheelie walker or, for ultimate freedom, a wheelchair. My argument is *once you give in, there's no coming back from that*. The obvious question has been asked, "Come back to what?" My answer is always the same "To hope and a body that is still able to do most things." Denial? Yes, but I reckon I'm onto something with exercise, and it's part in staving off for me the unthinkable.

I embark on a serious amount of exercise most days—always with the oversight of an exercise physiologist—for which there is a definite upside of fitting into my clothes. And the best exercise I have found to date was discovering the benefits of pole dancing, which is perfect because you hang onto a pole, and the core exercise is radical. I remember the first day I showed up with my limp and walking stick. I was worried I wouldn't be taken seriously, and the owners of *Pole Park* in Townsville are the ultimate *kindness of strangers*. However, at 18 months, they are no longer strangers. They have had grab rails installed and continually come up with alternatives to accommodate any limitations I have. No matter how many times I complete beginners, they are continually encouraging and enthusiastic about my progress.

One of the most exciting things for me has been doing stand-up comedy for which I have an alias—Eliot Ness—pretending to be someone else is sheer joy. My bio describes me as *performing since 2019 wherever they allow her—mostly in bars—and easily adapts to any venue as long as she can get on the stage....* I've been asked why I don't talk about MS in my stand-up, and quite simply, I answer, "Because it's not funny."

In 2020, something happened that I could never have anticipated. My beautiful first-born son, Valentine, 19, died unexpectedly in a tragic accident. When it happened, I did so much of nothing—mostly sitting alone in my beautiful garden drinking all the wine I could find—and wondered what effect it would have on MS. So far, I choose to believe I am no different, and honestly, I am still so filled with grief. MS is not a priority right now. I often see him in my dreams, and just the other night, I asked him, "Why did you go?" His answer was, "Mum, I had to go first to make sure it was safe." He was the light in the room, the echoing laughter and the life of the party, yes, all the cliches. With the coolest name and the best birthday, we had set him up so that no one would ever forget him. Yes, Valentine was always easy to remember.

To the doctors who see me as not taking this seriously, please forgive me. I have been waiting to get better since this all began. With that in mind, I have barely scratched the surface in terms of covering everything that has happened, good and bad. But honestly, it's been so long that I have forgotten what life was like without MS and remain blindly optimistic that the cure will come. In the meantime, I will follow up on every random diet, superfood, miracle drug, meditation technique, and manifestation ritual that becomes available in the hope that it's the magic bullet. I am gullible and, at times, naïve when it comes to the possibility of full functionality. In the meantime, I am the most resilient person I know. To the bystanders who see me and offer assistance, because my difficulty is anything but invisible, I thank you for your kindness. You are amazing! Please keep offering.

Please, please, please, friends and family, don't comment when you notice I get worse; please only tell me when I improve.

Watch the VLOG/Podcast of Elizabeth on YouTube

ABOUT ELIZABETH

Elizabeth Neal, a woman of unwavering strength and optimism, has faced life's challenges with determination and a sense of humor. Diagnosed with MS in 1991, she endured misdiagnosis and hostility in the RAAF. Despite constant fatigue, dizziness, and falls, she found joy in her marriage, motherhood and pursuit of higher education.

Through it all, Elizabeth's resilience continues to shine exploring various treatments and exercise routines to manage her condition. She discovered the empowering benefits of pole dancing and even ventured into stand-up comedy to embrace life fully.

Tragedy struck in 2020 when her beloved son Valentine passed away unexpectedly. Amidst the grief, Elizabeth remains hopeful, seeking a cure for MS while cherishing her son's memories.

With an unwavering spirit, Elizabeth faces each day with optimism, refusing to let MS define her. Her determination, support from friends and family, and love for life inspire those around her.

20

Kristi Paschalidis

YOUNG, ALONE AND HOPEFUL

Being 13 years old, I was trying to navigate my way through life and learning how to be a teenager. I couldn't stop talking about the Backstreet Boys, and my focus was getting the latest lip smacker lip-gloss.

Suddenly, things weren't feeling right. I started to have a tingly feeling in my toes, and I couldn't feel my feet. Hmm... probably nothing. Then I started having the same tingly feeling up my legs. Strange. It'll pass. My arms now have the same pins and needles feel to them. This can't be right.

The tingly feeling made its way across my entire body; even my gums felt tingly. I mentioned it to my Mum, and from there, a barrage of tests with different doctors began. I even visited my dentist to ask about my gums. He gave me the same confused look most doctors gave me, telling me they couldn't see anything. By chance, I was sent to another specialist who mentioned that perhaps I should get an MRI done. At the time, there were only a handful of MRI machines in Sydney. It was far from common practice; no one I knew had heard of them or had experience with them. Luckily, a machine was in Kogarah, which wasn't far from my house.

The procedure at the time cost about $900. I was fortunate to be in a position where I could afford to have this conducted, but I always wonder what would have happened to me if I couldn't get the test done.

My Dad had taken me to the MRI appointment after school, and looking back, I really had no idea what I was walking into. I was in a long tube, covering my entire body with very little space. There was barely any space between my nose and the surrounding wall. I couldn't move, and there were loud noises, all very confronting. As this was a new procedure, I was in the machine for a lot longer than expected. They were still working on the process. This meant more time in the tube with the loud noises, not knowing what was going on. I was confused and scared. I was alone, shivering from the cold. I've had MRIs every year for over 20 years, however, my first experience still haunts me.

I am claustrophobic, and I always wonder if this was caused by this first experience. I now come *prepared* for all my MRIs. I bring my eye mask, I ask for a blanket, and I've found a location that offers to play music through headphones while I lie there.

From there, the results were sent to the Royal North Shore Hospital, where I'm told a panel of 12 doctors deliberated on the results before coming to the verdict that I had MS. After hearing many stories of other people going years without MS being diagnosed, I'm grateful that they were able to identify this so quickly.

MS usually affects people between the ages of 20 and 30 years. I was 13 when I was diagnosed, making me the third youngest person in the state at the time to have been diagnosed with MS. MS is different for everyone. My symptoms were fatigue and the feeling of pins and needles, with stress and heat, particularly steam, bringing on an *episode*. I have always avoided baths and saunas for this reason.

When you're 13, you seem to know everything about the world, and I was convinced that the doctors had it all wrong. There was nothing wrong with me; I was just like everyone else. I had completed the MS readathon at school, and all of the people on the posters were in wheelchairs. That wasn't me.

I didn't want to know about MS or even talk about it. I went into a state of denial and tried to shut it all out. My parents went to MS support groups without me, as they were also trying to cope with the news. What I didn't realise at the time was that my diagnosis didn't just affect me; it was something that affected my family just as much. They were at every single appointment. They were trying to understand how to manage it and helped me to understand it.

The following year, a nurse visited me at home to teach me how to self-inject three times a week. It was uncomfortable, a bit painful and overall, I didn't enjoy it. As a result, I wasn't consistent with my medication. I would maybe take one injection a week instead of three. I still didn't think anything was wrong at this stage. I would pretend to self-medicate and instead squirt the medication down the sink. I look back now and am embarrassed at how foolish I was. This went on for a while until I finally saw the impact and strain this was having on my parents. I think this is what eventually woke me up.

I was having issues with my bladder and was constantly needing the bathroom. I remember visiting a urologist and explaining my struggles. A procedure was scheduled to see how much liquid my bladder could hold, which led to me having to use a self-catheter. My principal knew about my condition and catheter and organised for me to use a staff bathroom for privacy. But it was awkward trying to secretly visit the staff bathroom without staff or students seeing me. This was extremely uncomfortable, and it didn't last long.

Looking back, the feeling of isolation and loneliness were my biggest hurdles. It was a lot of information to take in and process. It was decided that it would be best not to share the news with any of my friends. Children can be cruel, and I didn't want to be treated any differently or excluded.

That mentality stayed with me throughout the years. I've never been very open and forthcoming about my condition. It was only once I became a mother that I started telling people about my condition.

I was doing my year 9 exams when I went through an *episode* of MS. I was so tired that I didn't have the energy to lift my pen to write my answers. How do you even begin to try to explain that you're too tired to lift a pen? It was such a confusing time. It indicates exactly why I chose not to tell any classmates, as this certainly would have been met with much laughter and ridicule. From then, I sat all of my school exams in a separate room with a scribe, just in case I needed them. I was also given some additional time for bathroom breaks.

University life was a bit more intense. I studied full-time, worked part-time, and had an active social life. Instead of doing four subjects a semester, I did three, which meant it took longer to finish my degree. In an effort to speed this up, I did a few summer school and winter school classes. It meant that I graduated after three and a half years instead of four. I continued to sit in a separate room for my exams.

It was also a time when I wanted to go out all the time and socialise. My body had other plans. Although I tried my best to listen to my body, I often pushed myself to its limits. I would go to a bar or a party when I should have been at home resting. I reached a point where I couldn't move, and the fatigue really took over. By this, I mean I couldn't lift my arms or move from the couch. The smallest movements can be a big effort for me.

I have always worked since finishing university and battled with the notion of whether I should share my condition with my employer. There were days when I struggled to keep up; I just wanted to sit and do nothing. I did hide in meeting rooms when I

could, but that wasn't ideal. My fear was how the company would react, whether it would affect my employment or if I would be treated differently. I felt the quality of my work spoke for itself, and I didn't want to be seen as getting preferential treatment.

A past relationship taught me the dangers of *Dr Google* and the importance of asking questions about a person's condition. I was in a serious relationship for a few years and had shared the details of my condition with my partner. They decided to share the news with their family. Not knowing much about MS, they turned to Google for information and came across some misleading articles, one explaining that people with MS couldn't have children. They forced my partner to end the relationship. This took me a really long time to move on from. My condition was out of my control, and I felt I was being judged on a misconception.

Luckily, I met someone two years later and told him on our third date about my MS. Like a crazy person, I gave him pamphlets and instructed him to tell his family and not to contact me if there was an issue. We just celebrated our eighth wedding anniversary and have two beautiful children, so clearly, that article was incorrect.

Over time, my symptoms have grown. I've had blurred vision, loss of balance, and brain fog, in addition to fatigue, and suddenly entire parts of my body go numb. My arm or my leg suddenly *won't work*, or I can't lift my arms to drink some water, or I'm stuck in a chair and can't get up to go and lie down. I remember trying to drink my coffee through a straw because I couldn't lift my mug. It's all spontaneous and will completely hit me out of nowhere.

The best way I can describe my fatigue is by saying that I feel I have sandbags over my body, preventing me from functioning. I can feel a weight on top of me and can't move, regardless of how much I might try to concentrate.

This makes it extremely difficult to plan and commit to events and functions. I'll have an event I had organised or confirmed weeks ago, and suddenly I'm hit with an excessive wave of fatigue, or I can't feel my arms. I feel silly cancelling because *I feel tired*. I feel people don't realise that my definition of *tired* is not the same as theirs.

The biggest struggle with MS I have had to deal with would be motherhood.

I always had a fear of being a mother with MS. What if I don't have the energy to hold the baby? Will I be able to run after them? Will I be a good mother? These thoughts ran through my head constantly.

I read articles and brochures and spoke to a family friend that has MS and was a mother. I spoke with my neurologist a few times. Being a mother herself, she was very empathetic, and we talked through different scenarios for my concerns.

After months of trying, I finally fell pregnant and gave birth to a beautiful, healthy baby girl.

Nothing can truly prepare you for motherhood. The exhaustion is like nothing else you have experienced. For someone living with MS, this is even more difficult. Like most new mums, you are tired and emotional, but on top of that, you genuinely can't move. I was lucky and had a very good pregnancy. A few months after my daughter was born, my MS resurfaced to a level that was more intense. I genuinely was running on empty and couldn't move. There was a morning when my daughter was screaming in her bassinet, and I don't know how I did it, but I had to muster what little energy I had and look after her. Looking after myself was not a priority, BUT as my husband often told me, if I didn't look after myself, I wouldn't be able to look after her. It was a real struggle.

When I tried telling someone how tired I was, the usual response was, *we're all tired, or you're a mum, what were you expecting* or something else along these lines. People meant well but didn't truly understand what being tired meant for me.

My husband is a shift worker, working 12-hour shifts, and often isn't there at night or on weekends. I love being a mother and spending time with my children, but the days can be extremely long when I'm entertaining them on my own. It also means the nights are unkind. The dinner, bath, and bed routine is left to me. Getting up and rocking my baby while they suffer from teething, sitting with them when they have nightmares, or when the dreaded croup decides to grace us with its presence. Regardless of how weak I am or how little energy I have, I help with whatever situation has arisen. I am lucky that I have support from my family, though when it's 1:00 am or 3:00 am, I'm the only one.

I made the decision to speak up and advocate for people with MS and to share my story where I can once I became a mother.

Just before my daughter turned one, I rejoined the workforce, working three days a week—a big adjustment on so many levels. At the time, I had to catch two trains to get to work and two trains to return home. This meant that before I had even logged in for the day, I was exhausted. As MS is an *invisible disease* and I may not look like anything is wrong with me, there is no reason for anyone to offer me a seat on the train. I had to stand the entire way, get off one train, and walk across the platforms to get to the next train, where I had to stand again. This might sound like an ordinary work commute, but the energy required was quite high. Once I got to work, all I wanted to do was put my bags down and rest. As I was part-time, it was quite a busy role where I tried to get as much done during the time I was in the office before having to rush off, begin my train commute again and begin my dinner, bath and bed routine.

I always assumed that my daughter would be my only child. Could I put the strain on my body all over again? I had one healthy baby, and my body was feeling pretty consistent. I hadn't had an epi*sode f*or a while. When my daughter was two, I desperately wanted her to have a sibling, a forever friend.

With both of my pregnancies, the decision as to when to start trying was never left with me. I had to do many tests before we even got to that stage. My neurologist had to review my progress, body and treatment. It was all very thorough, but what is such a personal and special decision for most was not my experience. I had to be given the all-clear before I could even begin my pregnancy journey.

I was not optimistic the second time. Much to my surprise, I was told that the test results were looking positive and I could try for another child. I was over the moon!

Within a year, I had a beautiful baby boy. Again, a good pregnancy. When he was older, I truly started to feel the effects

on my body. I might add that my son was born during the Covid lockdown. All the help and support I had planned instantly went out the window.

Once I was chasing after two children, it really took a toll on my body. The frequency of when I can't feel my arms or legs is more constant. I often need to go for naps and rest during the day. I try to keep up, but I also need to plan our days and activities. Our outings and big games are for the morning while I have a lot of energy, while the quieter independent activities are for later in the day. This sounds easy, but not everything sticks to plan. My plan also doesn't account for the extremely dark, hard days. The days when I can barely move and even getting up to get some water is something I need to consider if I can spare the energy. This is where the mum guilt kicks into overdrive.

Both of my children have a love for books and will happily sit there while I read to them. This is a big win for me. When I have limited energy, sitting still and flicking pages sometimes is the only thing I can manage. I do remember making up the *sleeping game*. We would lie on the ground pretending to sleep, and the other one had to wake them up. My daughter loved the game, squealing with delight as we played. She was too young to realise this was a game of necessity for me. It gave me a chance to rest my body, and she was safe. I felt like the worst mother because I believed she deserved more than that.

It's often said that being a mum is the hardest job in the world, and being a working mum is even harder. What about if I take it up a notch and explain that I'm a working mum with MS, and my main symptom is fatigue? There is no category for that. I don't fit into a box.

I was so young when I was diagnosed, and I often wonder what would be different if I was diagnosed later in life. Having a different way of looking at life, what would that have meant for how I handled my diagnosis? Would it have made a difference? Would my life have been different? What about if my children were older and less reliant on me?

When I tell my story, I'm often looked at with pity and told how awful it must have been. I have always found this frustrating, as I consider myself extremely lucky. I grew up with MS. I didn't have to shift how I lived my life, change my diet or learn a new way. I don't know any other way. I have also had a really wonderful neurologist who has been with me since the start, who genuinely cares and who has helped keep me on track. My condition has not stopped me from living a full life. I have studied, I have married, and I have had children. I have also had some incredible experiences. I have been white water rafting in Austria, have sipped limoncello in Positano, have danced until the wee hours of the morning with friends, watched a sunset in Santorini, climbed the Sydney Harbour Bridge and swam in the ocean in Hawaii, to mention a few. My condition

has not stopped me from enjoying life. I've just done things at a slower pace, but I have still gotten there. I have never tried to hide behind my condition to progress in life. I want my children to see that when they grow up, and I hope, in some way, I can inspire them to be the best they can be.

Watch the VLOG/Podcast of Kristi on YouTube

ABOUT KRISTI

Kristi Paschalidis is an accomplished senior internal recruiter with over 11 years of experience across multiple industries. She holds a B. Social Science degree, majoring in Human Resource Management from UNSW. Additionally, Kristi is a qualified Diversity and Inclusion specialist.

In 2015, Kristi married her husband and they have been blessed with two beautiful children who bring immense joy to her life.

At the age of 13, Kristi was diagnosed with Multiple Sclerosis (MS) and has since faced the challenges of living with this "invisible disease." Despite the obstacles, she successfully completed high school and university while actively maintaining a social life and travelling. Over time, as her symptoms progressed, Kristi learned to adapt, and remains hopeful for a cure. Initially, she kept her diagnosis private, however, she has now embraced her role as an MS Ambassador, speaking at various MS community functions to educate others and raise awareness of MS. Kristi also provides support to individuals who have been diagnosed with MS, understanding firsthand how overwhelming the journey can be. Her mantra for others has always been, "We can't be a superhero every day. There are days when being human is more than enough."

21

Clare Reilly

THE DICHOTOMY OF DISABILITY

The day I was finally given my diagnosis was one of the worst days of my life. Many years later, the haze has lifted, and I now see this as a pivotal day in my life. I wouldn't say it was one of the best days of my life—although that would flow nicely—but definitely one of significant positive impact.

Bent over at the outdoor tap, folded at a 90 degree angle from my waist, I washed my hands and then struggled to stand up. My core had no control as I struggled to return to standing. I turned to my husband after a morning of gardening and asked, "What if it's MS?" With no reason to think that, I'm not sure where the thought had come from. No family history of multiple sclerosis, no chronic illness, no disability, and no autoimmune conditions. All I knew of MS was the MS Readathon from primary school. I had little to no experience with disability.

This questionable revelation had come after months of no answers from various professionals. I had been dealing with an intensely painful lower back for some time and had noticed my walking was *weird*. As I struggled to ignore the pain, afternoons were spent lying on my dining room floor in tears after calling my mum to come and supervise my toddler. I saw a physiotherapist who said they had never seen anything like the way my legs moved on a Pilates reformer machine. An osteopath who could see *that things were improving.* A spiritual healer who told me that my lower back pain was evil spirits inhabiting my body from childhood trauma.

After living in pain for months—not long in the scheme of a multiple sclerosis diagnosis—and waiting for six weeks after my neurologist told me that my symptoms were caused by either multiple sclerosis or a benign brain tumour, I received the results. I was given both answers and uncertainty. Six weeks of anxiousness—anxious stomach aches, bouts of anger and fits of heaving and sobbing tears—only to be thrust into more unknown.

A wave of relief caused by finally being given a name for what I was living with was immediately crushed by the fear of the unknown. I could treat it with medication, but I didn't know how much longer I could run around after my toddler. I now knew what I was living with and yet still wanted to put my head in the sand and ignore it.

The dichotomy began that day.

The highs and lows, the tos and fros, the ups and downs—the dichotomy of the emotions brought on by the diagnosis. One of the biggest things I have learned from my diagnosis is that two things can be true at the same time. You can be both happy and sad, excited and grieving, proud and ashamed, and many other dualities.

Disability and diagnosis are HUGE and also nothing. Your diagnosis can define you and also have no influence over who you are.

Disability is value-neutral. It's neither a good thing nor a bad thing—it's just a thing. After that initial shock and the daily navigation of managing life, it becomes life.

The remarks of, "Oh, that's so sad," or "I'm lucky enough not to have anyone with a disability in my family," or "How brave you are for spending the day in Melbourne all alone; I don't know how you do it," are so blindly uncritical of the larger social problem. What am I expected to do with life, sit at home and feel sad and sorry for myself? Are the people raising these concerns going to do something about the difficulty I face when accessing public transport? Or are they just going to consider me inspiring for merely existing? Disabled people don't purely deserve respect for *overcoming* our disabilities. We are not inspirational for just living our lives. Many disabled people are inspiring, but this is because they share their stories. They advocate and speak proudly for what they believe in. This is not a requisite for being disabled.

My disability has, in fact, shaped me. It's changed me in almost every way for the better. I feel as though I am more empathetic and more aware of things others are going through, whether that be more awareness for people living with chronic illness and disability

or awareness for others not living as part of the mainstream. Or simply just empathy that everyone is living with something they find difficult behind closed doors. My disability has changed how I see the world, how I interact with those around me, and how I choose to participate in life.

But, on the flip side, my disability doesn't define me. I don't introduce myself as a wheelchair user, as someone living with MS.

I am so much more than that; I am so much more before that. I am a mother, a wife, a friend, a creative, a logistical queen, a sourdough bread baker, and a dress wearer. This leads me to my next point.

You can be happy, living a brilliant full life and still be grieving what you have lost—and this can go on forever.

I am studying, working, an active mum and a loving wife. I am a good friend, a creative with too many hobbies, and I love to travel and go on big or small adventures. I live an incredibly full, satisfying, active and adventurous life. I can honestly say that I am happy *every day, not all day every day, but every day*—anyone else comfort watch *Sex and The City*?

Grief can hit you when you least expect it. I can be in the middle of a grand adventure. A day out in Melbourne city, where I have ridden Wendy—my power wheelchair—down the street, onto the Portarlington to Docklands ferry. I could have visited art galleries, seen a musical and then arrived at the front door of a divine-looking shop, only to find there are stairs for entry. I can feel the frustrations and anger wash over me. The internal battle of *why me* screaming inside me.

Or I can wake up one day and not hold back the tears. Every step, slowly, with my trusty indoor walking frame, Rusty can bring tears to my eyes and add to the growing lump in my throat. The sobs can erupt, tears flowing uninterrupted down my face, over my swollen cheeks and down my neck, hitting the collar of my dress. Gasping breaths between inhaling before the next wave hits. Being unable to answer *what's wrong* because it's everything and nothing.

The sadness doesn't have to be caused by anything in particular.

It's important to notice, to remember that life is wonderful and not get stuck in grief and frustration. Frustrations of uncertainties, of having lost the ability to do things you were once very able to do, the frustration of the word sitting on the tip of your tongue, or

completely losing phrases into a puff of smoke from your mind. Frustrations of the inaccessible world we live in. The grief of the life you have lost.

It's important to have these thoughts, but it's also important to think, why not me. My life is fabulous! Rainbows, smiles from strangers, visits to art exhibitions, theatre productions, unfurling leaves on indoor plants. Wonder really is all around and can weave through, around and in between frustrations.

Using mobility aids is both devastating and liberating.

For a long time, I avoided using mobility aids. I felt as though by needing them, I had failed. The decline in my mobility, seeing and feeling my legs ache, and my hips and knees not bending as they were supposed to. Feeling less and less able. The distances I was able to walk was decreasing. I was in pain, missing out on life and seeing my world becoming smaller.

Getting your head around using a wheelchair can be a huge emotional strain. Admitting to myself that I needed one was the hardest part. I'll never forget the day when I realised a wheelchair would be a benefit to my life. I was sitting at my office desk, mid-podcast interview. My guest spoke about how they use a wheelchair to make the world a more accessible place for them. They spoke about how when they go out with their family, using a wheelchair means they can spend more time out and about and get more involved with their children's lives. They spoke about how it saves them from pain and fatigue. And they spoke about how it was like changing between a car and a push bike, runners, and high heels.

A revelation, a light bulb moment. If I added a wheelchair to my arsenal of aids, I could spend more time out and about. I could

spend more time with my community. I could go on adventures that I thought might have been lost to me for good.

When I started back at work after starting to use a wheelchair, my workplace was large, so I contacted JobAccess to see what they could do to make my workplace more accessible. Their recommendation was a power chair—a WHILL power wheelchair meant I could get quickly around the large site. We—my family and I—named her Wendy, and she changed my life. Not only was I able to get around at work, but I was able to walk with my son to school. I was able to spend full days solo adventuring in Melbourne. I was able to go on bush walks with my friends and family, a throwback to my outdoor education background.

Using mobility aids, particularly wheelchairs—I now have two, a manual and a power chair—has changed my life for the better.

I now have an aid for every situation and every outfit. That's right, aids can be a fashion accessory.

After getting past the fear, frustration, and shame, I embraced the mobility aid and it has given me so much independence and freedom.

Big adventures and small adventures are the same.

I've travelled around the world. I've built a house. Birthed a baby. I've spent four years working at an off-the-grid outdoor education centre. I've lived some big adventures. But just like *growing up*—I now have a child, husband, bills to pay and responsibilities—MS can impact my ability to take grand adventures.

I now get a thrill out of *smaller* adventures as much as I do *big* ones. A day out using public transport while using mobility aids, a drive into the country, a theatre performance or a visit to the local pub for a cocktail. In a podcast I listened to recently, the guest spoke about how no individual in the world can experience 100% of what there is to offer. When you get diagnosed with MS, when your mobility declines, some doors may close, but your eyes become wide to the doors that you may never have seen prior to diagnosis. These are new doors that can open and contain experiences you may never have considered before.

I have a degree in outdoor education and a passion for long multi-day hikes. I've done 10 and 20-day bush walks. I've hiked the Overland Track in Tasmania, sections of the Australian Alps Walking Track that winds through the high country of Victoria, New South Wales and the Australian Capital Territory and a chunk of the Bibbulmun Track in Western Australia. But until I had a disability and access to a power wheelchair, I had never seen a musical.

Pride and guilt can co-exist.

A relatively *short* walk of 700 metres can feel like a multi-day hike of epic proportions. The conflicting feelings of pride for coming such a long way and frustration and guilt for it being so much effort and for taking so long while the non-disabled friend or family member totters beside you can be confusing. My patronising thoughts encourage each step as though I am a toddler learning to walk.

The feeling of failure is real. I hadn't done enough exercise. I hadn't tried hard enough. I haven't been able to beat the progression of multiple sclerosis. It was my fault. But then, the sneaky, sunshiny feeling of pride can force its rays through.

I am working on it. Three times a week, on a good week. Exercise physiology, clinical Pilates, work with a therapy assistant and every second week with a neuro physiotherapist. I do stretches up to three times daily.

I am proud of who I am, what I do and who I have become despite and because of my diagnosis.

Being grateful and frustrated by the myriad of appointments.

Each minute of each day is a choreographed dance of epic proportions. Each step of the salsa, the fast tempo, intricate footwork, fluid movements, and beat of the music, synchronised to the daily dance of managing my schedule. Work, school hours and after-school activities set the rhythm section, considered the foundation of salsa music. The horn section consists of physical therapy appointments squeezed into lunch breaks before or after work. Piano, playing complex montuno patterns that add harmonic and rhythmic interest, support workers and cleaners coming into my home, shushing the vacuum for regular Zoom meetings, and outputting my social energy to supportive strangers. Bass, the low-end foundation of self-care, regular hair washes, and maintaining my valuable energy for more important things than time spent in the shower. Finally, I pepper in percussion, adding texture and interest to life, days out with my family, wines with friends, lunch dates and big and small adventures. The music is a choreographed performance, each element balancing in music notes, threatening to create harsh, jumpy beats instead of the beautiful rhythmic flow of the salsa music.

Each appointment is important, maintaining my ability and improving my quality of life. Conversely, they fill every minute of my day, allowing little time for spontaneity or rest.

I am so grateful for these supports, professionals, and aids. But I tell you what, I'm exhausted by my full diary.

You can be exhausted or physically unable and yet completely mentally alert or vice versa.

While my body may be moving slower every day, my mind feels almost as sharp as ever. The conflict of waking up in pain, of stiffness and spasticity radiating through my body, or my dropped foot scuffing along the ground, all the while my mind working a million miles an hour, can be an incredible frustration.

To have the mental capacity for social events but be unable to get dressed, stand straight or take a safe step can feel so unfair. To be physically stuck at home but feel my mind whirling is a prison for my thoughts. I'm one of the lucky ones. I have found a job where all the staff work from home. Those days when my mind is active, but my body not so much. It only requires me to make it to my desk to feel I am contributing to society.

Conversely, others living with MS experience extreme brain fog. Cognitive dysfunction, forgetfulness, the feeling of having a word constantly on the tip of their tongue. All the while looking *fine*. Living the life of an invisible illness.

Multiple sclerosis is a disease of duality.

Those of us living with MS are all linked and yet all completely different.

How many of us have heard something like, *I knew or know someone who had MS; they were fine or died or really struggled....*

Joining the international MS community by sharing my story online, on social media and via the MSUnderstood podcast, even just joining the local MS coffee group, helped me connect with incredible and understanding people worldwide. The people were living with the same diagnosis that I was, but often with completely different symptoms.

I've talked to people who had numb fingers, mobility issues, pain in certain spots, loss of sensation in particular body parts, loss of taste, brain fog, and fatigue. The symptoms that are experienced by MS are as varied as the people who are diagnosed with it.

Comparing people's experiences is generally insulting, while we understand that it is often meant with kindness. I don't want to know that your aunt twice removed died from MS. First, because we know you don't die from MS, but from complications it can cause. Second, I hope that won't be my experience.

Not one person living with MS experiences the same symptoms as another. But we do all have a level of camaraderie and understanding. We relate to each other with a knowing nod. A secret club. The password is our diagnosis.

The blessings and burdens of a multiple sclerosis diagnosis are innumerable, are forever in opposition, and are all true at the same time. MS is a conflicting, confusing disability. It's invisible, it's very visible, it's a disease, it's a disability, it's in your mind, it's in your body, it affects every aspect of your life, and it changes nothing of who you are at your core.

The dichotomy and dualities are infinite and consistent. Black and white, frustration and calmness, positivity and anger, inclusion and exclusion, exhaustion and working harder and harder to prove your worth, excitement and exhaustion, anger and acceptance, loneliness and connection, successful and struggling. You could ask any person living with this progressive, debilitating autoimmune disease, and they could list 100 dualities they live with and through every day, and everyone is different.

My experience is one of daily duality. Happy and sad, tears and joy, compassion and anger. Every day is different and unpredictable. The constant unending, unwavering battle of living a life of dichotomy.

Watch the VLOG/Podcast of Clare on YouTube

ABOUT CLARE

Clare Reilly (she/her) was diagnosed with Multiple Sclerosis (MS) in April 2017. With a background in outdoor education, Clare loves spending time outdoors. Clare lives on the Bellarine Peninsula, near Geelong, with her husband and son. Clare explores various arts and crafts, is passionate about environmental sustainability and enjoys sharing good food with loved ones.

She is an advocate for those with MS and chronic illnesses, sharing thought-provoking posts on social media and hosting the podcast MS Understood. Clare's podcast has nearly 100 episodes, providing hope and understanding to newly diagnosed individuals and their families. Notable guests include Tim Ferguson of Doug Anthony All-Starts, Chantelle Otten sexologist and Emily Padfield from Netflix's Win The Wilderness, along with individuals sharing their MS stories. Clare has received awards for her business excellence and has now contributed to three published anthologies. With a Bachelor's degree in Psychological Science in progress, she aspires to provide therapy and counseling for people with new disabilities or chronic illness diagnoses, and dreams of writing her own novel. Find the MS Understood podcast on all major platforms.

22

Tanya Rountree

DO I LIVE WITH MS, OR DOES MS LIVE WITH ME?

I was diagnosed with relapsing-remitting MS in May 2006. I was 19 years old. At the time, my parents were going through a messy separation. I was working fulltime and reflecting; life was probably stressful. I hope people can take a few things from my story. First, everyone with MS leads a different path, but we all have similar symptoms, and when you are ready, having support from people leading similar paths is comforting. When you don't feel comfortable with a neurologist or don't think they have your best interests at heart, find a new neurologist. People without MS do not get it. I've had it for 17 years, and I don't even get it sometimes, but that doesn't stop them from expressing their opinion or telling you a story about *someone they know who has MS*. It generally isn't a nice story. I hope my story reaches even one person and helps them.

In May 2006, I was still living at home, and I remember my right thigh feeling *weird*. I rang my mum, who was at work and told her, and she told me to *put an icepack on my leg*. This is funny to this day because we often joke about my mum's *icepack* or a *hot pack remedy* for most injuries. If you've ever seen *My Big Fat Greek Wedding*, she is akin to the father's *Windex* medical miracle. Bless her.

It turns out that when I put that icepack on; it was the catalyst to change my life. I couldn't feel it; nothing at all. When I told Mum this, she said *that's odd*, clearly thinking, *how could an icepack not work?* I don't remember, but I'm sure she probably told me to try a hot pack.

This led to a doctor's appointment. Some sort of luck booked me in with a doctor who was familiar with MS, and he referred me to a neurologist for an *urgent appointment* with no mention of what might be wrong. It's been a long time, but I remember being at that appointment with the neurologist, sitting in his very clinical office, and being told I have multiple sclerosis. I know in there somewhere I had an MRI. He said they don't normally diagnose people who haven't had two relapses, but I told him about losing sight in one of my eyes a year earlier, with a decent amount of pain. He said that was *optic neuritis* and counted as my other relapse. I was told I had *a lot of lesions on my brain and spine*. I didn't feel lucky about that, but I also had no idea what that meant.

My sister was with me at the appointment, and I remember turning to her to ask what multiple sclerosis was. She replied, "My friend's cousin has it. He was driving one day, and when he stopped and got out of the car, he dropped ..." She got interrupted, and I was thinking, *he dropped what—dropped dead, dropped his wallet?* It turns out he dropped to the ground because he had lost feeling in his leg. I hope he's doing okay!

I can't say I handled my diagnosis well, but I'm not sure there is any great way of dealing with something like that, especially at such a young age. Here I am, 17 years later. I have been married for a number of years, and we have a beautiful threeyearold, but it has been one hell of a journey, and I'm very sure it is only beginning.

Back in 2006, I was learning how to inject myself with medicine every second day, still working full time and dealing with the questions, the relapses I was having and medical appointments. I avoided anything MS related. I was asked if I wanted to speak with someone from MS Queensland, and I declined. I remember my mum trying to find every cure possible—natural or not. She got me into drinking spirulina, taking cow's milk tablets and a few other *cures*. As a mother now, I can't imagine how hard it was for her to see her daughter inject herself every second day, be sick all the time, and try to push through it all, pretending it was funny and not all that bad.

I have been on countless medicines since my first medication. The first two were injections. Both caused me terrible side effects, and I was still relapsing, working and partying through the relapses. I distinctly remember losing the ability to use my right arm and learning to use my mouse at work with my left arm. I remember walking to work from the bus stop and being so slow that I couldn't cross the road before the redflashing lights stopped flashing, and the lights went green. I remember putting sticky tape on my fingertips so I could type because they felt so weird and horrible. Going out clubbing with my friends with a crutch because my right or left leg, who knows, was so weak I could barely put weight on it. Getting drunk and being very unstable, having to wee a thousand times and not just because *I broke the seal*. It turns out I had a terrible bladder.

I met my now husband in 2012 at a mutual friend's wedding on New Year's Eve. After we started dating, I struggled internally with knowing when to tell him I had MS. I did not want to leave it too long as it also scared me that our relationship would end because it would scare him away. I remember asking my friend what I should do and asking my mum—I think I asked everyone.

I remember telling him one morning when we were lying in bed. I said, "I have to tell you something, and I really want you to think about it and take it on board, and if you don't want to continue this, let me know. It's okay". I told him. I think he asked questions. But I distinctly remember him saying, "That's not a reason to break up.

If we're not getting on or we are fighting a lot—sure, but you being unwell doesn't make me want to break up with you". I sometimes wonder if he regrets that statement 11 years later.

In later years, I had a relapse that made both my eyes shake—*nystagmus*. I had a job where I read documents all day, and I would go to work, and I could not focus on the words, but if I closed one eye, it was a bit easier. I ended up visiting my neurologist for this relapse, and for the first time, in what I think was eight years of having MS, he put me on steroids.

I would catch the bus to the hospital, have my steroid infusion, and then catch the bus to work and continue working for the day. The comedown from the highdose steroids was horrendous. I remember thinking I was dying. Each time since, after having a few days of furiously cleaning my house, I always end up sitting on the shower floor, crying, with my husband telling me it's okay. I yelled at him, but they always shortened my relapses and made me feel pretty great for a few months.

Fastforward to 2015, my husband and I wanted to try for a baby. With that came neurologist appointments to change to a medication that was safe if I got pregnant. My neurologist at the time, whom I didn't love, put me back on an injection that I had reacted badly to years earlier. He said it was the only safe option, and I was to come off it if I got pregnant.

While we're on the topic of neurologists, I definitely stuck with my original one for way too long. He was abrasive, had very little bedside manner and was well known for being an excellent neurologist who specialised in MS; he wasn't for me. I distinctly remember when I was a few years diagnosed and needed to change treatments. We discussed an option—he explained the risks involved with the treatment, namely an extremely rare side effect called PML, which was a brain infection with not great outcomes. Sitting in his office, I was very against going on this treatment, and he said to me, "It's either this treatment, or you end up in a wheelchair and die". I definitely left his office crying that day—but I didn't go on with that treatment, as I'm very stubborn.

In 2015, I was on injections again, and we were trying for a baby. I had a reaction to the injections one night, and my now husband called the ambulance to say I was having an allergic reaction. But after 20 minutes, before the ambulance arrived, the reaction passed. I stopped the injections. I also fell pregnant not long after.

Unfortunately, I miscarried, and along with that came an onslaught of relapses, and the moment finally came when I changed neurologist. When I met with my new neurologist for the first time, he seemed panicked looking at my MRI. It was odd, as he had a genuine concern for me. I can't remember the timeline, but he told me, with no choice, really, that I needed to go back on strong medication because my MS was *angry*.

I had two choices, the original medication, Tysabri, which my old neurologist had suggested years earlier, and come off it if I fell pregnant again. Or Lemtrada, a fairly intense chemo treatment dosed over two years, and I would likely not need treatment for a long time and could try for a baby four months after my last dose. What a decision. After having an emotional miscarriage and being thrown into making a decision that felt quite urgent, I wasn't in the best space.

I researched Lemtrada, joined Australian and American Facebook groups, and asked all the questions. It consumed my life. By the time I saw my neurologist again, I had another MRI, and he told me he wasn't giving me a choice. I needed to do Lemtrada—my MS was too aggressive. I was happy he made the decision for me.

After the first round of Lemtrada, I improved drastically. I remember walking into my neurologist and him saying *holy shit*. I stayed stable for the entire year and was ready for my second round a year later. Unfortunately, I contracted pneumonia during the second round of infusion, so it was a rough journey. I had to stop the infusion and stay in the hospital for a week, and then once I was better, they finished the infusions. My dad also passed away from cancer around the same time I was going through my second round of treatment, which was stressful for me.

Unfortunately, I didn't fare so well after that. I returned to work, but a few months later, I remember talking to my husband about maybe having to take some time off to recover. I ended up having an MRI, and I had more lesions. I think I had about five relapses in the space of a few months. Unfortunately, it only takes one relapse to change things, and I was progressing towards a wheelchair—something I have actively avoided since being diagnosed.

I was giving up work, as all my specialists told me it was time. It was a really hard time in my life, both because of what was happening to my physical self and because my brain couldn't conceive what my life would be without work—I was only 30. My neurologist went back and forth about what he wanted to do, but we ended up agreeing that I would have a third round of the Lemtrada treatment.

I had the third and last treatment in December 2016. I struggled with every round of the infusions. It seemed to go to my lungs, but this round was particularly hard for me. I improved after this round and was back walking with a cane again, unsure if that was my stubbornness and determination or the treatment doing what it was supposed to do, maybe a bit of both. I got back to work parttime after a year off, and my director at the time was quite supportive in her own way and told me later *I knew you would get back.*

Looking back, I think I had progressed a little without realising—denial—but kept living life as usual. I started to have to lift my legs up to put my shoes on. Brushing my teeth was hard, and I started to mostly wear dresses and other things I adjusted. Subconsciously, because it was harder, but I mostly lived in my denial world.

The problem with living with a chronic illness and being in denial is that you never truly understand how the disease works. After the first round of Lemtrada, when I improved, my husband and I purchased and built a twostorey home. What were we thinking?

I had always wanted children, or at least one child, but as we got older and my treatments became more and more, I had settled on the idea that we wouldn't have children. I remember struggling to babysit my sister's children, who were fairly independent, thinking I cannot have my own child; it would be too hard. It was definitely a hard time emotionally for me, but I think I eventually came to terms with it. Of course, with all things in my life, when I finally came to terms with the fact that we would not have children, I accidentally fell pregnant!

My emotions were torn. I was so happy, scared and petrified, but mostly petrified. I strongly considered an abortion—which I hate writing about now, but it is the truth. Living with MS is really f**king hard, and at that point, I had had aggressive MS for a long time. Adding a child to that equation wasn't something I could fathom. Strangely, my husband, who wasn't ever really fond of having children, was the one who said he'd like us to have a child, and we discussed it, and I went through with the pregnancy.

I had a pretty terrible pregnancy, my MS was stable, but I got sick from the water. I lost 15kgs during my pregnancy and got gestational diabetes, even though I wasn't keeping much down—go figure. I don't think you could say any labour was great, but mine was definitely not great and did not go to plan, and my poor baby boy was born with medical issues.

By this stage, I had been with my husband for over eight years, but boy, did our relationship take a hit. Someone once told me people with MS are more likely to get divorced or be single than people without MS. It wouldn't be easy to live with me; I know that. I live in pain and complain about it. I can't do anywhere near the things I used to do, and most days, my fatigue can be bad, but I think I'm lucky that I married someone who, for the most part, is understanding—for now, anyway.

That aside, my MS seemed to be okay after our boy arrived, but the lack of sleep killed me. It was 2020, which meant *the village* wasn't as available as it normally would be, but we got through it. Thankfully, in 2021, an occupational therapist from MS Queensland reached out and helped me to get NDIS funding—something I had applied for previously and was rejected.

I could write an entire chapter on NDIS, but I will say I am lucky to live in a country with the NDIS, and when it works, it definitely works. Unfortunately, in 2022, while I was struggling with the possible progression of my MS or struggling because I was a new mum and had MS, I began to have troubles at work.

I don't want to go into that much in this book, but I have reflected on my career a lot lately. I realised that I have always, always felt like I needed to work harder or more to counteract my disability. Yes, I had to have days off because I couldn't *push through*. Yes, sometimes I wore sunglasses at my desk because the lights bothered my eyes. Yes, sometimes I would lie my head on my desk because of my fatigue. It wasn't until recently that I realised I was being discriminated against often. Things that have been said to me throughout my career when I've asked to progress have included, "It's not the right time for you", "You're young. Your time will come", "I need someone in that role that doesn't take time off", "I don't think, medically, it's the right time for you to change roles", and that is just a few.

I wouldn't change anything looking back. I was young and grateful I even had a job, but deep down, I really hope employers start to actually change. I am currently volunteering for a notforprofit that has been designed to assist Australians living with a disability to start their own small businesses or do gig work. I think that may be the path for many with disabilities—be your own boss. One day I emailed the director saying, *I'm so sorry I cannot do this or that today. I'm having a bad day.* He wrote back and said, *never ever say sorry. I completely get it. This is the whole reason for the notforprofit.*

I was recently having a conversation with an old friend from work who left around a similar time to me, and she said something to me that really stuck. She said, "I don't think anyone ever realised how difficult it must have been physically and emotionally to become unwell at the age you did. I don't think enough was done to support the emotional side of this, and that's a huge problem. One you will no doubt focus on in your volunteering career".

I really hope my volunteering role and this book open the eyes of at least a few employers, friends, or family of people who have MS. I hope that newly diagnosed people get the support and help they need when they are first diagnosed and don't disregard their diagnosis the way I did.

Psychology has definitely been a huge help for me, talking about having a degenerative disease, learning coping mechanisms for the ups and downs that come with this disease, realising that I need to prepare for my future and accepting what that future may look like. In other words, don't build a twostorey house, don't be blind to the truths of MS, and not feel like I need to push through another event or workday and try to enjoy my life.

I was diagnosed with MS a long time ago—IT IS NOT a death sentence. I have had a great career, and I do believe that people's thinking is changing, and inclusivity has come a long way. I have and will continue to live a nice life. I have a beautiful threeyearold boy, whom I love more than anything, and it's hard, definitely, but I wouldn't change anything if I could.

ABOUT TANYA

Tanya was born and raised in Brisbane, Queensland. She still lives in Brisbane with her husband, son and fluffy puppy. She actively attends physio weekly and enjoys (sometimes) hydro fortnightly.

She is currently volunteering for a wonderful start up called **Enabled.vip** was created and is run by people with a disability for people living with a disability. It is an online platform dedicated to engaging with disabled Australians to become their own entrepreneur! Tanya feels strongly about Enabled.vip and believes it is the way forward for disabled Australians for employment in Australia.

Watch the VLOG/Podcast of Tanya on YouTube

23

Kerrie Sculac

RISE ABOVE ADVERSITY

I am loving my life and who I am now. This didn't happen overnight, and I have been through a lot of changes and challenges to get to this point. I come from a very close and supportive family. I am the second daughter of four girls to my amazing parents. The stable foundations of a loving family, great friends, and external support have enabled me to overcome the diagnosis of multiple sclerosis that I faced at 22 years of age.

In my early 20s, real life was just beginning. My Fiancé and I had just bought our first home, and I left studying in my second year of university to embark on a career as a banking officer. My life was great and moving along well when I started to notice some health issues. I remember one of my first symptoms was a strange tight *hug* feeling around my waist. It felt like I had a wide band sitting around it, but of course, nothing was there. This symptom would come and go, and I eventually told a female doctor about it, to which she gave me a puzzled look, tilted her head, and said nothing. I did wait for her to address it, but I felt she thought I was being a bit weird and didn't question me further about it. At the time, I was about 20 years old and didn't push it further and put it down to *I must have been imagining it,* and I never mentioned it again. About a year later, I started to experience other symptoms, such as blurry vision. I spoke to my branch manager about this, and we both thought the tiny terminal computer screen and the lighting in the room may be affecting my ability to see well. I went to an optometrist who persuaded me that I needed glasses, but in reality, after spending $400 on them, I did not need them at all. Months after, I experienced pain and tightness down one side of my body every morning as soon as I opened my eyes from sleeping. I knew this should not be ignored, so I asked my female colleagues at the bank if they could recommend a good female doctor to me. There was no way I was going back to the doctor I saw who dismissed the hugging sensation when I told her. A few of my colleagues told me about a lovely female doctor whom I now have stayed with for almost three decades. My first appointment with this doctor involved many tests and a referral to a neurologist who sent me off for an MRI.

I walked with my parents into the neurologist's building, a little nervous as to what I would hear from the results of the MRI. I was young and didn't really understand any disease or condition. I didn't know what to expect or how to react to any diagnosis. The neurologist was not very friendly and sat behind his large antique desk with an open fireplace behind him in his imposing consultation room. He didn't seem to have any compassion when delivering the diagnosis of multiple sclerosis to me. I was glad to have my Mum there for support so she could hear what was being said by the doctor because I think my brain went into *what the* mode, and I had no idea what to do next. My Dad, who stayed in the waiting room, was amazing, and not long after, he arranged a visit to our closest Multiple Sclerosis Australia office. My fiancé was also very supportive, and on the day of diagnosis, he left work immediately to come and see me. When he hugged me, he said, "We will get through this together." For months and months, questions would pop into my mind like what have I done wrong, how should I be reacting, can people notice, or do they know? This whirlwind diagnosis set off many other medical appointments and research.

It was important to me to keep my chin up and not let it impact my life as I knew it. I continued to work for as long as I could with the support of my colleagues. When I reflect on my early diagnosis days, I was in denial, but I knew there was no point in worrying about the *what if*? I would look at any book I could find that had multiple sclerosis in its contents and listen intently to anything on the news that spoke about multiple sclerosis developments. Living like this can become overwhelming and get in the way of the great experiences life has to offer. I found solace in practising yoga, which taught me so much about my body, health, and life. I still attribute yoga teachings today to my health and wellbeing outcomes. I always listen to my body, be aware of how I am feeling, and adapt as I need to.

The medical therapies that were available for relapsing-remitting MS at the time of my diagnosis were regular injections. I had no intention of being in a race to stab myself with a needle daily. There was never a great push from the neurologist to choose a therapy. Due to the large gap between appointments, this may have contributed to the MS flare-ups and progression. I experienced more and more symptoms such as tingling, numbness, weakness in limbs, balance issues, incontinence, fatigue, and walking difficulties. Many people could see the difficulties I was having. However, I was very good at hiding the invisible symptoms and not expressing their impact on me. I didn't feel comfortable with the neurologist that gave me my diagnosis. After a year or two, I started seeing a new neurologist in my area. This neurologist promptly prescribed me one of the disease-modifying injections. I became unwell from the side effects of this injection, and after an admission to hospital, it was decided to stop that type of therapy and try a new type instead. I could see from the MS attacks that the symptoms would still linger, even though I tried such things as Prednisolone. The second therapy was also an injection, and the MS nurses were brilliant in assisting my husband and me in administering these therapies. It was difficult for me to work out and understand if I was having a temporary flare-up or bad days, so I was always reluctant to let my neurologist know because I could also see that not much was helping. The neurologist gave me the option to switch to a daily tablet which was much easier to administer. It was difficult to work out what was going on because I was reliant on the professionals, and I felt that there was only so much they could offer. During this time, it was more about masking the symptoms, and the first drug that comes to mind is Baclofen. I was prescribed Baclofen by the neurologist, and the dose was increased over many years. In hindsight, I wish I never started it. I believe this drug was numbing nearly every muscle in my body, and I couldn't really tell the difference between the progression of the MS symptoms or its horrible effects on my physical and mental health. It wasn't until my husband left me that I found the strength to take control of what was happening to me. The depression took its toll, and my brain and body had had enough. My therapies needed to be managed in a different way.

This is where the physical support of my family increased and became very important. I also sought professional help, but this only took me so far, and thank goodness for my loving family. I felt it was necessary to take control of my health, but I discovered not to go down rabbit holes, as this only caused more harm than good to my wellbeing. I also turned to MS Australia to reach out for some help. My family was my full-time carers, and the MS social worker was able to arrange a small amount of relief hours of in-home support. It was minimal support hours and was not very efficient compared to what is now available through the National Disability Insurance Scheme (NDIS).

In 2017, I was awarded an MS Go-For-Gold Scholarship in the category of the Arts, which enabled me to pursue my interest in mouth painting and writing short poems. I have immensely improved my mental health through creative arts, together with regular exercise, involvement in my community, and taking an interest in healthy eating.

I slowly built up my strength and daily courage to get through my days, drawing on what I had learned through yoga, my family, and my own research. I started to become aware and questioned my own thoughts and what I was telling myself. I had to be kind to myself and know it was okay to shed some tears and allow myself to grieve but reassure and remind myself that there was so much more to be happy about. When going to bed each night, I would say out loud five things that I was grateful for that day. I would also make sure the simple pleasures, such as sipping a hot chocolate on a cold day, were reinforced into my brain that enjoying such simple things in life is what makes life worth living. It is not about what material things I have or impressing anyone else; what matters is a happy and healthy me. Ultimately, I get to choose how I feel about situations and focus more on what I can do rather than what I cannot do.

To enable me to live my best life, I use assistive technology such as a wheelchair and voice-controlled devices. These are great, providing that the structure of my surroundings and immediate environment, as well as the person I am engaging with, is forthcoming and adaptive to this technology. For example, I was super excited and spent a lot of time preparing to go out to my local cinemas with one of my sisters and two of my aunts. Upon arriving at the cinema and heading towards the lift, we were confronted with an *out of order* sign. There was no other lift to be utilised in the building. The only way to get to the next level was the stairs or the escalator. As we discussed our situation with the cinema staff members, I was determined to watch the movie with my family. I asked the staff members what other options I had

for getting upstairs. The only option they were offering me was a refund on my ticket and to check when the lift would be in use again. At the time, I felt disappointed as they didn't realise how much time, effort, and energy it took me to not only arrange the social outing but the physical logistics of actually getting there. As I continued to discuss the predicament with my family, a lovely couple appeared and asked if they could be of any assistance. The strong gentleman and my aunts carried me up the escalator while my sister and the lady carried my wheelchair up separately. Thanks to their help, I got to watch the movie with my family. Throughout the movie, I had to keep reminding myself to stay in the moment and appreciate the movie I was there to watch as my mind kept wondering about the stressful situation I was in just before the couple came to my aid. The kind couple even arranged to help me back down after my movie had finished despite their movie still running. I will always be grateful to them and was inspired to write a short poem about them entitled *Angels Appear* and sent it to them in a poetry calendar I had published as a way of saying thank you.

Over the last six years, as a form of therapy, I have immersed myself in creative writing through short poems at different times. I have found that putting words on paper helps my brain process my thoughts and the highs and lows we all encounter along the way. I have also used poetry as a gift from my heart. This is an example of a poem I wrote for my regular carers that helps me on a daily basis so I can remain living in my own home.

The Support Worker
Never underestimate the work that you do,
Sometimes I would not be able to get out of bed if it was not for you.
Feel free to smile, laugh, dance & sing along with me. In my moments of quietness, thank you for respecting my space and privacy.
You wear many hats during your shifts.
Caring, compassion & commitment are your gifts.

Through my NDIS plan, I have been able to engage with different service providers to help me work on and reach the goals I would like to achieve. In order to continue to pursue my passion for painting, one of these service providers listened to the challenges I had around mouth painting, and together, we created a chin-cup paintbrush holder. This has made it a less strenuous task when I paint and has enabled me to enjoy the experience of painting as it should be enjoyed.

Having MS has opened up many opportunities to meet others going through diverse challenges themselves. It has made me look at situations from a different perspective rather than looking at them at face value. Networking with others with similar challenges has enabled us to bounce off each other and create solutions to navigate our way through what is generally a non-disabled world. As the world continues to embrace new technologies for good, we also appreciate the voice of high-profile disabled sports persons

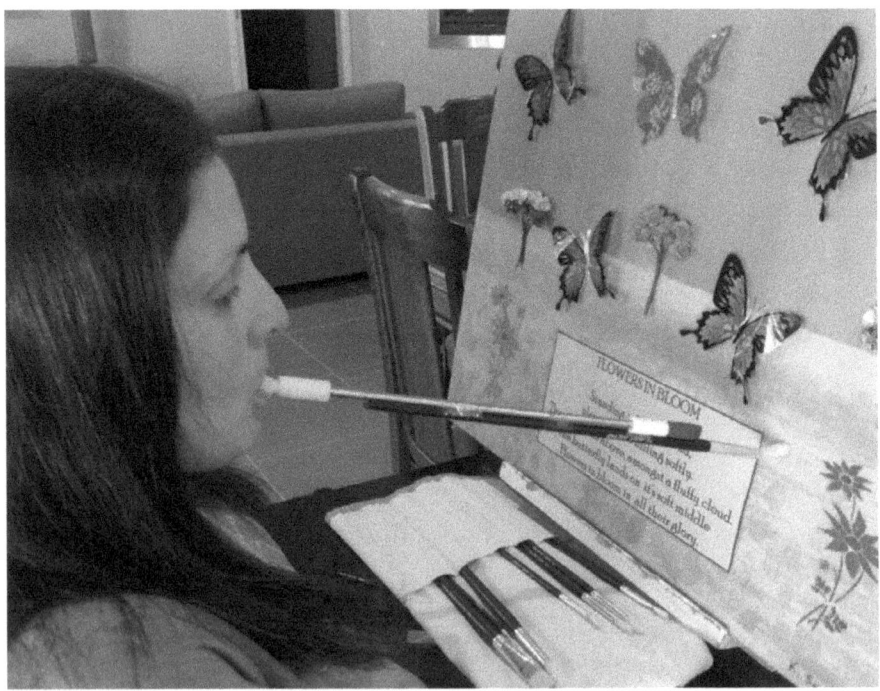

who have helped open up conversations around providing such solutions. Sharing these experiences with others allows conversation, which leads to positive change. This is why I continue as a community member of my local Council *Disability Access and Inclusion Committee* in order to make changes on a local level.

I am grateful to be able to share my MS journey thus far and hope that it can help even just one person manage any similar issues they may face.

Watch the VLOG/Podcast of Kerrie on YouTube

ABOUT KERRIE

Kerrie was born in the South Eastern suburbs of Melbourne, Victoria, Australia in 1975. She is a disability advocate and uses her lived experience of disability to help perform her role as a community member of her local council Access and Inclusion Committee.

Kerrie writes short poems and is a chin cup painter and will be publishing her first book soon. She is passionate about arts and uses this as not only a therapy for herself but a way to give back to others.

Kerrie excelled in her education years and was on her way to fulfil a career in corporate banking until the progression of Multiple Sclerosis changed her pathway. Through Kerrie's perseverance, strength and courage she continues to share her life experience with others including this MS chapter.

24

Lachlan Terry

MY PLeaSe EXPLAIN JOURNEY

A thousandmile journey has a lot in common with getting out of bed in the morning. It always, always started with that first step and then followed up with putting one foot ahead of the other. That philosophy applies to everything in life, even neurological conditions that sap your strength and enthusiasm to continue. The thoughts about the past and what has happened to me over the last 25 years are reflected in my chapter title. It is a tongueincheek play on words combining my condition with the well-known quotation *PLeaSe explain?* Why me? Why now? Why not someone else? Why can't they find a cure? Why can't I disappear? Why can't I die right now? Why does it have to be so hard? Why, why, why, why, why, oh so many bloody why's. In spite of the treatments and medications that help alleviate symptoms, pain and infirmities, there is no cure and no explanation for any neurological condition apart from this one. You can only play the hand that you have been dealt, and that has been my way of dealing with my condition. Get up, get out there and get on with it.

I was the eldest of seven children born in 1957 on a western Queensland sheep station between Hughenden and Winton. Mum

and Dad worked hard, and while we were comfortable, that only came about through hard work and learning to handle tough conditions. Between hot, cold, droughts, floods, bushfires and low commodity prices, there was usually something happening to keep us hoping and thinking of the next move. Our correspondence schooling was usually fairly flexible to enable us children to help with the stock work, either mustering or in the yards. All the siblings had jobs around the house and learnt to drive farm vehicles by nine or 10 years old and were sent to do jobs around the property on our own. The art of thinking for oneself, together with a little resilience to overcome difficulties or obstacles, was instilled at an early age and constantly used throughout life. For many years I took it for granted, but little did I realise what an attribute it was going to be in later life.

I completed Grade 10 level at school and then did a plumbing apprenticeship in Townsville on the advice of my father. I attained my trade certificate in 1977, married shortly after, and returned to the West to help run the family property. The work on the property kept me very busy, and apart from the odd job, I never returned to my plumbing trade. Unfortunately, after seven years, my wife Pam and I went our separate ways. Our sons, Joseph and Daniel, remained with me on the property and visited their mother during the school holidays. There was a lot of stock work involved with cattle and sheep. The management of animal parasites and weed control necessitated the use of lots of chemicals. This fact came back to haunt me in later life. It was one of the many *oh why's* that I mentioned before.

Over the next 10 years, my father died, we leased and then eventually sold the property, and I remarried. Joanne, my wife, and I had ended up in Mount Isa contracting on the redevelopment of a mine site 150 kilometres south of the town. Phosphate Hill was a huge project with a hundredodd contractors and over a thousand men on site. We were also involved in freight services and waste removal and had water trucks. We were extremely busy employing three or four other people to help us handle the required workload. Each day thinking on your feet and resilience was still a big part of my life because, with our many clients, your plans had to change by the minute every single day. The business had grown very quickly, so we bought a larger property with a house and a large shed on it. Family wise, two had become three with the addition of our daughter Prudence.

Phosphate Hill had been very good to us financially and set us up, but eventually, it came to an end. Unfortunately, I was unable to source more contracts for our equipment, so in the interim, we bought a local parcel delivery business in Mount Isa. Their business had taken a nosedive in the previous 12 months that was not reflected in their books, so I looked at taking a job with Mount Isa Mines (MIM) to make ends meet. To get a job at MIM, you had to undergo a medical assessment, so I presented at their medical centre. It was all going well until the doctor asked me to duck waddle across his room, which I failed to complete. I thought it was a joke, as when I had been doing mine site deliveries, I had never, ever seen anyone duck waddling around the mine site. The doctor was adamant, however, that I had failed the test and there was going to be no wellpaid job at MIM for me.

Anyhow, his next words to me were very disconcerting. He suggested I should go see a specialist because, from what he observed, I may have neurological issues. That caused me to think back over the previous six months about some things that had been happening to me during the deliveries that I didn't pay much heed to. I sometimes had an odd gait; I used to trip over the slightest undulations in the pavements or road surfaces. Also, I couldn't lean over and grab the combing rail and leap down to the ground from the back of the truck without feeling awkward and unbalanced. In the past, that was something I could do with ease time and time again. I began to realise then that I had a serious problem.

So, I visited a doctor in Mount Isa who, while not a neurologist, looked at patients with neurologicallike symptoms and referred them to specialists in the big cities. She diagnosed me with an umbrella term of Spastic Paraparesis and referred me to a neurologist in Brisbane by the name of Peter Silburn. After tapping all my joints for a reaction, multiple questionnaires, all sorts of blood tests, a lumbar puncture and MRI scans, he was no wiser as to what I had either. He suggested two things. One, it was probably not hereditary. Two, although none of the tests provided any evidence, it was a possibility that the use of the chemicals over the last 1020 years could have caused my symptoms. I returned to Mount Isa with a Clayton's diagnosis, Spastic Paraparesis. I had a condition that they could not identify. Great, I was by now becoming more than a little worried about our future.

The big question now was what to do, what to do, what to do. I had a friend who owned a cab that needed a spare driver, so I did the driver induction course, and the police character check. Fortunately, they didn't do a medical. I was ready to go, in a sitdown job with air-conditioned comfort, for the most enlightening experience of my life. The next thing that I did I had to swallow a lot of pride. When we had the local parcel delivery business, each week, we would get at least four pallets of Amway products to deliver around town. In doing this, we became friendly with the local Amway platinum distributor, who also owned a cattle station out of town. Of course, he was spruiking about how good this Amway was. Ten years before, my cousin and some friends had tried to enlist me into Amway, and I had scoffed at the idea and turned them down. There was no way I was going to flog soap suds to the neighbours. Now there he was, a cattle station owner telling me I could earn $50,000 a year from getting other people to use Amway. Here I was, staring down the barrel of being in a wheelchair for the next few years. So it was, *stone the crows, this can't be that bloody hard, here give me the pen, where do I sign.*

By this time, we had a son Stephen and another one on the way, but Joanne and I were still both working hard at trying to build this internet business, Amway. I was working long hours in the cab six days a week. Joanne had success with her cosmetics and jewellery. But as hard as I tried, I could not get people to join us in the business, and as I saw it, I could not sell a box of matches. We thought perhaps Mount Isa was oversaturated with Amway distributors and we should move to a bigger centre. We moved to Townsville in mid2004 after six and a half years in Mount Isa and two years as a cab driver. In Townsville, I picked up another job driving cabs on 12hour shifts and pursued Amway again. However, after another twelve months, I was totally disillusioned with Amway. We had met all the KPIs, and attended every meeting possible for four years. It had returned us nothing, so we let Amway go as experience learned. My earlier assessment had been correct. The stress and trauma of our move, packing everything up, shipping to Townsville, moving the family and finding another house and job in Townsville also triggered a relapse in my mobility. I had noticed a significant decline in my mobility during the move.

By mid 2006, two years post move, and six years post failed mine medical, I was using a walking stick for mobility. I relied on it to the degree that I was of no use to an elderly or disabled passenger with luggage or groceries. I left the taxi driving and started working in the taxi dispatch centre on an irregular rotating shift. I persevered with that for about 12 months but was never, ever going to acquire the keyboard speed to reach the job quota per hour on busy nights. One night I made a dispatching mistake that cost me my job at the call centre.

So, it was once again back to what to do, what to do, what to do. I did not have a clue what I was going to do after that. I did not have any admin skills, I did not have any clerical skills, and I did not have any IT skills. All the skills I had were in hard work and long hours. My opportunities in that area, either with employment or selfemployment, were rapidly diminishing by the day between mobility issues or fatigue. I approached a firm that specialised in disability employment and even knowing my issues, all they wanted to put me into was more of the same. They wanted me to drive a bus, a bus of all things! I eventually managed to get the

Disability Pension, but only after three applications, and that was with all the doctor's reports and test results. My original diagnosis of Spastic Paraparesis was a millstone around my neck because, according to the *powers that be*, I actually had to have a specific condition. So, I visited a Townsville neurologist that diagnosed me with Multiple Sclerosis, but I suspect that was just so I could collect the pension. Then the government halved the pension because Joanne had fulltime employment. It was all becoming too hard, and I would not consider that I had ever suffered from depression. However, I was getting pretty disillusioned with certain aspects of my life.

So, we decided that for the time being, I would be the stayathome mum and do the school pickups and meetings, afterschool activities, the meals, the washing and the cleaning. Joanne would be the income earner with my meagre pension, adding a little to the side. I was investigating other possibilities for developing some form of reasonable income. I looked at worm farming using our backyard, and I looked at a photography course, as I had always been a keen photographer. It would have to be a selfstarting backyard business because we had no equipment and absolutely no capital. I became involved with Scouts Australia as a volunteer as my children were attending, and the Scouts were understaffed. Through a friend, I became involved in community radio, thinking this may lead to an income. Subsequently, I did announcer training, eventually DJ'ing my own twohour show once a week. I was there for five years doing the *Blues Show*. However, while it was community involvement and enjoyable, it was not an income earner.

Like everyone else, I had seen lots of really simple ideas that anybody could have thought of and suddenly become a very popular landslide marketing innovation that made someone a multimillionaire. There were none of those ideas floating my way. However, in mid2008, Joanne decided she was going to go her own way, and 12 months later, we were divorced. I had attended marriage counselling previously at her request but thought the whole thing was a bit onesided. Perhaps I was wrong, but I felt I was no more than snappy, cranky, or unhappy with my lot in life. There was no domestic violence, child abuse, drunkenness, or drug addiction. At worst, I was not a major breadwinner for the family, but through no fault of my own.

I have always held a disregard for divorced parents, male or female, who totally disconnected themselves from their children after a family breakdown. I found myself a tiny flat not too far away, bought a small secondhand car, and maintained contact with my children at every possible opportunity. At the start, because I only had a tiny onebedroom flat, it was only every other weekend to stop over. Then during the week for a couple of hours after school a couple of days per week. I really missed having my children in my life and hoped that our divorce would not affect them too much. Even though I tried to remain positive, my selfconfidence regarding my employment opportunities had taken a huge hit.

Over the next few years, my time revolved mainly around the community radio and the Scouts—of which I had now become

Group Leader because no one else would take on the role. These two activities required a lot of my time as there were the actual hours of handson time as well as the organisational aspect and the committee meetings. I also spent as much time as I possibly could with my children with their activities, as well as activities I conjured up to give them a broad scope of interest.

In about 2013, a new neurologist arrived in Townsville from the United Kingdom. Mike Boggild quickly rediagnosed me with Primary Lateral Sclerosis (PLS), a condition more closely related to Motor Neurone Disease than it is to Multiple Sclerosis. He'd had previous experience with PLS in the United Kingdom. He diagnosed my symptoms swiftly and visually without the aid of any testing. He also told me that there was no medication or operation that would improve my situation. I was at least a jump ahead of a lot of people in the fact that I was in no pain, and it was a slowly progressing condition.

The rest of my time I spent trying to develop a source of income in different avenues. I tried my hand as a teacher's aide at my children's school. I tried to market my photography at local markets.

At considerable expense, I enrolled in a proofreading course. I tried to develop a secondhand business from home through social media as well as a homebased barbering business using community notice boards and social media as my promotional tools. Another idea I tried was registering my kitchen as a commercial food preparation area to sell homemade food at local markets.

Although I still had the aptitude to have a crack at anything, I no longer had the resilience to go the distance if it was not somewhat successful early on. As the reception of my ventures was, at best mediocre, they usually did not last longer than a few months.

The big enjoyment in life was spending time with my children, especially during the school holidays when we would take trips away from Townsville to visit other places. To keep costs to a minimum, I utilised bush camping, cabins, and caravan parks and relied on relations and friends in the areas we were visiting. In 2015, I discovered a superannuation policy on which I had not claimed personal insurance, which temporarily solved my financial situation. I traded in my little town runabout car on a Nissan XTrail and had a fair amount left over that would supplement my pension

for a few years. Having the XTrail meant we could go and explore more remote regions, which I loved. My children and I made trips to many great destinations, including Cape York Peninsula, Darwin, Gulf Country, Birdsville Track, Ayres Rock, NSW and Victoria.

I had been editing my photography and posting on Facebook as a hobby for some time and receiving favourable responses from friends, some of whom suggested I should market it. From those comments, *Art Leasing & Sales*, my new business was born. Much of my editing was radical to the extent that a lot of my images resembled artwork more than photography, so I started targeting business premises promoting my local artwork with a difference. NDIS worked with me to help build my business. My plan was a rotation of artwork for every business every three months to keep things looking fresh and different. I eventually had 120odd canvases on rotation as well as sales. I developed a website, an Instagram page and Facebook. I became a member of Business Networking International and LinkedIn. I did a number of exhibitions and open houses at my home. I used business cards and letter box drops around Townsville. Through the business networking organisation, I promoted myself as a great idea with a difference for any occasion. The leasing aspect of the business was great as a promotional tool, but it was labour intensive. Viability was in retail sales, and I couldn't seem to make that happen despite my efforts with the time invested and dollars spent.

Then COVID19 happened, and over the next two years, I lost some of my bigger customers. It became an issue accessing businesses to do the rotations and even to promote my business. Then in 2021, my XTrail had a major engine malfunction. Despite all the effort and time I had invested in my business, I could not afford to repair or replace my vehicle. I had a closing down exhibition with canvases priced to clear, and I donated the remaining canvases to charities for their fundraising use.

By this time, I had become involved through the internet with a Brisbane based Disability Support Agency going by the name of MND & Me Foundation. Terrific support advocates who are also heavily involved in fundraising as well as being involved in research programs in which I now participate. Next year heralds another big adventure for me on my journey. I can't say too much at this stage, as some key elements have yet to be put in place before a public announcement about our plans. I can say it involves the MND & Me Foundation, fundraising and my good self.

Over the years since I have had this condition before and after my diagnosis, people have said to me what an inspiration I was to them and others. I have never set out to be or even seen myself as an inspiration. Even in times of disillusionment, I have only done what needed to be done to achieve my goal. If I failed, I would then pick myself up, dust myself off and have another go, use another angle of attack, or perhaps choose another goal. People have often asked me how I feel about having the condition and how disappointed I must be. My philosophy is, as stated previously, *you can only play the hand that you have been dealt*. Achieving goals does take a lot more effort and is more often than not done at a slower speed than others would to accomplish the same task.

Never ever give up, ever.

Watch the VLOG/Podcast of Lachlan on YouTube

ABOUT LACHLAN

Lachlan Terry led a vibrant, active life until the unsettling prospect of being confined to a wheelchair emerged. In his 42 years, he had avoided debilitating injuries, relying on a mix of good luck and management. The gradual and unexpected onset of his condition hindered job opportunities and even mundane tasks like picking up a coin.

The question "Why me?" lingered, but Lachlan learned to accept life's unpredictable nature during 13 years of uncertainty, misdiagnoses, and hurdles. His upbringing on an outback station instilled a pragmatic outlook, and he embraced the idea of playing the hand he was dealt.

Despite his undiagnosed condition, Lachlan remained mobile, using a walking frame or electric mobility scooter, covering an impressive 5,500 kilometers in a year. He remained devoted to various roles as a Scouts Australia leader, radio DJ, home barber, traveler, photographer, and Art Leasing business entrepreneur. Grateful for opportunities, he eagerly shared his story, embracing the power of politeness and gratitude that had always guided him. Determined and resilient, Lachlan Terry showed the world the strength to seize every chance life offers.

Instagram: **www.instagram.com/art_leasing_and_sales/**

25

John Van De Putt

WHAT A DREAM

What a dream my life has been. It's not always been a good dream, but it's been a dream. It doesn't feel like I'm here. I'm on the outside looking in as if it's not the life I was supposed to live.

I had a great childhood with four brothers: Herman, Robert, Frank, and David and three sisters, Annamaree, Maryanne, and Chantel. My parents, Johannes and Ria, immigrated from Holland in 1965 and arrived by boat for a better life. She was a schoolteacher, and he was a fitter and turner. We spent many school holidays on trips away to Scotts Head and Port Stephens. In seeing the eastern seaboard, nine people would be in a Holden station wagon. I'd sit in the front excited to see the ocean and spend time away—totally illegal these days with no seat belts—towing a caravan, plus one red cattle dog was thrown in the back.

At 17, I won GOLD, the Duke of Edinburgh Award. I was a very good swimmer and an A-grade rugby league player with the North Sydney Bears. I was very energetic, young and arrogant—probably the Dutch coming out in me. I was married by the age of 21 to Pedr. I started my own business in the industrial waste and services industries. At this stage of my life, all I thought about was making money and supporting my family. I had started to experience symptoms of MS, such as I couldn't run as fast and had extreme fatigue. Thinking I was getting old, even though I was only 21, I dismissed it and never sought medical attention. In the following years, we had two children, a girl Britany and a boy Kaleb.

In between the birth of my older children in 2001, I became ill with vertebral osteomyelitis, an infection in the spine. One day, I came home from work and could not get up the stairs. I was admitted to the hospital and had heavy doses of steroids for a week. Then I had to learn to walk again.

The specialist informed me that this could be the start of MS. I worked hard to get back to walking with hydrotherapy and, after approximately four months, went back to my business. I tried to live as if nothing happened, like an ostrich with their head in the sand.

With the birth of Kaleb, my wife had postnatal depression. I did not understand it or was not willing to accept her condition. In hindsight, it was because she was battling an invisible condition,

just like I am now. At the time, I was more interested in making money than supporting the family mentally.

After a lengthy discussion with Pedr, we decided it would be better for us to separate. I took on the role of primary caregiver for our children. I had great support from her parents and other family members. It would have been one of the hardest decisions for Pedr to make, leaving her children.

Around 10 years ago, I apologised to her for the way I did not support her and said that I was sorry. I did this because I am now more understanding of the battles she faced by having a condition that people cannot always see but is very real.

After my vertebral osteomyelitis, I had no relapses for the next few years. However, I never got back to being one hundred per cent, and I always knew something else was wrong.

During that period, in 2003, I concentrated on the business I was building and was not worried about my health. I drank too much and partied way too hard. I had employed the services of a nanny to help with the children. Then, suddenly, like a freight train, everything came crashing down. My feet were burning. I could hardly see what I was typing on the computer screen. My fingers were numb. So, I went and saw a neurologist in 2005.

I was diagnosed initially with RRMS.

For the next few years, I would have a relapse once a year. They would not give me any disease-modifying therapy because I was told I had to have two to three relapses in a 12-month period. Mine were only happening once a year. They would just give me large doses of steroids by IV over three days. The side effects of the steroids were terrible. You can't sleep on them, and you are consistently hungry, which then causes weight gain. Then they discharge you and send you home to recover, which takes weeks as it's not an instant fix. There were no MRIs available to diagnose someone if they had MS.

When I was diagnosed with MS, I did not change my lifestyle

much at all. I was still running a very stressful business, employing around 100 people. It felt like a kindergarten on steroids, and then throw in there looking after two young children as a single parent. Life was very stressful.

I did not take my illness very seriously at all. I used alcohol as a coping mechanism to numb the pain from the MS, which had the opposite effect and made my MS symptoms worse. At one stage, I was constantly in and out of the hospital for two years, and with every relapse, I would become worse. I had many relapses that would fall around my son's birthday, always ending up in the hospital for another dose of steroids and repeating the aftermath from that round. At one stage, the family joked that dad must be going into hospital soon as my son's birthday was coming up again.

During this time, I drank a lot of alcohol, and my health was deteriorating rapidly. I was still a very young, arrogant man at 34. My children had to stand by and watch my body deteriorate in front of them. I could not kick a ball or throw them around in the pool. I couldn't do any rough play with my children that most fathers enjoy with them. It made me very sad.

Life was changing, and it was changing quickly. During this time of my life, I felt like an outsider. I did not know where to turn to or whom I could ask for help. There was no NDIS, and disability support was state government funded. Besides, I was too arrogant to ask for help. However, it would have made a big difference in our lives. I now know that asking for help is a sign of strength, not weakness.

When I was around 35, I met a woman named Melanie through work, and we fell in love. I was very hesitant to commit to a new relationship, as I knew my body was deteriorating. I informed her of the situation, and she totally understood.

After a very deep, soul-wrenching conversation regarding my illness with Melanie, we decided to have a child. Our biggest concern would be how we would be able to look after our child. I knew I was going to get worse and worried she would leave me; however, Melanie reassured me that would not happen.

The birth of our daughter Lily came in 2008, and at the same time, my business was failing due to my health. I was very ill and became a stay-at-home parent during this period. The plus side was that I had a great time with my daughter, and we went out often together. As a dad, we look after children differently than mothers and let them take more chances.

I can remember times when my daughter was stuck up a tree, and I could not help her get back down as I was in a wheelchair, so she had to find her own way down. We often went to a soccer field in my wheelchair, and I would get bogged, and we had to ring the fire brigade to get me out.

Around six years after being diagnosed, I became more emotionally aware and reached out for help. I needed help to do simple things around the house, as my partner was at work.

I found it to be gender biased in what funding was available to certain people at the time, since I was a male needing help, such as cooking and cleaning the house. They did not give me funds for this, as they would say the wife could do it when she got home. Then I asked, can I get funding to help me get the lawns done, and they said *no, we don't fund things like that*. This became a repeated conversation I would have, asking for help from state government organisations.

It became a constant battle to get help, even when I contacted the MS society. They would bring out an occupational therapist and inform me what I needed, but there was no funding.

What was the point of knowing what I needed when there was no funding to supply these services? It did not help me in my situation. If anything, it made me feel more unworthy to be around. My depression got worse and worse. My youngest daughter was my saviour. She made my life worth living for, and I had an absolute ball bringing her up, taking her to places in my wheelchair, her sitting on my lap, or holding her on the back with a skateboard.

When you have MS, you try to live with it. At the start, I tried to fight it, but I am too exhausted now.

Having MS is shit. There are no rose-coloured glasses with this disease, and I tip my hat to anyone that has made a go of living with it. I struggle every day. As soon as I open my eyes in the morning until I close them at night, I live with it. I wake up looking at a ceiling hoist that gets me out of bed every day and reminds me of my disease, the places where I can't get into, to the way people look at me. But these are challenges I accept every day when I wake up.

Having MS for me has changed me as a person, not only physically. I am now permanently in a wheelchair, my MS has moved to SPMS, and I am totally dependent on other people, and emotionally as well. I regularly see a counsellor to help me with my emotions and cope with my body failing me.

During the time spent with my daughter, I became more empathetic, understanding and patient with everyone around me. Having MS has taught me to be humble.

As my daughter grew up, my MS progressed. During 2013-14, I became a board member for a community organisation, Community Pantry, based in Bargo, and I used my skill set to get them to become compliant to be a charity.

This was the first time I was confronted with my disability, as one of the board members wanted to know what could someone in a wheelchair possibly contribute to this organisation! I had ongoing battles with this person, and in the end, I resigned. It was wrong to treat someone with a disability so poorly. We are still valuable members of society. By this time, I knew how to control my MS a bit better, such as keeping away from very stressful situations.

The major saviour in my life has been the introduction of NDIS, where before, you had to beg for services, such as getting new tyres for a wheelchair. In the past, the provider was a state government funding body that would say *we have just given you a new pair of tyres this year; you should use your wheelchair less.* What the f**k! I was a father looking after a young child, so I would do a lot of park hopping and catch trains, and we often went to the beach. They replied *I should instead take a taxi rather than roll everywhere.* Well, I'm sorry, does that mean people without a disability should not get new shoes and take taxis everywhere and not walk? It made no sense.

With the introduction of NDIS, I can still remember the first meeting; it was very emotional. With the questions they asked, however, I can totally understand why. For the first time, it made me realise how much assistance I needed. My first plan was not the best, although it was a start and made me go on to have a totally different mindset. With this extra help, I can go out into the community even more. It has enabled me to study, and I became the president of a little athletics club Lily participated in.

Each stage of my MS has had challenges, and little incidents in one's journey make it more challenging than others. I remember, not fondly, a few incidents of shitting myself in public with my daughter and her saying *don't worry, Dad, I will get you home.* Another time falling on the floor, my daughter put a pillow under my head and said, *it will be okay; I will ring the ambulance.* My MS affected my bladder to the point it constantly leaked, and I hated smelling like piss all the time. It's weird, I don't care about my wheelchair or the way my left arm doesn't move, even the way I forget things or get very tired easily in the heat, but I hate smelling like piss! So, I decided to get the suprapubic catheter.

Unfortunately, my relationship with Melanie totally changed, and it was the final nail in the coffin of our relationship.

I was battling mentally, and there were thoughts in my mind, such as, *am I really a man?* This was because I wasn't a financial provider and now was a full-time parent. The catheter affected our relationship sexually.

When the NDIS came into play, it was a godsend. I got extra

services and even went to respite so my wife could have some time with our daughter without me around. The only problem with respite was, yes, I have a disability, but I really do not like spending more time on the weekend with other people that have trouble communicating. These weekends away for me were torture, but I knew it was important to continue going there, just to keep the family together.

We lived together for the next few years, not as a sexual couple, but just as a couple. In 2019, we travelled to Austria to watch my daughter perform in gymnastics. We took a support worker to assist me while on our travels. There are certain moments in your life that you think about, and this trip definitely makes me think about the difficulties I had travelling due to my disability.

This included my hoist, wheelchair, shower commode, and other aids with me, let alone transport and accommodation that were disability friendly while visiting that country. It was an effort, but we managed it. The thing that I remember most is when they were transferring me from the aeroplane seat to the aisle wheelchair; they dropped me in the transfer and ended up dragging me along the aisle to the front of the plane and picking me up there. Here I was, getting dragged up the aisle with my daughter, looking on and crying.

Many hurtful things were said at the end of this relationship with my wife. I understand carer burnout, and I've seen it destroy people and couples. I just wished NDIS had come in earlier.

At present, I'm still rebuilding my self-worth. I re-entered the workforce as a support coordinator. I thoroughly enjoyed working with other people to better manage their NDIS plans. It is stressful but can also be very rewarding.

I was getting up at 6:00 am with two carers, catching a train to work until 5:15 pm, and then taking a train back home. As soon as I got home, I was so extremely fatigued that I had my support worker ready to put me to bed and have dinner; it was a full-on big day.

On the way to work, the trains were out at one stage, and they instead supplied a bus. I ended up having an incident on the bus where my wheelchair wasn't tied down like it should have been because there were no facilities for it. My wheelchair fell over, not just once, but a few times. I had to get help from the other passengers to lift me back up and into my wheelchair. I do not get anxiety very much. However, this incident has now caused me much anxiety about catching any buses in the future.

At present, I'm working with the SRA for a safer alternative for people in wheelchairs to go on country trains, and we are trying to sort out a solution for the buses.

With my MS, I have memory problems because of cognitive issues. I really struggle to remember names; I know everything about someone but, for some reason, cannot remember their names. I was working for a disability organisation. It was incredible how some people I work with found it offensive that I could not remember their names. It wasn't done on purpose, but it was just one of those things. They made me feel inferior, so in the end, it was a six-month contract, and I did not ask to get it renewed.

When you are in a wheelchair, people look at you differently. Then they are, for some reason, surprised that you can communicate and talk. They don't even see you as a human being, and you don't get asked to go to parties or outings. One good thing about being in a wheelchair is that your conversations with people are unbelievable. The wheelchair breaks down some communication walls, and they feel safe. Conversations range from someone selling their used undies online to help the child go from school to people dying of cancer. Sometimes, I think I should do a podcast with people I talk to.

The thought of living by myself for the rest of my life I was at peace with, after the separation from my wife. However, after accepting being alone for the rest of my life I fell in love with a great lady. I understand the challenges I have with this relationship, such as carers fatigue and many other issues which do not relate to my MS. however, this lady has taught me how to love again and has given me the strength for me, not to be embarrassed about my wheelchair or even my catheter i am in a relationship I thought I'd never be in or worthy to be in , as I tell people i'm definitely pulling above my weight LOL I truly believe my past has made me the person I am now.

During my lifetime with MS, I've done nothing spectacular. I've gone to hell, and I'm working my way back. I cannot sugarcoat this disease, but I can tell you one thing: this disease changes you as a person, some of us for the better, and some of us for the worst. It is traumatic yet fulfilling, and your inner soul can be totally drained, but you wake up in the morning wanting to be part of the world.

This disease has changed me dramatically. It has given me the mental strength to live day by day. It has helped me live with the loss of my daughter, Lily, who passed away in a car accident 12 months ago. It's made me become a more understanding and forgiving person.

Stuffed if I know what I'd be doing if I didn't have MS, but I know one thing. There's hope for all of us as we all take a different path. There is no right or wrong. Live that dream of yours to the best of your ability, and f**k what other people think. Enjoy the ride as best you can.

Watch the VLOG/Podcast of John on YouTube

ABOUT JOHN

John Van De Putt's life has been a rollercoaster of highs and lows. Born to Dutch immigrant parents, he had a great childhood with many siblings. He achieved success in sports and business, but his life took a turn when diagnosed with multiple sclerosis (MS).

Ignoring the early symptoms, he faced numerous relapses and hospitalisations. His marriage struggled due to his health, but he found love again and embraced fatherhood. MS changed him physically and emotionally, leading to self-discovery and humility. The introduction of NDIS improved his life, allowing him to work as a support coordinator.

Despite challenges, he cherishes each day and encourages others to embrace their dreams.

26

Beth Wurcker

THROUGH WORDS

The 1960s

"The day they decided that Sneetches were Sneetches. And no kind of Sneetch is the best on the beaches." – The Sneetches by Dr Seuss

We run free on the family farm, pull apart old engines, and conduct solemn funerals for ants we entomb in empty matchboxes. We feed our poddy calves and lambs with milky Denkavit, all the time aware of their inevitable fate. Our Aunty Ruth records our adventures in black and white, and I sometimes sit quietly in her darkroom to watch the magic happen.

When the creek swells after rain, we build makeshift canoes out of discarded wood and have races, ducking under barbed wire fences at the last moment. Miraculously, we all survive our childhood.

Saturday mornings, I go into town with my beloved Pa in his Morris Austin. After we have everything on Gran's shopping list, we stop by Mr Ell's shop in the main street to buy a bar of Cadburys dairy milk chocolate that we share in secret. "A little bit of what you fancy does you good", Pa always says with a smile, and he gives me the lion's share.

I love school because it has a whole demountable building lined with books. I go there every lunchtime with my best friend Sue Coleman and read one book every day. Sue writes poems in my autograph book, and this is my favourite.

I love stars, pink stars, purple stars.
When the night is dark and stormy, the stars show me my way.
I love stars.

I see children argue in the playground, doing the dance of enemies one day and best friends the next. I think I would like to bring people together so that no one ever feels left out. I have a composition published in the New South Wales School Magazine.

I finish this decade by being awarded Dux of my primary school out of 30 Year 6 students. I get a certificate, and a book called *Around Australia on Highway* 1. It sits in a bookcase alongside some of my favourite books.

I am safe.

The 1970s – Eight Great Comedies

"Experience is merely the name men gave to their mistakes." –The Picture of Dorian Grey by Oscar Wilde.

Merriwa does not have a high school that goes to Year 10, so like my siblings, I go to a posh school in Sydney. I stand at the bottom of the grand staircase in the former mansionturnedboarding house and tell Mum and Dad that I will like it here. This is the only time I use these stairs, as from then on, we are only to use the back stairs designated for the former occupants' domestic staff.

I am no longer a big fish in a small pond, but rather a medium fish in an Olympicsized swimming pool. I love the huge library that even has individual study nooks—I learn they are called carrels. This school also has lots of tennis and netball courts, a gym and a swimming pool that I do my best to avoid. My nickname is

Bessy Book. In 1st form, I spend my prep time writing stories and pass each scribbled page around the room to be read. A favourite among my fellow boarders was one about a man who has his brain gradually replaced with cotton wool.

During school holidays back in Wonnarua country, we play Scrabble and 500 after dinner. I am paid $1 an hour to paint fences on the farm.

I leave school thinking I will become a nurse like my mother. Instead, I take up a mechanical engineering traineeship with the Department of Defence at Garden Island dockyard. This is 1976—I am 17 years old and quite naïve in many ways. I am the first female in this role, and this brings with it a fair amount of misogyny, sexual harassment and resentment. I do enjoy some parts, and the best rotation is with the quality team working on a submarine refit on Cockatoo Island. The other memorable rotation is with the firstyear fitting and turning apprentices. I learn welding, metal lathe work and having to hand sand a bit of mild steel to an incredibly small tolerance. My father proudly keeps one of my best test pieces on his desk. I am resilient.

The 1980s

"Happiness is making the most of what you have, and riches is making the most of what you've got." – The Shell Seekers by Rosamunde Pilcher 1980

I leave the Department of Defence to start my own contract drafting business. I marry a wonderful man, but I am too young to make it work. For the first time, I see glimpses of my potential, and my path to selfdiscovery is sadly not compatible with this marriage.

Opportunities open up to me. I am tapped on the head to lead a technical, administrative team for a medical device manufacturer, moving to a specialist role with a nowdefunct computer company before landing a role with an American bank.

I run with work colleagues in Lane Cove National Park at lunchtime and at night around my home in Artarmon. I especially love to run up the hill towards Channel 10, encouraging and urging my legs to go just that little bit further. I run in local fun runs, including a City to Surf, and I relish my strong body.

From time to time, my friends set me up with their superficially suitable male friends. I also spend time with a former firstgrade rugby league player who cannot quite decide whether he is actually single or just temporarily separated. I decide for him and move on.

I am restless.

The 1990s

"I never cease to be thrilled when entering my own gateway... and always feel that entrance gardens should give the first sensation of rest to those returning home...." – Gardens in Time in the footsteps of Edna Walling by Trisha Dixon and Jennie Churchill

One night I see my future at a Toastmasters club meeting. Tall, dark, with broad shoulders, wearing a blue Holstein Friesian Association jumper. It takes Steve a couple of years to see our future, but we get there. Apparently, the decision point for Steve was when he saw me swimming underwater for 25 metres in one breath and with no fins.

I give birth to two fine sons, Max and Jack, who give Steve and me enormous joy and the exquisite anguish of their mortality. In a moment of serendipity, I swap my wellpaid job that now has a view of Sydney Harbour to work in the notforprofit aged care sector. My tiny office is in a decrepit old building in Ryde. I am finally at home.

I swim laps at lunchtime and enter my one and only twokilometre ocean swim at Dee Why on an overcast day and fairly big waves.

We move to Canberra in the middle of winter and buy an older house in a great street in a perfect suburb. It was love at first sight. The house is affordable only because John Howard has sacked almost every public servant in Canberra. It needs a lot of work but has great bones. We put on an extension, renovate the interior and landscape the garden.

We flourish in this oftenderided city and talk among our friends that Canberra is the bestkept secret ever. We sometimes fail to wait until ANZAC Day to put our heaters on but do not care.

I am happy.

The 2000s

"It is perhaps when our lives are at their most problematic that we are likely to be most receptive to beautiful things." – The Architecture of Happiness by Alain de Botton 2006

I wake up and cannot feel anything on my right side. It feels very odd when I brush my hair. Did my feisty 4yearold son Jack kick me and accidentally hit a nerve? In just a few weeks, I am hiding behind a pillar, sobbing uncontrollably as I read the emotionless sentence confirming I have Multiple Sclerosis. All I see is the face of the only person with MS that I know. Confined to life in a bed in a small back room of her house and alone all day while her husband worked long hours. Her only escape is a visit to the local shops on Saturdays. In my mind, this is ME tomorrow.

The neurologist tells me there is no cure, no treatment, to go live my life and come back if anything changes. I write to my parents with the news, unable to do it by phone. They call, and for the first time in my life, I hear my mother crying.

I refuse to take my neurologist's view as gospel and start to research. The internet is full of crackpot theories and approaches, but I find a promising book by American physician Dr Roy Swank. His theory is that by eliminating saturated fats from your diet, you reduce inflammation. I go cold turkey. Absolutely minimal amounts of mono and unsaturated oils, no red meat for a year, only white meat from chicken and totally avoid all foods with saturated and trans fats. Being a person who tends to see things in black and white, I easily adapt.

A year later, I came across an Australian professor of emergency medicine who has successfully managed his own MS through an approach that also has a focus on nutrition. Dr George Jelinek's approach to diet is stricter than Dr Swank's, and I move to a permanent fisheating vegan diet. Diet is just one aspect of his approach, and the only one I struggle with is the daily meditation.

I am now employed with the Red Cross, still in community aged care. Volunteer opportunities with Red Cross Emergency Services see me support communities affected by bushfires, floods and equine flu across Australia.

My sister Sue and I enter the Tour de Femme cycle ride and blitz it.

I do not have relapses as such and only once need a course of IV steroids. No other symptoms that I can attribute to MS have appeared for several years. Needing a fresh approach, I engage a new neurologist who starts me on diseasemodifying treatments that consist of daily injections—no big deal. I completed a degree in community education, majoring in *counselling*. I become an MS Ambassador and talk to groups of newly diagnosed people at Gloria McKerrow House in Deakin. I travel to Sweden with my son Max's soccer team, where they play in the Gothia Cup.

I am hopeful.

The 2010s

"Just living isn't enough, said the butterfly, one must have sunshine, freedom and a little flower." – Hans Christian Andersen

It is 2010, and we travel to Vietnam and Japan, where despite Jack studying Japanese for five years, he refuses to speak it.

On World MS Day in 2012, I climbed the 463 treacherous steps to the top of Il Duomo in Florence. Two weeks later, I am in a Paris apartment with my sister Sue packing to go home after four weeks in Italy and France. The sole under the toe of my right walking shoe is completely worn through.

As an MS Ambassador, I promote the Canberra MS Swimathons, and in 2013 my team, Miss Betty and Friends, actually entered it. My friend Penny, her daughter Sophie and I volunteer at the 2014 MS Colour Dash, and we gleefully cover the runners in brightly coloured powder.

A letter arrives from MS Australia to tell me how to apply to the NDIS. I throw it away because I don't have a disability.

I notice things start to change. This is subtle, at the edge of my consciousness, almost like when you try to recall details of your dreams. The heat of a Canberra summer is oppressive, and my new symptom of severe heat intolerance means I do not cope; fans and cold cloths are not up to the job. My right leg is heavy, at times uncooperative, and I start to limp when I am tired.

A second letter arrives from MS Australia, and this time I do not throw it away. I am accepted into the NDIS with a suitably modest package. I now officially have a disability.

My new neurologist puts me on different immunotherapy because Copaxone is causing some injection site problems. Betaferon is still an injection but only every second day.

My hobby of designing and making jewellery using polymer clay sees me hold two exhibitions with two artist friends. The proceeds contribute to spending money for more trips to Europe and the US, where our son Jack studies. I am in New York's Port Authority when I start to trip a lot, probably because there are so many people all in a huge hurry, a world away from my sedate Canberra. I buy an ugly black walking stick, and suddenly everyone parts in front of me like the Red Sea.

I now have an occupational therapist. Handrails appear on the steps to my home, and Steve says he is willing to lose the rose bed if a ramp is ever needed. The bathroom gains grab rails and a handheld shower.

I now need more time to comprehend complex material, and sometimes I struggle to find the right words. These symptoms are the most personally challenging to acknowledge, and I take too much time before seeing a neuropsychologist. I spend hours and hours completing a hoard of tests. Some I blitz, especially the one where I put obscure words in a sentence to demonstrate their meaning. Others are very stressful and upsetting. The worst one is where I repeat strings of numbers that get longer and longer before reciting them backwards.

The test results are in and, as I expect, reveal MS related cognitive changes. The first piece of good news is that my IQ result is good, so I have a good base to work off. The second and most important thing is that I now have an understanding of the changes as well as strategies to minimise the effects and play to my strengths. Don't be fooled into thinking I accept this development with maturity and acceptance. This is by far the most difficult and uncomfortable part of my story to write. I feel shame and a deep sense of loss. Shame because I do not want anyone to know and, god forbid, pity me. Loss, because I am afraid of who I am if my mind does not work. Again, I go to the worst possible scenario where I am unable to work, medically retired and worthless. The only person I tell is Steve; he is his usual wonderfully reassuring and supportive self. I work very hard to compensate for this loss, and it seems I do this quite well.

I am so sick of injections, and my latest neurologist prescribes an oral immunotherapy drug. I am having awful bouts of muscle spasticity, especially at night, so I now take a muscle relaxant. Botox into my calf muscle is another treatment I try, but with no improvement.

After too many lessthansatisfactory neurologists, I come across Professor Michael Barnett from the Brain and Mind Centre in Sydney, who is everything the others are not. He tells me I have probably transitioned from relapsingremitting MS to secondary progressive.

I am anxious.

The 2020s

"The future is real. The past is all made up." – Succession Season 2, Episode 5, Logan Roy.

My limp is now pronounced, and the wornout soles resulting from my foot drop see me on a firstname basis with my local shoe repairer. I start to use a walking stick more often as I have a few falls. It only takes a height difference of a mere millimetre on a footpath to see me topple over in a very inelegant manner. Storebought walking sticks are boring, so I spray mine bright red. I buy a very fancy red one from a business in England whose byline is *made to stand out, not to fit in*. I like it so much I buy another one, this time an orange one that lights up like a Christmas tree.

My wellinformed neuro physiotherapist refers me for something called a Functional Electric Stimulation device. In simple terms, a mobile phonesized device on a cuff worn around my upper calf that stimulates my right foot to lift at the right moment. It is lifechanging and only affordable due to my NDIS funding.

More handrails appear in my garden and along my back steps, although they are so steep I can no longer safely use them. My poor balance and a concrete right leg mean I can no longer venture safely into much of our garden, especially the deep garden beds. Once I get down, I find it very difficult to get back up.

When I travel, I have to plan very carefully. If flights between Canberra and Sydney are on a Dash 8 turboprop, I need to arrange the use of the lift at Sydney Airport because they don't use an air bridge. Hotel accommodation needs to be on the ground floor or have a lift. Bathrooms have to have a separate shower. I support the South East Queensland site of my organisation, and travel during summer is horrendous. Travelling anywhere where I will be mostly outdoors and the temperature over 25 degrees is no longer an option, especially in high humidity.

And, of course, MS is the gift that keeps on giving. My left thumb now has arthritis; it hurts to use a walking stick, so I now have an occupational therapist who specialises in hands to add to my team of allied health providers.

I am OKAY.

June 2023

"I can see clearly now, the rain has gone, I can see all obstacles in my way."
– I can see clearly now – Johnny Nash (1972)

So far, I've made the conscious decision to write my story totally from my perspective. What this approach did, however, was not address the supports that have enabled me to live the happy and productive life I have. My husband, Steve, is an unwavering source of love, support, and encouragement. Our sons, Max and Jack, are kind, considerate and thoughtful, as is Max's beautiful partner Hillary. My extended family and friends also respect and actively support the choices I make to manage my MS. Just last week, a former colleague visited the office with a vegan lemon cake she had made just so I could share it. This sums up how caring and thoughtful just about everyone has been.

What I most appreciate from my family, friends, and colleagues is that they just let me *be me*. My MS and disability are simply not a factor unless it has to be.

So, where am I today?

Life is wonderful. I'm at a time and place in my journey where I have done and continue to do all I can to manage and influence the course of my MS. I feel at peace and nowhere near as anxious about my future as I was five years ago.

I can't climb the 463 steps to the top of Il Duomo anymore or the 100metre staircase to SacréCoeur, but there are still so many walkable parts of my favourite cities.

I can't walk on soft sand, but Steve will piggyback me to where it is firmer.

I can't run or hop or skip, but I still get around independently and have maintained my daily 10,000step goal for over a decade.

I can't see myself doing any more higher education studies though I still work fulltime in a mentally challenging role with the best organisation I've ever been with.

And at least for the foreseeable future, Steve's rose bed is safe!

ABOUT BETH

Beth was born in a small town in the upper Hunter Valley in NSW, the third of 4 children. Her family lived on a property along with her beloved grandparents.

After finishing her schooling at a Sydney boarding school Beth had a number of career changes before serendipitously landing a not-for-profit community based aged-care position, where she remains today.

Diagnosed with MS at age 41, Beth focused on researching ways to reduce the impact and slow the progression. In the two decades since diagnosis her main issues have been a decline in her mobility, severe heat intolerance and some cognitive challenges.

2023 sees Beth still employed full-time in a challenging and rewarding role with aged and disability provider Annecto.

Beth lives in Canberra, has 2 adult sons, a wonderful husband and 2 lovely mini dachshunds. Beth has an optimistic outlook on life in general and her future in particular. She loves to read, travel and spend time with friends and family.

Watch the VLOG/Podcast of Beth on YouTube

MORPHEUS WRITING GROUP

Join the Morpheus Writing Group and embark on a transformative journey of self-discovery, creativity, and camaraderie. Our writing group is a haven for aspiring authors, a place where vulnerability and courage meet to craft powerful narratives.

In the Morpheus writing community, you'll find a space to unleash your imagination and explore the depths of storytelling. Led by multiple-published author, Justine Martin, the group discussions will nurture your writing skills, helping you find your unique voice and style.

The Morpheus Writing Group isn't just about writing; it's about growth. As you share your work with fellow writers, you'll receive thoughtful feedback, encouraging you to refine your craft and see your stories blossom. Our collective support bolsters your confidence, empowering you to push boundaries and embrace authenticity in your writing.

Beyond the creative exchange, Morpheus offers professional publishing services, ensuring your work is polished to perfection. From editing to cover design, we ensure your book meets the highest publishing standards.

Join us on this captivating journey, where dreams of becoming a published author become reality. We take pride in offering an affordable, Australian-owned space for writers to thrive without unnecessary hurdles.

Learn more at www.morpheuspublishing.com.au/writinggroup

JUSTINE MARTIN
KEYNOTE SPEAKER

The Queen of Resilience, Overcoming Adversities & A Survival Guide to Others!

Justine Martin, an extraordinary keynote speaker, presents a story that is not just unique, but profoundly courageous. Her narrative challenges the very notion of strength and determination, forcing you to reconsider your beliefs. A journey that commenced with an MS diagnosis 11 years ago, traversed three heart surgeries, and then three primary cancers. Against all odds and the discouragement of medical experts who deemed her unfit to work, Justine defied fate's decree. Instead of surrendering, she leaped into the realm of

business, not only reshaping her life with purpose and direction but also inspiring everyone around her. Her resolute stance in the face of adversities serves as a beacon of determination.

Justine's keynote talks on resilience are impactful and transformative. She imparts invaluable insights in sessions such as "The 10 Tips to Building Resilience," "How to Build Resilience When Faced With Adversities," and "Building a Resilient Workplace, Starts With the Individual." Navigating the challenging terrain of "Fatigue Management" and undergoing a transformation "From Victim to Victory; the Empowered Mind," her words resonate deeply.

A remarkable figure in medical and mental health circles, Justine's role as a former MS Ambassador for ten years, her continual awareness in media via newspapers, radio and publications and her consistent presence at Cancer Fundraising Events, showcase her commitment. Having battled numerous debilitating medical conditions, her tenacity, passion and resilience serve as guiding lights for countless individuals.

Her range of keynote talks caters to audiences grappling with medical and mental health issues. She dives into themes such as "How to Push through Chronic Disease," "Fatigue Management - Post Diagnosis," "Cancer Sucks, What Now?" and "Turn a Tragic Diagnosis into a Better Life than Before - I DID!" Justine's compelling story becomes a testament to the strength of the human spirit, inspiring listeners to transform their challenges into opportunities for growth.

Learn more and book Justine at www.justinemartin.com.au

MORPHEUS PUBLISHING SCHOLARSHIPS

Discover your writing dreams with Morpheus Publishing's commitment to giving back. We're delighted to offer two life-changing scholarships, empowering aspiring authors to realize their literary ambitions.

MS Book Author Scholarship: Are you passionate about sharing your experiences with Multiple Sclerosis? This scholarship grants an opportunity to become an author in our next anthology book. Share your story, inspire others, and make a difference.

Publish Your Book Scholarship: Unleash your creativity and hone your writing skills with our exclusive writing group classes. Learn the art of storytelling from seasoned authors and mentors. The best part? You'll get a chance to see your own book published!

At Morpheus Publishing, we believe in nurturing writers and empowering their voices. Our scholarships aim to support and uplift those who dream of writing and publishing their work. Embrace this unique opportunity to make your literary dreams a reality.

Learn more about our scholarships and join us on this exhilarating writing journey. Your story deserves to be told.

Visit our website for more information:
www.morpheuspublishing.com.au

Empower Your Pen. Shape Your Destiny.

GLOSSARY

ACDF: Anterior Cervical Discectomy and Fusion, a surgical procedure to treat neck pain and instability.

Acupuncturist: A practitioner who uses acupuncture, a traditional Chinese therapy involving inserting needles into specific points on the body to alleviate pain or promote healing.

ADHD: Attention Deficit Hyperactivity Disorder, a neurodevelopmental disorder characterised by inattention, hyperactivity, and impulsivity.

AFOs: Ankle-Foot Orthoses, medical devices worn on the lower limbs to provide support, alignment, and improved mobility.

Alzheimer's: Alzheimer's Disease, a progressive neurodegenerative disorder causing memory loss, cognitive decline, and behavioural changes.

Anterior Cervical Discectomy: Surgical removal of a damaged or herniated disc in the neck to relieve pressure on spinal nerves.

Anterior Discectomy and Fusion: Surgical removal of a spinal disc followed by fusion of adjacent vertebrae.

Anxiety: A mental health condition characterised by excessive worry, fear, and nervousness.

Art Therapist: A professional who uses art as a therapeutic tool to improve emotional well-being and self-expression.

Audiologist: A healthcare specialist who diagnoses and treats hearing and balance disorders.

Augabio: An oral compound that inhibits the function of specific immune cells that have been implicated in MS

Auto-ject daily needle treatment: A device for administering daily injections, often used in medical treatments.

Autoimmune: A condition where the immune system attacks the body's own healthy tissues.

B6: Vitamin B6, a water-soluble vitamin important for various bodily functions.

Baclofen: A medication used to treat muscle spasticity.

Bendamustine: A chemotherapy drug used to treat certain types of cancer, including lymphomas and leukemias.

Beta-Blockers: Medications that block the effects of adrenaline, often used to treat high blood pressure and heart conditions.

Betaferon: A brand name for interferon beta-1b, a medication used to treat multiple sclerosis.

Bipolar: Bipolar Disorder, a mental health condition characterised by mood swings between depressive and manic episodes.

Black Dog: A metaphor often used to describe depression.

Bowen Therapist: A practitioner of Bowen Therapy, a gentle hands-on technique for pain relief and relaxation.

Canadian Crutches: A type of mobility aid that provides support to the arms and shoulders while walking.

Cardiologist: A medical doctor specialising in the diagnosis and treatment of heart and cardiovascular conditions.

CAT Scan: Computerised Axial Tomography scan, a type of medical imaging using X-rays to create detailed cross-sectional images.

Catheter: A thin tube inserted into the body to drain fluids or administer treatments.

Charade the words: Act out a word, when your brain can't say it out loud or find it.

Chemotherapy: Medical treatment using drugs to kill or slow the growth of rapidly dividing cells, often used to treat cancer.

Chiropractor: A healthcare professional specialising in manual manipulation of the spine to address musculoskeletal issues.

CLL: Chronic Lymphocytic Leukaemia, a type of cancer affecting white blood cells.

Copaxone: A brand name for glatiramer acetate, a medication used to treat multiple sclerosis.

Corticosteroid: A type of anti-inflammatory medication commonly used in the treatment of various medical conditions.

Counsellor: A professional who provides psychological and emotional support through counseling sessions.

Cryoglobulin: Abnormal proteins that can cause blood to thicken and form clots.

Dementia: A general term for a decline in cognitive ability and memory that interferes with daily life.

Denkavit: Milk replacement for calves and lambs

Dichotomy: A division or contrast between two things that are or are represented as being opposed or entirely different.

Disease Modifying Therapies: Medications used to slow the progression of diseases, often referring to those used for multiple sclerosis.

DMD's: Duchenne Muscular Dystrophy, a genetic disorder causing progressive muscle weakness.

DMT: Disease Modifying Therapy, often used to describe medications used in autoimmune diseases.

Duke of Edinburgh Award: An internationally recognised program for young people that encourages personal development and outdoor exploration.

Dysplasia: Abnormal development of cells or tissues.

EDSS Score: Expanded Disability Status Scale, a system to measure disability in multiple sclerosis.

Endometriosis: A disorder where tissue similar to the lining of the uterus grows outside the uterus, causing pain and fertility issues.

Exacerbations: Sudden worsening of symptoms in a medical condition.

Exercise Physiologist: A specialist who uses exercise and physical activity to improve health and manage medical conditions.

Fungal Pneumonia: Lung infection caused by fungi.

Gastroenterologist: A medical specialist focused on the digestive system and its disorders.

Geepuz: Surprised, freaked out, unsure - in that moment. Slang.

Gestational Diabetes: Diabetes that develops during pregnancy.

Gilenya: A brand name for fingolimod, a medication used to treat multiple sclerosis.

Haematologist: A medical doctor specialising in the study and treatment of blood disorders.

Hip Dysplasia: Abnormal development of the hip joint.

HSCT: Hematopoietic Stem Cell Transplantation, a procedure used to treat certain cancers and autoimmune diseases.

Hullabaloo: A noisy or chaotic situation.

Humidity Crib: A temperature- and humidity-controlled environment for premature or sick newborns.

Hydrotherapists: Professionals who provide therapy and exercises in a water-based environment.

Hydrotherapy: Physical therapy conducted in a water pool for pain relief and rehabilitation.

Hypochondriac: A person excessively worried about having a serious illness.

IgM: Immunoglobulin M, an antibody produced by the immune system.

Immunosuppressants: Medications that suppress the immune system's activity, often used after organ transplants.

Infusion: Introduction of fluids, medications, or nutrients into the body through a vein.

Interferon: A protein that helps regulate the immune system's response to infections.

Interferons: A group of proteins that play a role in the body's immune response.

Interventional Radiologist: A medical specialist who performs minimally invasive procedures using imaging guidance.

Intrathecal Baclofen Pump: A device delivering baclofen to the spinal cord for muscle spasticity.

IVF Program: In Vitro Fertilisation program, assisted reproductive procedures to achieve pregnancy.

IVIg Therapy: Intravenous Immunoglobulin Therapy, using antibodies for immune-related conditions.

John Cunningham Virus (JC): A virus linked to a rare brain infection called PML.

Julia Gillard: Former Prime Minister of Australia (2010-2013).

Ketamine and Lidocaine: Medications used for pain relief and anesthesia.

L'hermittes Sign: an electric shock-like sensation that occurs on flexion of the neck

Lemtrada: A medication used to treat multiple sclerosis.

LESION: An area of abnormal tissue, often used in the context of neurological disorders.

Lumbar Puncture: A procedure to collect cerebrospinal fluid for testing.

Malingering: Deliberate exaggeration of symptoms for secondary gain.

Mania: Elevated mood and excessive energy seen in bipolar disorder.

McArdle's Syndrome: A rare genetic disorder causing muscle cramps during exercise.

Medi-port: A device implanted under the skin for intravenous access.

Meh Days: Days when one feels indifferent or unenthusiastic.

Melanoma: A type of skin cancer.

Meningioma: A tumour arising from the meninges, the layers covering the brain and spinal cord.

Methylprednisolone: A corticosteroid used to treat inflammation and immune-related conditions.

MND: Motor Neuron Disease, a group of progressive neurological disorders affecting nerve cells.

MonSter: A playful term used by some to refer to multiple sclerosis.

MRI: Magnetic Resonance Imaging, a non-invasive imaging technique.

MS Fatigue: Fatigue experienced by individuals with multiple sclerosis.

MS Hug: A sensation of tightness or pressure around the chest or torso, common in multiple sclerosis.

MS Readathon: A fundraising event encouraging reading to support people with multiple sclerosis.

NDIA: National Disability Insurance Agency (Australia), overseeing the National Disability Insurance Scheme.

NDIS: National Disability Insurance Scheme (Australia), providing support to people with disabilities.

Neuro-Physiotherapist: A physiotherapist specialising in neurological conditions.

Neuroimmunologist: A specialist in the interactions between the nervous and immune systems.

Neurologist: A medical doctor specialising in neurological disorders.

Neuropathy: Nerve damage often causing tingling or numbness.

Neuropsych Testing: Assessment of cognitive and psychological functions.

Neuroscience: The scientific study of the nervous system.

Nutritionist: A professional who provides guidance on nutrition and diet.

Ocrevus: is a medication used for the treatment of multiple sclerosis.

Occupational Therapist: A healthcare professional helping individuals improve daily life skills.

Omeo: A personal mobility device designed for balance and stability.

Oncology Clinic: Medical facility specialising in cancer diagnosis and treatment.

Ophthalmologist: A medical doctor specialising in eye health.

Ophthalmology: The medical field related to the eyes and vision.

Ophthalmology Eye Test: Examinations to assess vision and eye health.

Optic Neuritis: Inflammation of the optic nerve, often associated with multiple sclerosis.

Orthotist and Prosthetist: Professionals who design and fit orthotic and prosthetic devices.

Panadeine Forte: A combination pain medication containing paracetamol and codeine.

Paracetamol: A common pain and fever medication.

Paralysis: Loss of muscle function due to nerve damage.

Pelvic Congestion Syndrome: Chronic pelvic pain due to enlarged veins in the pelvis.

Peripheral Neuropathy: Nerve damage affecting the extremities.

PET Scan: Positron Emission Tomography, a type of medical imaging.

Physiotherapist: A professional providing physical therapy to improve movement and function.

Plasmapheresis: A process to remove and replace plasma from the blood.

Podiatrist: A healthcare specialist focusing on foot and ankle health.

Postnatal Depression: Depression occurring after childbirth.

Prednisolone: A corticosteroid used to treat inflammation and immune-related conditions.

Primary Lateral Sclerosis: A rare motor neuron disease.

Progressive Multifocal Leukoencephalopathy (PML): A rare brain infection often seen in immunocompromised individuals.

Prostate Cancer: Cancer affecting the prostate gland.

Psoriatic Arthritis: Arthritis occurring in individuals with psoriasis.

Psychiatric Ward: Hospital department for individuals with severe mental health issues.

Psychiatrist: A medical doctor specialising in mental health.

Psychologist: A professional providing psychological therapy and assessment.

Psychosomatic Illness: Physical symptoms with psychological causes.

Pulmonary Vein Ablation: A procedure to treat abnormal heart rhythms.

RAAF Doctors: Medical professionals in the Royal Australian Air Force.

Radiographer: A healthcare professional conducting medical imaging.

Radiologist: A medical doctor specialising in interpreting medical images.

Rebif Injectables: A brand name for interferon beta-1a, used to treat multiple sclerosis.

Rheumatology: Medical specialty dealing with musculoskeletal disorders.

Rituximab: A medication used to treat certain autoimmune diseases and cancers.

Roid Rage: Aggressive behaviour associated with steroid use.

RRMS: Relapsing-Remitting Multiple Sclerosis, a form of MS with relapses and remissions.

SCIg Therapy: Subcutaneous Immunoglobulin Therapy, a treatment using antibodies.

SLL: Small Lymphocytic Lymphoma, a type of cancer affecting white blood cells.

Spastic Paraparesis: Muscle stiffness and weakness affecting the lower limbs.

Speech Pathologist: A professional helping with communication and speech disorders.

Spirulina: A type of blue-green algae often used as a dietary supplement.

SPMS: Secondary Progressive Multiple Sclerosis, a phase of MS with worsening symptoms.

Sports Kinesiology: The study of movement in sports and exercise.

Stroke: A sudden disruption of blood flow to the brain.

Subcutaneous Injection: Injection under the skin.

Subpubic Catheter: A catheter inserted below the pubic bone.

Tachycardia and Cardiac Arrhythmia: Abnormal heart rate and rhythm.

Tegretol: A brand name for carbamazepine, used to treat seizures and nerve pain.

Topamax: A brand name for topiramate, used to treat seizures and migraines.

Tracheotomy: Surgical creation of an opening in the windpipe for breathing.

Transverse Myelitis: Inflammation of the spinal cord causing neurological symptoms.

TurboMed - Orthotic Mobility Aid: A specific orthotic mobility aid.

Tysabri: A medication used to treat multiple sclerosis.

Unilateral Mastectomy: Surgical removal of one breast.

Vertebral Osteomyelitis: Infection of the vertebrae.

Vertigo: A sensation of dizziness or spinning.

Walker: A mobility aid to assist with walking.

Wheelie Walker: A walker with wheels for improved mobility.

WINDEX: A brand of glass cleaner.

www.ingramcontent.com/pod-product-compliance
Lightning Source LLC
Chambersburg PA
CBHW040740020526
44107CB00083B/2806